Studies in Women and Religion /
Études sur les femmes et la religion : 9

STUDIES IN WOMEN AND RELIGION /
ÉTUDES SUR LES FEMMES ET LA RELIGION

Studies in Women and Religion is a series designed to serve the needs of established scholars in this new area, whose scholarship may not conform to the parameters of more traditional series with respect to content, perspective, and/or methodology. The series will also endeavour to promote scholarship on women and religion by assisting new scholars in developing publishable manuscripts. Studies published in this series will reflect the wide range of disciplines in which the subject of women and religion is currently being studied, as well as the diversity of theoretical and methodological approaches that characterize contemporary women's studies. Books in English are published by Wilfrid Laurier University Press.

Inquiries should be directed to the series coordinators, Eleanor J. Stebner (Faculty of Theology, University of Winnipeg, Winnipeg) or Tracy J. Trothen (Queen's Theological College, Queen's University, Kingston).

STUDIES IN WOMEN AND RELIGION /
ÉTUDES SUR LES FEMMES ET LA RELIGION

VOLUME 9

Linking Sexuality & Gender

Naming Violence against Women in The United Church of Canada

Tracy J. Trothen

Published for the Canadian Corporation for Studies in Religion /
Corporation Canadienne des Sciences Religieuses
by Wilfrid Laurier University Press

2003

This book has been published with the help of a grant from the Canadian Federation for the Humanities and Social Sciences, using funds provided by the Social Sciences and Humanities Research Council of Canada. We acknowledge the financial support of the Government of Canada through the Book Publishing Industry Development Program for our publishing activities.

National Library of Canada Cataloguing in Publication

Trothen, Tracy J. (Tracy Joan), 1963-
    Linking sexuality and gender: naming violence against women in The United Church of Canada / Tracy J. Trothen.

(Studies in Women and Religion ; 9)
Co-published by the Canadian Corporation for Studies in Religion.
Includes bibliographical references and index.
ISBN 0-88920-424-1

    1. Women—Crimes against—Religious aspects—United Church of Canada. 2. Violence—Religious aspects—United Church of Canada. 3. Sex—Religious aspects—United Church of Canada 4. Sex role—Religious aspects—United Church of Canada. 5. United Church of Canada—Doctrines. I. Canadian Corporation for Studies in Religion II. Title. III. Title: Linking sexuality and gender. IV. Series: Studies in women and religion (Waterloo, Ont.) ; 9.

BX9881.T76 2003   261.8'3315'082   C2003-901964-2

Cover design by P.J. Woodland

Order from:
Wilfrid Laurier University Press
Waterloo, Ontario, Canada N2L 3C5
www.wlupress.wlu.ca

∞
Printed in Canada

Table of Contents

Acknowledgements

*W*ith fondness and much appreciation, I acknowledge the contributions of several individuals:

My family, friends and colleagues who supported me with a firm belief in the value of this project. Particularly Ron Pearson, my companion, who shares my passion for justice; who listens to my frustrations and struggles; who sustains me with an ongoing commitment to play and enjoy life.

Special thanks to Ellie Stebner who has read drafts of different chapters and given her suggestions and support. Ray Whitehead has been teacher, colleague and friend and has always insisted that this book would come to fruition even when I had my doubts. Pam Dickey Young also has read several drafts of this manuscript and offered me unfailing wisdom and encouragement. Pam's friendship and guidance have been invaluable to me. Marilyn Legge, as trusted colleague and former Co-ordinator of the Series on Women and Religion guided me through the publication process. Roger Hutchinson has been dissertation advisor, mentor and friend. Through Roger, I have learned most profoundly how ethics are grounded in matters of everyday life.

Steve West and Linda Thomas, friends, editors and indexer, were instrumental in the completion of this book. Thanks also to the fine people at Wilfrid Laurier University Press. Any mistakes remaining in these pages are mine alone.

The men and women who have devoted energy, faith and courage to the writing of the documents I have described and analyzed have demonstrated a commitment to the Church's work in the areas of gender and/or human sexuality that goes beyond expectation. These have never been particularly easy areas in which to work; they have always been of great importance and have always required great risk.

All the women whose stories of past and ongoing violence have motivated me to more closely examine how the church is responding to this issue.

This project was made possible through the financial support of the following organizations and institutions: The University of Winnipeg, Queen's University, Queen's Theological College, Victoria University, Emmanuel College, the Women in Ministry Committee of the United Church of Canada, the Toronto School of Theology, and funds from the McGeachy Project of the Centre for the Study of Religion in Canada. This book has been published with the help of a grant from the Canadian Federation for the Humanities and Social Sciences, using funds provided by the Social Sciences and Humanities Research Council of Canada.

List of Abbreviations

ACTC	Atlantic Christian Training Centre
CASAC	Canadian Association of Sexual Assault Centres
DMC	Division of Mission in Canada
IWY	International Women's Year
MP&E	Ministry, Personnel and Education
NAC	National Action Committee on the Status of Women
NCG	National Coordinating Group
PCTC	Prairie Christian Training Centre
ROP	*Record of Proceedings*
SMF	Sexuality, Marriage and Family Unit of the Division of Mission in Canada
TAC	Therapeutic Abortion Committee
TFWM	Task Force on the Changing Roles of Women and Men in Church and Society
TPU	Theological Perspectives Unit
WA	The Dominion Council Women's Association
WIM	Women in Ministry Committee
WMS	Women's Missionary Society

Introduction

"*F*OURTEEN WOMEN DEAD, and one man. How many wounded?"[1] On December 6, 1989, a man carrying a gun separated the women from a group of engineering students. The women were told they had "no business" being there; he accused them of being "feminists" and began shooting. The man killed fourteen women simply because they were women. Some media reports following this horror depicted it as the result of an individual's pathology. Others recognized this massacre of young female engineering students as another manifestation of systemic sexism. Many years have passed since these women were killed at the University of Montreal's school of engineering, the Polytechnique. The memories remain. The pain, though perhaps dampened, remains; tears continue to be shed, and the culture in which we live and participate continues to sanction male violence against women.

Violence against women is not a new phenomenon. The Montreal Massacre spurred more people to recognize that Canada is not somehow immune to this systemic violence; the reality is, of course, that violence against women has been part of our culture for a long, long time. However, it was not until the mid-1980s that this violence was clearly identified as a problem—or issue—by most churches or by much of wider Canadian society.[2] Now that violence against women is on the agenda, it is important to ask why it took as long as it did for the issue to be named, how the problem is being defined, and how institutions such as the church are responding. In finding answers to these questions, we will come to a better understanding of why this violence continues and be able to address it more effectively.

This book arises out of my commitment to a vision—a hope—of justice and compassion for all people, particularly for those who experience violence and marginalization in our country and in our churches. As a feminist social ethicist, sexuality—and gender-related issues such as sexual orientation, and violence against women—are of significant interest to me. The ways in which these and related issues are understood are strongly influenced by the ways in which both human sexuality and gender issues are understood.

Notes to introduction are on page 123.

I will focus on gender- and sexuality-related issues in order to explore how our understandings of such matters may have contributed to our understandings of, and therefore responses to, violence against women. As the book's title indicates, sexuality and gender are the book's first concerns; in order to understand the dynamics of violence against women, it is first necessary to understand something of sexuality and gender. Such violence is perpetrated because of biological sex and socially constructed gender; women continue to be violated in a myriad of ways because they are women. Therefore, the findings in this book are relevant to the underlying dynamics of all types of violence against women (including emotional, spiritual, physical and sexual abuse), and more particularly to institutional responses to this systemic issue. This book can be understood as one moment in the broad discourse of violence. In keeping with the methodology of a feminist ethic, in order to understand the United Church's more contemporary approach to violence against women it is necessary to uncover and illumine the causal dynamics and relevant history. In so doing, this book adds another piece to this discourse. The question I will address is how the United Church's approaches to sexuality and gender contributed to the length of time it took for the issue of violence against women to be identified as a concrete issue on the agenda of The United Church of Canada.

The United Church of Canada is a uniquely Canadian institution that has a long tradition of grappling with issues of human sexuality and gender. I will examine the relevance and content of this tradition as it pertains to gender- and sexuality-related issues. Next, I will analyze three case studies that address the United Church's more contemporary approach to human sexuality and gender issues. Finally, I will show, as an example of the ongoing relevance of this history, how the historical approaches to these areas have both facilitated and obstructed the move to address violence against women.

The first chapter focuses on the methodology that I have chosen for doing this research and analysis. The decision to use the United Church *Records of Proceedings* (ROPs) as a source central for this book was a difficult one, due to the limitations of reliance on an official record. I will discuss these limitations and my decision to nonetheless use this source.

Also, I will clarify my understanding of some relevant issues and concepts to which I will refer throughout this book.

Chapters 2 and 3 provide an overview and critical analysis of the history of the United Church regarding sexuality and gender issues, as documented in the ROPs. An analysis of these ROPs shows the formative shifts in thinking, theology and the socio-cultural context.

Chapter 2 looks at the United Church's evolving understanding of human sexuality from 1925 to the 1960s. During this time, that understanding was transformed from a primarily *act-centred* ethic to a primarily *relational* ethic. By this I mean that, in the earlier years, issues concerning sexuality were defined primarily in terms of the rightness or wrongness of certain sexual acts, whereas in later years, sexuality has come to be understood primarily in terms of the quality of the relationships involved. Although the quality of the relationship gained importance in terms of a criterion for evaluating the expression of human sexuality, deontological claims have continued to play an important role in the evaluation of sexual relationships. The emphasis of this chapter is that over the years a paradigm shift has occurred in the understanding of human sexuality and is relevant to how The United Church of Canada has come to approach related issues such as violence against women.

In the third chapter, I examine the United Church's history of addressing gender issues and the family. Throughout the greater part of United Church history, women have been expected to follow vocations of wife and mother and to devote themselves to the care and nurture of their husbands—who were understood to be responsible for the economic well-being of the nuclear family—and, particularly, of their children. Women, in their designated roles, were considered central to the stability of the family unit. The preservation of this nuclear family unit was a constant concern for the Church particularly throughout the 1930s, 1940s and 1950s. The well-being of the family, which often was reduced to the preservation of the family, was believed to have been linked inextricably to the well-being of the nation. Moreover, as with sexuality, there was an eschatological component to this issue: the preservation of the family was believed to be essential to the coming "Kingdom of God." Since its formation, the United Church has struggled with the changing roles of women and, related to this, the changing understandings of the family. The Church's responses to gender issues and the family have tended to ambivalence; the dialectic between the recognition of women as moral agents with experiences that may not reflect those of the dominant men in the Church, and the desire to maintain order and traditional gender roles is a theme throughout United Church history. Further, the tension between the desire to preserve the sacredness of the traditional patriarchal Christian family and the growing recognition that within this sacred domain, destructive and even life-threatening behaviour can lurk, increased gradually over the years.

I next present three case studies from the 1980s. Chapters 4 and 5 examine the human sexuality studies entitled *In God's Image ... Male and Female* (1980) and *Gift, Dilemma and Promise* (1984). These studies attracted great attention and controversy. The ways in which they approached sexuality and gender issues reveal factors that both inhibited and aided the identification of related issues, including violence against women.

In chapter 6, I explore the development of one of the first officially formed United Church groups to explore gender issues: The Task Force on the Changing Roles of Women and Men in Church and Society (TFWM), its mandate and the issues with which it dealt from the late 1970s to 1984. This group's work on gender issues greatly contributed to the naming of violence against women as an issue on the Church's agenda. The differences between the respective approaches of the two sexuality task forces and the TFWM indicate factors that affected the United Church's later naming of and approaches to related ethical issues.

The closing chapter explores the issue of violence against women from the time of the Church's official recognition of the issue in the 1980s through to the early 1990s, and links the formative shifts discussed in previous chapters to the initial identification and ongoing approach to this issue. Also in this chapter, I situate the United Church's position in the wider Canadian context and pose critical questions such as: In what ways did this Church remain true to its tradition of seeking justice for the marginalized and of acting prophetically within society? Has the United Church been on the leading edge of Canadian society in its recognition of and response to violence against women? Or has it primarily followed other segments of Canadian society? The exploration of these questions leads to further questions and conclusions. In particular, I show that the United Church has become increasingly committed to self-critique: during the early years of the social gospel movement, the Church saw itself as part of the solution to the country's problems whereas in more recent years, particularly since the advent of the second wave of feminism in the early 1970s, the United Church recognized more clearly that in fact it could be part of the problem.

We carry our legacies with us—even as we create new ideas and offer new symbols—that continue to inform both our institutional and individual mindsets. Through the gradual uncovering and reconstruction of our stories and identities we can become more critically self-aware and can better understand both why we name issues in certain ways and what informs, encourages and blocks our responses to these issues.

This book begins a much-needed investigation of a Canadian Church's ethical approach to human sexuality and gender. Such investigation is essential to any understanding of the causal dynamics behind the Church's responses to the many related issues, including its communal slowness to stand clearly and definitively on the subject of violence against women. The findings in this book are not limited to The United Church of Canada; rather, many insights and questions arising from this research and analysis can be applied to other institutions and groups in Canada.

CHAPTER I

Methodology

Author's Standpoint

*F*EMINISTS HAVE ARGUED that objectivity demands intellectual credibility, a critical self-awareness of loyalties and biases, conscious emotional and spiritual engagement, communal engagement and ongoing self- and other-critique. Our identities are shaped by our context and experiences. As theological ethicist Sharon Welch argues, "Our vision is always perspectival. The problems we see and the solutions we envision cannot be separated from our social location. Interest is always operative and does need to be checked."[1] Neutrality, which is not the same as objectivity, is neither possible nor desirable; to profess it gives tacit support to accepted dominant norms, reinforces the status quo and keeps marginalized people in the margins. I assume a feminist understanding of objectivity and as such am committed to intellectual credibility, the clarification of context and loyalties, engagement and ongoing communal dialogue.

My experiences, biases and loyalties inform the standpoint from which my analysis begins. My experience and context necessarily inform how I understand social ethical issues. I am a white, middle-class Canadian woman. I grew up in southern Ontario, have worked as a professor in theology at The University of Winnipeg, and am now a faculty member at Queen's Theological College in Kingston, Ontario. I have a longstanding commitment to feminism. My first loyalty is to women, children and marginalized men.

As an ordained minister of The United Church of Canada, a professor of theology, and a passionate seeker of justice and right relation, I have chosen to explore the United Church's past, ongoing and present stands on ethical issues and policies. Our stories shape who we are, both individually and collectively. As Canadian ethicist Marilyn Legge insists, "Historical structures are *not* objectively 'out there' but are alive and well and forming the *ongoing* dynamics of the present."[2]

Ethical Framework

A feminist social ethical approach shapes this case study of The United Church of Canada. "Case study" is a relatively new way to talk about the historic discipline of casuistry, which is a way of approaching the study of ethics based on the analysis of particular cases. As ethicists Albert Jonsen and Stephen Toulmin explain, casuistry is based on the discernment of patterns and generally agreed upon assessments of related paradigmatic cases.[3] More problematic cases are then assessed by analogy to these less ambiguous ones. As more cases related to the paradigmatic ones are discovered and addressed, more factors arise for consideration in future, related cases. Both rules and changing contexts are relevant to this method of ethical decision making; as more voices or other variables are added to the mix, more complexities and pertinent factors are uncovered, and ethical decisions develop with each new case. As a result, although closure can be reached in particular cases, there are no final, once-and-for-all conclusions in larger issue areas. Consistent with the feminist social ethical approach of this book, casuistry presupposes a commitment to include a variety of voices and recognition of the relevance of context, including structures and systems.

The limits of casuistry are reached in relation to violence against women, for example, when abusers or others who participate in the silencing of this violence deny or attempt to justify violence against women. Dialogue regarding what constitutes violence against women can be pursued unless the subjects' agenda is to deny and silence the entire issue. If this is not the case but, rather, the conflict pertains to differing understandings of violence against women, then casuistry can be an effective method for opening dialogue. For instance, it is generally recognized that violence against women is wrong as it is a clear violation of the moral rule against causing harm. However, it is not always clear to everyone what constitutes violence against women. A paradigmatic case that everyone could accept might be a man using his fist to punch a woman. However, in different contexts many people have been less clear as to whether a physical push, verbal put-downs, or even rape in marriage constitutes such violence. My intent is to identify and clarify some of the factors that have contributed to this lack of clarity and agreement on an official level among the United Church community in particular.

One of my hopes in writing this book is that it will generate a greater awareness of the United Church's story in relation to gender and sexuality. Without an informed, critical, story-based awareness of our paradigmatic foundations, responses to violence against women and many other ethical issues related to gender and/or sexuality remain underdeveloped.

As I noted earlier, there are difficulties involved in the exploration of the past. Much of recorded history is triumphalistic; for the most part, the powerful have written the history books and the voices of the oppressed have been silenced or at the least distorted. In using the ROPs as a central source in my work, there are obvious limitations. The ROPs contain a partial history, written and recorded by those with institutional power, mainly white men, in The United Church of Canada. These records must be approached with a hermeneutic of suspicion, and the awareness that the history they represent is, for the most part, history as perceived by the powerful. Nonetheless, it must be approached if our lives and their meanings are to be transformed. Such a reconstruction is necessary to a fuller understanding of what in the Church has contributed to the current struggles of the marginalized to be heard by the more powerful. Having said that, it is important to realize that the case studies within this book do not address only powerful groups. For instance, as will become evident, the Task Force on the Changing Roles of Women and Men in Church and Society was an official United Church group and submitted official reports to General Council; however, they were arguably accorded little unofficial power within the wider Church.

The partiality of the stories I reconstruct here is a limitation that I hope others will address through the recording of more experiences before they are lost. No one work, including this one, will tell the whole story, but this book provides an essential piece of the puzzle.

The Church's dominant understandings of gender and sexuality must be studied and analyzed as part of justice work. As the official record of General Council reports and debates, as well as containing many official statements of United Church policy, the ROPs provide an excellent documentary record of the Church's thinking about such topics as gender and human sexuality, *at an official level*, since 1925.

As a feminist, I assume that women are full moral agents and have the right to be regarded as such. I also assume the patriarchal or "kyriarchal" (as coined by Elisabeth Schüssler Fiorenza to signify the interconnected systemic power imbalances that characterize North America)[4] nature of our North American culture, which compromises many people's moral agency through systemic marginalization. Simply put, I understand "patriarchal" to describe a culture that is characterized by interconnected systemic power imbalances. Patriarchal culture requires that one group—generally white, middle- to upper-class, able-bodied, heterosexual men—has power (desired or not) at the expense of all others. The meanings of sexuality, family, gender roles and the general social order are constructed according to patriarchal norms and values. If, indeed, violence against women and other abuses associated with socially constructed meanings of gender and/or sexuality are learned, then they are *not* inevitable.[5] This conviction undergirds the writing of this book.

Many feminist theologians, and certainly casuists, see history as open-ended in that they understand there is always the possibility of transformation as we learn and experience changes of heart.[6] This belief in an open-ended history is connected to belief in an eschatological future as well as in the redemptive power of memory. Since there is continuity between the past, present and the eschatological future, the promise of an eschatological reversal brings hope out of past hopes, struggles and pain. Without such a remembering and a conviction that the future will yield promise, there is neither point nor meaning in suffering. Christianity claims otherwise; there is hope and emancipatory potential in struggles and pains so long as we remember, reconstruct, and remain committed to a vision of God's radical and outrageous, inclusive love.

As have other institutions, the United Church has taken time to become aware of the painful consequences of some long and deeply held convictions. For instance, the Church no longer assumes that the preservation of the nuclear family unit as defined from a dominant white Anglophone perspective, takes precedence over the well-being of individual family members. Because of a too-common tendency to ignore suffering in order to maintain dominant truth claims, feminists rely primarily on consequentialist ethical arguments for ethical decision making. Principles are also considered important (and as such are explored below), but if the consequences of our principles are not considered carefully, we run the risk of reifying principles; principles can become rules that exist merely to buttress the status quo. We must hold our principles in an ongoing dialectic with the consequences of these convictions. Feminists tend to be most concerned with consequences but, nonetheless, are clear regarding the necessity and value of dynamic principles.

Most feminist theological ethicists, including myself, uphold the general principles of moral agency, embodiment, accountability, mutuality and justice. For instance, Legge outlines what she understands to be the key principles of a feminist ethical methodology: moral agency, embodiment, and accountability.[7] Margaret Farley stresses agency, embodiment, mutuality, equality and "equitable sharing."[8] Rosemary Radford Ruether focuses on the full humanity of women, mutuality, the connectedness of all creation and embodiment.[9] Carol Robb and Beverly Harrison understand the central principles of a feminist ethic to be moral agency, embodiment and justice. They argue that moral agency is a necessary precursor to accountability and, therefore, include accountability in their understanding of agency. Mutuality also is included as part of these three principles.[10] Although these principles may be named and defined somewhat differently, moral agency, embodiment, accountability, mutuality and justice, generally, are recognized as necessary to an adequate feminist ethic.

Finally, in asking about the roots of the United Church's approaches to gender and sexuality, I am asking not only a feminist question but also a theological question. The related issues of power, social construction and control are theological issues. The abuse of power is evil; as theologian James Newton Poling emphasizes, power used to control or dominate in any way

> Harm[s] the power of life itself within the relational web. Power so used stifles the possibility of mutuality and interdependence. Abuse of power not only destroys individuals, it also destroys the web of relationships on which all life depends…."Abuse of power is denial of communion and denial of freedom for self, others, and God."[11]

Engagement in the work of justice requires that we, as members of an institutional church, examine the ways in which we participate in the sanctioning of oppressive ideologies through our assumptions and worldviews. Only through critical reflection and analyses of how we use and abuse power, both collectively and individually, can we hope to break the silence and begin to transform our world into one that decries all injustice.

Our understanding of power is embedded in our understanding of God, and vice versa. The traditional image of God as a powerful white male seated on an elevated throne speaks of white male hegemony and glorifies power-over rather than mutuality. Our language and images of God are parts of our theology that shape and are shaped by our understanding of power; again, our theologies form and are formed by our context and experiences.

For instance, Karen Lebacqz and Ronald G. Barton claim that "for many women their concrete experiences of sexuality have had a significant impact on their theologies. Because of who they are sexually, they see God differently."[12] Further, one's bodily experiences can challenge the dominant understanding of hierarchical power: "Just as erotic love affirms the goodness of bodily connection, so it also affirms new forms of power. Erotic power is not the 'power-over' of domination and submission paradigms. It is a power of mutuality and life-givingness."[13]

In asking questions about power, gender and sexuality, I am asking theological questions. If we are to understand, develop and live theologies that most closely reflect what we desire, it is necessary to ask whose views are considered normative, and to challenge resultant assumptions. In spite of its many perversions and ambiguities, I remain committed to Christianity because of its root commitment to justice and hope, and because my faith and Church continue to inspire and impassion me.

In the following pages, I describe shifts in values and beliefs regarding the sanctification or demonization of institutions, roles and patterns of thought. Matters related to gender and sexuality evoke impassioned responses particularly when placed in a religious or other faith-based context. I expect that this book will do the same. My hope is that others will continue this social ethical work, particularly by pursuing first-hand stories from those who have lacked official voice. My intention is for this volume to contribute to this ongoing work, to illuminate areas for closer attention, and to generate discussion—including considered refutation.

CHAPTER II

The Development of The United Church of Canada's Approach to Human Sexuality

*T*HE UNITED CHURCH OF CANADA'S understanding of human sexuality, as reflected in the official *Records of Proceedings,* changed significantly between 1925 and the early 1980s.[1] Two relevant and intertwined paradigm shifts were in process: First, the United Church's understanding of the purpose of human sexuality moved from the conviction that such expressions must be limited to procreation and the strengthening of the union of married couples to the belief that intimate expressions of human sexuality are also important for the giving and receiving of pleasure and vulnerability within marriage. The former conviction was based partially on the fear that sexual pleasure can easily lead to temptation and, therefore, moral danger. This distrust of bodily pleasure has been bound up with distrust of women's moral agency. As Beverly Harrison points out: "In relation to...[women's] actions as sexual beings...there remains a lingering fear of affirming any genuine capacity to live responsibly apart from largely prohibitive and constricting action guides."[2] Second, the understanding of human sexuality has been transformed from a primarily act-centred ethic to a primarily relational ethic. Although the quality of the relationship has gained importance as a criterion for evaluating the expression of human sexuality, certain deontological ethical claims continue to play an important role in the evaluation of sexual relationships. By this I mean that in the earlier years, issues concerning sexuality were defined primarily in terms of the rightness or wrongness of certain sexual acts whereas more recently, sexuality has come to be understood primarily in terms of the quality of the relationships involved, allowing that these relationships fall within certain overarching parameters. These two paradigmatic shifts are interrelated in that, as United Church official records began to reflect an understanding of human sexuality as encompassing more than procreation and union within marriage, a greater concern for the overall quality of the relationship began to emerge.

Whether a sexual ethic is primarily act-centred or primarily understood in relational terms has influence on the ways in which related issues are defined and, therefore, acted upon. For instance, primarily act-centred sexual ethics have often functioned to blur the distinction between sexuality and violence. A theology that limits sin to specific acts—particularly sexual acts—often reduces victims of crimes of a sexual nature to tainted goods; a primarily act-centred sexual ethic has tended to define the victim as impure rather than to focus attention on the violent assault on personhood and relationship:

> Victims of so-called sex crimes often are more stigmatized than the perpetra-
> tors of the crimes because such offences stereotype victims as sexually
> "impure." It is time to recognize that those who are recipients of violent
> "sexual" acts are not sexually polluted; they have been victimized by ugly acts
> of human retribution, evil because of the contempt for persons they express
> rather than the genital contact they involve.[3]

This confusion between sexuality and violence slowed the naming of violence against women as a pervasive ethical issue that the church must address.

Dualistic theologies have contributed to this historic tendency to a primarily act-centred sexual ethic. Dualisms such as male/female and spirit/body, respectively, have characterized much of Christian history. Not only are the two components split apart and, therefore, rendered absurd, but also the first component is valued through the negation of the other. Historically and theologically, men have been associated with the mind and spirit whereas women have been identified with the carnal, bodily side of humanity. Further, the mind and spirit have been separated and elevated above the body, sexuality and nature. While the latter have been viewed as mutable and to a large extent uncontrollable, the mind has been perceived as the locus of rationality, reason and control. This hierarchical dualistic approach has served to both reflect and perpetuate negative and fearful views of the body, sexuality and women. The lower half of these dualisms are usually projected onto women and other marginalized people. When a theology of sexuality is grounded in these hierarchical dualisms, the ramifications are numerous and often deadly.

A patriarchal dualistic theology often holds women responsible, as temptresses, for "the basic dynamics of sexual interest and temptation."[4] Therefore women, from the perspective of such a theology, are responsible for any expression of sexuality or any violence that is expressed sexually.

However, not all women are seen as temptresses within a patriarchal theology of sexuality. Another facet to this dualistic theology is the Eve/Mary dichotomy. Traditionally, Eve has been seen as temptress, leading man away from all that is good and pure into the realms of bodily passions, out-of-control lust, sensuality and eventual death.[5] Eve represents these repressed and renounced elements of our existence. Mary, on the other hand, has been portrayed as Eve's redemption and fulfilment. She is the nurturing mother and faithful wife who, paradoxically, abstained from sex. Within this dualistic model women tend to be seen as either Mary- or Eve-like.

A dualistic worldview systematically induces further alienation—

These dualisms, symbolized by sexism, incarnate a heritage of self-alienation and social projection of inferior and auxiliary humanity onto women. Racism, the subjugation of lower classes and colonized people, and even anti-semitism operate out of much of the same language of sexist dualism, i.e., the elevation of the "head" people over the "body" people. This same psychology also blinds us to our ravaging of nature and the amorality of technology.[6]

The association of women with nature means the abuse of nature as well as the abuse of women. Traditionally, both have been seen, particularly since the Enlightenment, as needing to be "mastered" and controlled in order to avoid chaos and a redistribution of power. In a patriarchal culture, white, able-bodied, heterosexual, middle- and upper-class men generally hold the preponderance of power. This is not to say that we design our theologies deliberately to preserve the established order; however, theology often functions to preserve the status quo. The task of the church as faithful community is to continually discern, what values are most consistent with appropriate sources of authority such as scripture, tradition, reason and experience.

This rapid overview of a traditional theology of sexuality points to a few theological issues that particularly influenced the early United Church, and further illuminates the issues that will be discussed during the rest of this chapter and the next.[7] Topics examined in this chapter are birth control, the marital relationship and sexuality, redemptive homes, pornography and abortion. These topics were defined by contemporary, official Church records as topics related to human sexuality. Over time, as the definition of human sexuality changed, the topics identified as being related to human sexuality also changed.

The Canadian social purity movement was a primary voice in framing and defining issues related to "the sexual and moral aspects of social life" throughout the years 1885-1925.[8] This movement was concerned not simply with the outward behaviour of individuals but particularly with the inner life. The state was often called upon and expected to take a primary role in the shaping of this inner morality. Organizations such as women's groups and churches were attributed much greater recognition than similar organizations are now, as bodies whose members offered much needed and respected knowledge. Those whom we would designate as professional and expert voices today, such as doctors, psychiatrists and social workers, were not recognized as authorities regarding moral issues. Therefore, there was a far greater degree of collaboration among women's groups, the church and the state.[9]

Although this movement was nearing a close by 1925, the United Church embraced many of its concerns. One concern of the social purity movement was to restrict sexual intimacy to marriage but not to silence or deny the value and existence of this aspect of the marital relationship: "Purity educators certainly denounced sexual excess; but they also denounced prudishness and warned parents that the road to sexual hell was paved with well-meaning attempts to keep children 'innocent.'"[10] This focus on sexual acts and purity shaped the Church's early years but gradually gave way to the social gospel movement and its emphasis on social justice within the dominant paradigm.[11] This is not to say that this concern with purity simply disappeared. Rather, it was eventually superseded by other concerns around order and stability, and still surfaces from time to time.

Birth Control

From a moral standpoint, sexual expression was limited to the marital relationship. Within marriage, sexual activity was seen as important and appropriate primarily for procreative purposes but also for the well-being of the relationship. The authors of the 1932 report, *The Meaning and Responsibilities of Christian Marriage,* contended that though one of the primary purposes of marriage was to procreate, there were some conditions under which sexual intercourse did not have to hold the possibility of conception. These conditions included the inability to conceive for biological reasons; instances when "it is reasonably certain that any offspring...will be in the form of a stunted humanity and a burden to society" (*ROP* 1932:279, 80); if the woman's health would be seriously endangered; or if too many children would undermine the care the parents could give to each of them (280). In all but the first case, contraception is necessary. As the report indicates, after interpreting Christian tradition, scripture and particularly the gospels, as well as experience, the authors concluded that: "conscience should prevail, and by conscience we mean not some selfish or capricious opinion, but a considered judgment based on the recognition of all the facts and obligations inherent in a situation" (280-81). Each married couple was to mutually agree on the best way to be true to the will of God regarding sexual intercourse, contraception and the rearing of children. The ultimate responsibility devolved from the institution to the couple. This position could be understood as either one that recognized and trusted the moral agency of heterosexual couples or as one that refused to take a clear stand on the use of contraceptives. The primary purpose of marriage continued to be procreation, but the United Church acknowledged that some cases and circumstances allowed for the use of contraceptives. This was a radical stand at that time; the use of contraceptives was illegal in Canada until 1969.

A second report received in 1936 (*The Report of the Commission on Voluntary Parenthood and Sterilization*)[12] addressed the question of voluntary parenthood. The authors of the report constructed their arguments on the basis of religious tradition, particularly Jewish and Roman Catholic traditions. The Roman Catholic Church approved of abstinence from intercourse during fertile periods with the purpose of preventing conception.

The authors deduced that the Roman Catholic Church "approves of voluntary parenthood" (ROP 1936:326). The Central Conference of American Rabbis declared in 1932 that, in families where there were at least two children, the wife could use birth control. This choice and interpretation of sources indicates that the authors of the report probably had decided on their ethical position before they investigated other sources of authority. The intent does not seem to have been to open debate through an examination of related religious traditions, but rather to substantiate an ethical position that had been arrived at on the basis of consequentialist reasoning.

This report stated that the use of contraceptives could protect the physical well-being of the mother, lower the infant mortality rate and, most important, strengthen family life (ROP 1936:326-27).[13] The commission claimed that the purpose of sexual intercourse included, but was not limited to, procreation: "There is no religious obligation to have intercourse only when no precaution is taken against resulting conception; but, on the contrary, marital intercourse brings its own contribution to Christian life when it is definitely divorced from the quest of parenthood" (326). The reason undergirding the decision to support the practice of birth control was not a recognition of women's moral agency but a desire to strengthen the family which was seen to be in serious danger. The primary purposes of sexual intercourse in marriage had come to be understood as procreation and the strengthening of the marriage. In the context of a destructive economic depression—"a time of difficulty and distress hitherto unknown in Canadian history"(ROP 1932:100)—the protection of the basic family unit assumed a new priority. By using all available resources to keep the family intact in this time of distress, the Church saw itself as protecting the survival and purity of the entire nation. As the Board of Evangelism and Social Service later noted, "As fares the family so fares the nation and her citizens overseas and at home" (ROP 1942:83).

The sources of Christian tradition and, most important, experience and social consequences, supported the ethical conclusion that contraception should be available to married couples. Theology and scripture were not used as explicit authoritative sources in the construction of this ethical argument (ROP 1936:326-29). As Angus McLaren and Arlene Tigar McLaren observed, the "protestant clergy's arguments in favour of birth control were always based more on social, economic, or eugenic preoccupations than on theological considerations. Birth control came to be but one more issue that would find a niche in the Social Gospel."[14]

Regardless of the ethical criteria used, the United Church had affirmed that sexual interaction purely for the purpose of pleasure and bonding could be virtuous and desirable if it served to strengthen the family and society. Generally, bodily pleasure has not been trusted as a moral good in classical Christian theology. As James B. Nelson reasons, "Long ago, when the two sexual dualisms (spirit over body, and man over woman) joined together, the antipleasure stage was set. 'If it feels good, it must be wrong.' Pleasure of all sorts seemed bodily, hence suspect."[15] Although this report did not advocate marital sexual intercourse for purely the purpose of erotic pleasure, it endorsed this pleasure as a means to the greater end of familial and national unity.

Sex outside marriage, however, was forbidden and was perceived to threaten the moral fabric of the entire nation. For this reason, the decision to support the availability of contraceptives also created serious concern: would this move serve to promote extramarital sex and therefore lead to national moral disaster? (See ROP 1936:328; ROP 1948:132, 362). Were women able to be sexually responsible without the fear of an unwanted pregnancy to control their behaviour? ROPs from the years following this decision supporting the use of contraceptives express serious concern over whether women could handle this new responsibility (ROP 1946:112-13, 132; ROP 1936:328). The authors of the 1936 report argued that the availability of contraception is not the real problem: "The prospect of immunity may indeed strengthen the lawless disposition; but the problem lies in the fostering of a disposition which is subject to moral law" (ROP 1936:328). As noted by the Board of Evangelism and Social Service, it was feared that the sale and availability of contraceptives augmented this threat to the nation's morality. In 1946 these concerns continued: although sex was celebrated as God-given between married men and women, it was believed to pose unlimited peril to all of society if not prohibited outside marriage (ROP 1946:132, 134). An increase in venereal disease—understood as a consequence of immorality—was cited as evidence of the sinful nature of sex outside marriage (see 379). The Board of Evangelism and Social Service noted the fear that the sale and availability of contraceptives increased this threat to the nation's morality:

> There are certain statistics that have a bearing on the moral situation in Canada and which present an unhealthy picture...divorce statistics have risen to 7,942—the highest in Canadian history. The sale of contraceptives and the sale of drugs have reached alarming proportions. Illegitimacy has been rising each year....Abortion is on the increase....(ROP 1948:362)

The subject of birth control generated discussions, reported in the ROPs, that indicated a distrust of women's moral agency and a desire to protect the sanctity of the family. As long as women "foster a disposition which is subject to moral law," order was perceived to be maintained and the basic unit of society, the family, strengthened (ROP 1936:328). The authors of the ROPs understood moral law as consistent with traditional gender roles and the acceptance of marriage as the only appropriate context for sexual intercourse. When women strayed from these dominant moral norms and, therefore, threatened the order and stability of a society predicated on the maintenance of the nuclear family, confusion resulted and preventative steps were sometimes taken.

Redemptive Homes

The United Church participated in the support and work of redemptive homes which functioned to rehabilitate girls and women who had deviated from accepted sexual morality. In an effort to preserve the family and therefore the country from moral decay, the United Church continued the "rescue and redemptive work" begun by the Methodist Church in 1910 (*ROP* 1925:125). Until 1935, when the number was reduced by one, there were eight redemptive homes supported and overseen by the United Church (*ROP* 1936:361). These redemptive homes were for young women and girls although the superintendents attempted to help misguided boys by referring them to other resources, such as The Farm Centre for boys (*ROP* 1938:307).

These homes were under the oversight of the Board of Evangelism and Social Service, and the direction of a superintendent who, in all cases, was an unmarried woman (e.g., *ROP* 1930:108-10). A report of the Board of Evangelism and Social Service described the nature of their work:

> In Toronto for several years we have employed a lady of special training, mature experience, good common sense and deep Christian sympathy, as a social worker. She…searches out young girls from the country who through lonesomeness and other causes have drifted into questionable company and often into wrongdoing, many of whom have been saved from moral disaster; finds new environments for young lads who have fallen into bad company, thus helping them to build better character; discovers little children, homeless, orphans, neglected for adoption into good Christian homes. (*ROP* 1925:127)

The reasons for deviation were often understood to stem from the faults of other women. For instance, single mothers, having violated sacred family and gender norms by not having a husband, were at high risk of being suspected of moral neglect. Moreover, most single working mothers were of a low economic class and were often immigrants; classism and racism compounded their plight. As Mariana Valverde writes regarding the Toronto Victor Home, a redemptive home primarily for unwed mothers: "The Home forced single mothers to stay for six months and their babies for one year….No rationale is given for the rule about babies, but it probably was designed to prevent what was known as moral neglect of children, the type of child abuse of which single mothers were automatically suspected." Moreover, as Valverde observed in the deaconesses' reports, there was a particularly vituperous attitude toward "working-class and immigrant mothers" stemming from the classist and racist assumption that these mothers were unable to provide adequate nurture for their children.[16] The belief was that besides indicating a general deterioration of the family, these morally neglectful mothers passed on their faults and produced sexually delinquent girls who could corrupt young men. The girls and women in these homes were referred to as "inmates" (ROP 1930:109) and the nature of most of their sins centred around sexual acts; their crime being deviation from the sexual moral code for females.

The motivation for the operation of redemptive homes was complicated; the purpose was not simply an overt attempt to maintain control and order. In most cases these young women had become pregnant and therefore had special needs. Although they were not judged favourably regarding their sexual conduct, they were given a place to live and to have their babies. Clearly, compassion and a desire to help these young women to get on the right path were the predominant concerns behind the functioning of the homes. The ethical difficulty lay in how one defined the right path. In this case, right meant that which was consistent with the dominant social norms.

In the redemptive homes no distinction was made among the so-called inmates between those violated and those who chose to engage in sexual intercourse: "The women were considered to be 'fallen' by virtue of the fact that they were in a Rescue Home....The practices of rescue work continued to treat all women in rescue homes as requiring conversion and reform, regardless of their guilt or innocence."[17] Any sexual involvement outside marriage, whether the women were victims or willing participants, was seen as a moral evil committed by the women involved.[18] The example of women and girls rescued and redirected on to the right moral path from prostitution, the white-slavery[19] trade or incest illustrates this point well. Valverde and historian Linda Gordon both point out that, although white-slavery rhetoric—particularly as promulgated via the church—condemned the willing prostitute and spoke protectively of the innocent victim of white slavery or, less frequently and vehemently, the victim of incest, all were considered guilty of sexual immorality and in need of redemption.

This threat to the nation's moral and spiritual well-being continued to be perceived into the 1960s. Further, the decreasing age and increasing number of girls admitted to redemptive homes was cited as further evidence of an ongoing and growing threat to Canada's morality (ROP 1958:411). Since morality was equated largely with sexuality and females were seen as the primary caretakers of the sexual moral code, it was through the redemption of deviant girls and young women that the entire country could be redeemed (ROP 1946:112-13).

The Marital Relationship and Marriage Breakdown

As the force of the social purity movement slowly faded, followed shortly by the decline of the centrality of the social gospel movement in Canadian society, the church gradually lost its position as the authority in the regulation of sexual behaviour. Increasingly, society had become defined by professional, expert voices. For many Canadians, the church was no longer the ultimate ethical authority.

In the 1960s, greater concern for the relational quality of sexual acts within marriage emerged. This was not a new value. For instance, the 1936 report *The Meaning and Responsibilities of Christian Marriage* stated that women have the right to not be exploited. However, the importance of relational concerns as compared to the rightness or wrongness of sexual acts began to shift. Concern shifted from promiscuity outside marriage to the quality of the marriage relationship itself. Ultimately, both were addressed to emphasize the importance of maintaining the family. However, the ethical values underlying this concern changed; earlier, the United Church had been concerned with the sinfulness of any sexual act outside of marriage, but the marital relationship itself was de facto good. Further, sexual intimacy within marriage, as indicated by the Church's stance on contraception, was considered a private matter between husband and wife. As a result, there was little scrutiny of the quality of sexual expression between husband and wife.

By the 1960s, this changed. Divorce became understood as necessary in some marital relationships if, for example, the relationship had reached a point where it was destructive to all family members as well as the neighbourhood. Further, the issue of mutual consent was raised in the 1960 report on "Christian Marriage and Family"—*Toward a Christian Understanding of Sex, Love, Marriage:* "Mutual consent is an important element of that sexual union that fulfills the intent of creation and satisfies the needs of both partners. Where consent is not mutual, the personal integrity of both partners is desecrated. Harm is done to both victim and violator" (ROP 1960:157).

This concern for mutual consent within the marital relationship is significant in that it indicated recognition that mutual consent was not automatic within marriage. Rather, this position recognized that marriage is an ongoing process in which there is potential for both growth and destructive behaviour. It is also important to note, however, that the harm experienced by both the "victim and violator" was not differentiated, and the report did not define this issue in relation to sexism. Indeed, at that time the United Church had yet to identify the relevance of systemic gender power imbalances (although the analysis and existence of systemic power imbalances was familiar to the United Church, there was as yet no awareness of sexism indicated in the ROPs). While the Church raised the issue of consent, the roles of husbands and wives were described in the same report and it was stated that within marriage "women are expected to accept men as lovers" (ROP 1960:174). Paradoxically, consent was important but the wife should not refuse her husband sexually.

The emphasis on the dangers of sex outside marriage and the goodness of marital sex had given way to a closer scrutiny of the quality of the marital sexual relationship. The recognition of consent indicated that the goodness of all sexually intimate acts within marriage was no longer assumed. Though it was the mere beginning of a dialectic between a growing recognition of the complexities of relationships and an ongoing desire to keep things as they had been, the quality of the relationship had become an important ethical concern.

Pornography

By the mid-1970s, concern was directed more toward the quality of the relationship than sexual acts. Illustrating this claim is the United Church's changing approach to pornography as an ethical issue. The United Church's 1977 General Council agreed that pornography was sinful not because it dealt with sex but because it was abusive and objectified people. Saskatchewan Conference, through a memorial, which is a request for action, to General Council, decried the tendency of advertising to reinforce sexual stereotyping. Furthermore, this memorial contended, advertising was particularly harmful to women, citing *The Feminine Mystique* by Betty Friedan as a source in support of this argument (ROP 1977:93-95). Two more memorials called violence and pornography in movies and television deplorable because they exerted an "unhealthy influence"; the criteria for "unhealthy," however, were not defined. A fourth such memorial, from Toronto Conference, offered two more detailed reasons for its concern: the increasingly violent nature of pornography including the "hatred and abuse of women and children," and the threat posed to the Christian marriage and family (112-13). The authors' reasons for thinking that Christian marriage and family were threatened by pornography are unclear, but one may suppose that the moral values assumed to underlie marriage and family were contrary to those assumed to underlie pornography. This fear had first appeared in the ROPs in the early 1940s, when the Board of Evangelism and Social Services expressed its concern regarding the moral "challenge" to the family and nation posed by "printed and photographic material and movies of the baser sort" (ROP 1942:312), whereas specific recognition of the abuse of women and children in pornography was quite new.

The United Church General Council approved the request of Toronto Conference for the establishment of a task force to investigate both theology and social research as they pertained to pornography.[20] The Council noted that pornography "involves exploitation, hatred and violence; the buying and selling of the human body; and the degradation and dehumanization of our bodies and persons" (ROP 1977:154). Although this comment is supportive of the concern raised by Toronto Conference, it, unlike the actual memorial, does not name pornography as a gender issue, shaped by sexism.

Pornography came to be defined primarily as an issue of violence connected to systemic oppression, particularly sexism. This change is related to a shift in the understanding of sin. Previously, when "indecent literature" or "pornography" was discussed, it was in the context of a primarily sexual act-centred morality; such literature was sinful because it depicted and encouraged unacceptable sexual behaviour. Reports to General Councils in the late 1970s and 1980s defined pornography as sinful on the basis that it is "degrading, abusive and/or violent" (ROP 1984:63) to the human person and to women and children in particular. Sin, in this context, came to be understood primarily in relational terms.

The 1980 General Council recommended, in response to a memorial from Alberta Conference (ROP 1980:756), that "in any further work on the issue of human sexuality, that sexploitation (sex and violence) be a matter of serious concern for both the Division of Mission in Canada (DMC), and the Division of Communication" (ROP 1980:964). The Alberta Conference memorial defined pornography as an issue of sex and violence but it was considered to fall primarily under the rubrick of human sexuality. At the same Council, the Division of Communication submitted a study paper that critiqued contemporary advertising as often degrading to all people and particularly to women by "treating...[them] as sex objects and nothing more" (ROP 1980:106-7).

In 1983, in response to grassroots concerns such as those named above, the Division of Mission in Canada established the Task Force on Pornography. The task force produced a report and an educational kit on pornography. General Council (1984) received and supported the report, endorsed the recommendations and requested widespread distribution of the kit. The task force report, which forms the core of the study kit, was foundational for two reasons: it defined pornography in *relation to sexism,* and as *violence not sex.*

The authors of the report defined the purpose of sexuality as an "expression of love and a form of intimate communication between equal human beings"(ROP 1984:311). This expanded the traditional United Church understanding of sexuality: it implied that sexuality is more than intercourse and the purpose of sexual expression is more than for procreation and strengthening the family. Pornography "negates" these purposes and "is about injustice toward women and children" (311).[21] The main criteria that the task force relied on to formulate this ethical position were their interpretations of the teachings of Jesus and of human experience, particularly women's experiences of suffering.

The authors stated that pornography was becoming increasingly violent and that this increase was both a cause and a reflection of a general increase in male violence against women (ROP 1984:311-15). They also said that the perpetrator of violence was almost without exception male, and the victim was almost always a woman or child (313). Building on these claims, the authors suggested that the central ethical question was this: "Is the right of male gratification more important than the rights of women and children?" (314). The authors asserted that all people, and in this case particularly women and children, have the right to "walk the streets unafraid" (314) and to not be abused or objectified. Moreover, when this right was weighed against the right of some men to sexual gratification, it was the consequentialist claim that pornography contributes to male violence against women which tipped the balance in favour of women's right to safety. Although men may have the right to sexual gratification, the authors reasoned that when this right was expressed forcefully, it was no longer valid since it infringed on the right of women and children to safety. Principles alone were not sufficient to make ethical decisions in this case.

The task force queried why there was such a large market for pornography. They reasoned that since we live in a society defined by hierarchical dualistic thought in which maleness is seen as normative, gender stereotypes are perpetuated. These stereotypes prescribe certain roles for both men and women that lend themselves to the violence of pornography:

> Society encourages men to express anger and aggression through sexual violence. Pornography sets up women as scapegoats for male anger with its obsession with rape, bondage, snuff films, mutilation, dissection of female anatomy; its fascination with humiliating, conquering, penetrating, sodomizing and objectifying women....Pornography lies about men in that it says they can only be violent, angry and hateful. Pornography also promotes the lie that women get sexual pleasure from pain. (ROP 1984:315)

The task force posited that stereotyping was the primary cause of male sexual violence against women. Control and power, as issues that underlie stereotyping, were not directly addressed. The *Pornography Kit* became one of the first resources available that examined pornography in a theological context, and the task force disbanded after the kit was produced. DMC established an ad-hoc committee on pornography to continue work in this area.

In subsequent years, the General Council continued to receive and respond to memorials regarding pornography[22] and related concerns such as nude female "entertainment" (for example, ROP 1986:683-84; ROP 1988:114, 731). A concern with sexual acts continued to influence and shape the approach to ethical issues of many of these memorials. At the 31st General Council it was recorded that the DMC "plans to continue its anti-pornography work, which is seen as part of an overall opposition to violence against women" (ROP 1986:533).

The 25th General Council (1972) affirmed the need for further study and education concerning human sexuality and mandated the Executive of General Council to appoint a committee to explore this issue (ROP 1972:70). Also indicative of the shift toward a primarily relational ethic of human sexuality was the recognition that human sexuality was to be understood as "interpersonal rather than merely technological or physiological" (70, 164-73).[23] This paradigmatic shift from a primarily act-oriented ethic to a primarily relational ethic precipitated celebration, resistance and confusion throughout the 1980s.

Abortion

After receiving memorials concerning abortion, particularly in the latter part of the 1960s, the Joint Committee on Abortion was established (*ROP* 1966:88-89; *ROP* 1968:104). In 1971, the DMC Joint Committee, comprised of members of the Board of Evangelism and Social Service and the Board of Women, submitted a report to General Council. The United Church's General Council accepted this report and its recommendations with one amendment (*ROP* 1971:68-69) indicated below by italics, which are mine; Section 1(a) and (b) of the accepted report stated that the General Council recognized the complexity of ethical issues surrounding the abortion question and claimed that sometimes abortion was justifiable:

> I (a)...1. The value of the foetus; 2. The right of the child to be wanted; but nevertheless affirm that abortion is morally justifiable in certain medical, social and economic circumstances. [and] (b)...that an abortion should be a private matter between a woman and her doctor, *without prejudice to the need for consulting her male partner, where possible.* (*ROP* 1971:160)

It was not considered necessary that the woman consult with her male partner but was preferred when possible.

The authors of this report used ethical reasoning similar to that of the 1936 contraception position in that they were concerned with "medical, social and economic circumstances." Consequentialist ethical reasoning remained most important. Also similar to the 1936 position was the conclusion that abortion was a matter of "personal conscience." The 1971 report assumed women's responsible moral agency—"We question the right of any committee to intervene between a woman's careful decision and her right to act accordingly" (*ROP* 1971:157)—and clearly claimed women's well-being as an important criterion when considering abortion.

A DMC report received by General Council one year later (*A Statement on Birth Control and Abortion*) clarified the authors' concern regarding the use of therapeutic abortion committees. The report noted that almost three years had elapsed since the Criminal Code had been changed to allow for the sale and use of contraceptives as well as for the implementation of the therapeutic abortion committee system. "It is now possible to see four distinct trends in Canadian abortion practice." The trends cited were: a "rapid rise in the number of legal abortions," a "decrease in the number of hospital admissions for incomplete or septic induced abortions," "unnecessary late termination," and "profit making" on abortions by physicians (*ROP* 1972:164, 165). Because women who wanted an abortion would probably get one whether or not it was done by a competent physician, and because therapeutic abortion committees served both to slow the process to the point where the fetus had become much further developed and often to limit access to abortions to those women with more power or money, the authors concluded that the law was unjust and unworkable (168).

The issue of abortion had become defined as a justice issue concerned primarily with equal access to abortion for all women. The main difference between the 1936 argument for the use and availability of contraceptives and this one regarding the accessibility of abortion, is that the consequences in 1936 were defined more in terms of the preservation of the family whereas those cited regarding abortion were defined more in terms of women's well-being.

In 1972, the United Church's General Council received *A Statement on Birth Control and Abortion*, which affirmed the position of the 1971 report. Later, at the 26th General Council (1974), the General Council Executive appointed a commission to study and review the United Church's position regarding abortion. This commission consisted of two women and three men. (One must wonder why a group addressing an issue so clearly related to women did not consist of at least as many women as men.)

General Council approved the commission's report in 1980. The report, *Contraception and Abortion*, again defined the issue primarily as one of equal access: there are many unwanted pregnancies in society, and the committee system was "unjust in principle and unworkable in practice" since it prevented equal access to abortion for all women. The authors argued that in order for abortion to be more accessible, it "should be a personal matter between a woman and her doctor...permitting the woman to bring to bear her moral and religious insights into human life in reaching a decision through a free and responsive exercise of her conscience."[24] The ethical claims underlying this statement were first, that no woman should be coerced into enduring an unwanted pregnancy, and second, that while the decisions reached by every woman will not be equally responsible, this must not prevent equal access to safe abortions for all women.

Difficulty with this position concerns not only the physician's role but also the Church's role. In order for a woman to make her own decision as an autonomous and relational agent, the physician must help her clarify which factors are morally relevant and to weigh them. One cannot ensure that physicians function in this way rather than asserting their own agendas, any more than one can claim that all women will make equally "responsible" decisions, whatever that means.[25] Further, by defining abortion as primarily a matter of "personal conscience," the Church gave women what might be perceived as grudging permission to choose abortion but, at the same time, refused an official role in this decision making.

The 1980 United Church report claimed that abortion may be justified as the "lesser of two evils."[26] The ending of human life was defined, theologically, as an evil. However, it was also claimed that people have the right to well-being. If a continued pregnancy would harm a woman's well-being, then abortion may be justified as a lesser evil. Hence, the harming of a woman's well-being is an evil. Abortion, too, is defined as an evil, albeit a lesser evil.

The United Church requested that the federal government remove abortion during the first twenty weeks of a pregnancy from the Criminal Code on the basis of these 1980 ethical arguments. The Church recognized women's abilities to act as responsible moral agents; women should have the right to choose in consultation with a physician. This report was a significant step toward an adequate feminist ethic of abortion, since it recognized women's moral agency *and* systemic barriers to equal access.

The United Church had decided to support the availability and use of contraceptives in 1936. By 1971, the Church's policy regarding abortion supported the availability of abortion to women, in consultation with a physician. Through the 1970s that position was extended to respect women more clearly as responsible moral agents while recognizing the claim that the well-being of women must in this issue be regarded as a significant moral good. Further, by 1980, systemic oppressions were recognized as relevant factors that unjustly prevented equal access to abortion.

A significant shift had occurred in the ethical reasoning that undergirds the conclusions that contraception and, subsequently, abortion should be available to all women. In 1936, the main concern was the preservation and well-being of the family. By 1980, the family was no longer perceived to be de facto good and there was no longer only one understanding of the appropriate constitution of a family and gender roles, as will be seen in the next chapter. This emerging critique of the family, coupled with a changing approach to human sexuality, resulted in a growing recognition of women's autonomy and well-being as norms necessary to Christian reproductive ethics. The family continued to be valued, but that women's well-being sometimes conflicted with the assumption of the family as automatically salvific had become clearer. This increased clarity necessitated ethical choices. Regarding abortion, the United Church, at an official level, chose to value women's well-being and capacity to function as responsible moral agents over the value of producing more children at any cost. In the 1930s, regarding contraception, the United Church had chosen to value the unity and well-being of the family over unlimited procreation. These choices and the identification of relevant values, of course, hinged on the ways in which the issues were defined.

Concluding Remarks

The United Church of Canada has traditionally valued the well-being of community. The struggle to value community while at the same time recognizing that some communal voices have not been heard or valued to the same degree as others has made change considered and slow. The meaning of community, reflected in the ROPs, has changed over the years. During the Depression, the second world war and its aftermath, the preservation of the nuclear family represented hope in what must have seemed, at times, an otherwise hopeless world. At the same time, the United Church has always expressed a commitment to the well-being of individuals including women. As women began to challenge more loudly the perception that women were either pure—married mothers and committed first to their families—or fallen and in need of redemption, and as general awareness of the sometimes harmful consequences of certain theologies and ethical stances related to human sexuality issues continued to unfold, the *ROPs* reflected responsive change. These changes in ethical reasoning did not consistently issue forth in a different position. For instance, the United Church has always judged pornography as a moral evil but the reasons for this judgment have shifted. By the 1970s pornography came to be seen as wrong because of its harmful consequences to women and children, not primarily due to the earlier reasons.

The United Church has struggled with women's agency. There was great suspicion and distrust of women's abilities to remain in monogamous marital relationships after the approval of the use of contraceptives. Typically, women were both perceived as responsible for and having control over sexuality and distrusted in that role. The mission of the redemptive homes illustrate this point.

In the 1960s, concern shifted from the dangers of sex outside marriage to the relational quality of sex within marriage. Although this was always important to the Church insofar as the sexual relationship between husband and wife affected the family and therefore the nation, prior to the 1960s the quality of the marital sexual relationship was not often questioned. Issues such as consent and the necessity of divorce began to be raised in the early 1960s; the well-being of individual family members began to assume more importance as an ethical criterion for the assessment of marital relationships; and it was becoming apparent that the family could not be assumed to be a good or healthy community if one or more members suffered because of other family members.

By the late 1970s pornography was considered sinful primarily for relational reasons: it objectified women, violated their personhood and damaged the quality of relationship between men and women. Also indicative of an increasing regard for women's agency as embodied subjects was the United Church's 1980 stance on abortion; the well-being of all women, as experienced and defined by the women directly and immediately affected, constituted the most important criterion.

The United Church's gradual change from a primarily act-centred sexual ethic to a primarily relational sexual ethic has been tied to the perception of women's status as moral agents and to the relationship between sin and human sexuality. As women's subjectivity and agency became more trusted and respected, there was not the same need to control sexuality. As feminist theologian Carter Heyward points out, "understanding sexuality historically involves making connections between the social control of sexuality and the social control of women."[27] Earlier, certain sexual acts, particularly all those outside marriage, had been understood as sinful in and of themselves. Eventually, the quality of the relationship came to be understood as a more relevant factor for assessing the acceptability or value of sexual acts.

CHAPTER III

The Development of The United Church of Canada's Approach to Women's Roles and the Family

Definition of Family and Gender Roles

*T*HROUGHOUT THE GREATER PART of United Church history, women were expected to follow the vocations of wife and mother and to devote themselves to the care and nurture of their husbands and, particularly, their children. The preservation of this family unit was a prevailing concern for the United Church throughout the 1930s, 1940s and 1950s. Moreover, there was an eschatological component to this concern: the preservation of the family was seen as essential to the coming Kingdom of God (*ROP* 1940:89).

The 1932 report *The Meaning and Responsibilities of Christian Marriage,* contended that the "primary function of marriage…was the rearing of children and the protection of the mother during the period of infancy" (*ROP* 1932:277). The bearing and rearing of children by women were considered the best examples of the then-lauded virtue of sacrificial love: "The Church believes that the highest values can never be attained in the pursuit of selfish ease and pleasure at the cost of a childless home" (279).

This 1932 report defined the Christian family as consisting of two parents—a woman and a man—and their children. The wife, as stated above, was expected to be the domestic caregiver while the husband was to provide economically for the family. This normative definition placed the traditional family beyond scrutiny. It was not so much that the maintenance of the nuclear family unit was valued above the well-being of individual family members, but that the very question of the well-being of individual family members, within an intact nuclear family, was posed rarely.

Ideally, within these prescribed gender roles there was mutual care and love between family members (*ROP* 1932:280). The authors of the report were so convinced of the value of this mutuality that they claimed that a severe breach of this norm meant the end of a marriage: "We cannot think that Jesus, with His affirmations of the worth of every person, would sanction the subjection of a wife to a loveless, cruel husband, or vice versa" (284). This understanding of the nature of the Christian family as a heterosexual married couple committed to procreation and mutuality within traditional gender roles was repeated in the 1946 report submitted by the Commission on Christian Marriage and the Christian Home (*ROP* 1946:118) and in the 1960 report by the Commission on Christian Marriage and Divorce (*ROP* 1960:174).

From the time of the United Church's formation, the ROPs indicate that it supported, in principle, women's well-being. For instance, the 1932 report on *The Meaning and Responsibilities of Christian Marriage* asserted the mutuality required in Christian marriage: "Marriage has created a situation in which unique privileges are constituted and recognized….The exercise of these privileges calls for constant mutual considerateness; and the Christian husband will readily repudiate every assertion of claim resting on a tradition of proprietary rights in his wife" (*ROP* 1932:280).

The report further acknowledged that women have the right not to be exploited "either within or outside marriage." It also recorded appreciation for the changing status of women: "The Church would view with the most serious misgiving any practices which menace the slowly acquired gain of centuries in enhanced respect for womanhood, especially in the emancipation of womanhood either within or outside marriage" (*ROP* 1932:282).

On the other hand, there was a tension in that respect, for the "emancipation of womanhood" was supported as long as this emancipation did not threaten to disrupt the basic social order, in particular, the order of the family.[1]

Women and Ordination

The United Church made two significant moves in the 1930s that could be interpreted as responses to a growing recognition of women's agency: the admission of women to ordained ministry (*ROP* 1936:224) and the approval of the use of contraceptives (*ROP* 1932:279-81). The motivations behind these moves, however, are debatable. Lydia Gruchy was the first woman to be ordained in the United Church, in 1936. Notably, at Gruchy's ordination service, a speaker attributed her ordination to the efforts of a man: "We have come tonight to mark a step in our church's history—a development which we owe, not to the intransigent demand and agitation of women, but in the first instance, perhaps to our revered and affectionately esteemed Dr E.H. Oliver. His knightly and chivalrous attitude and advocacy have finally prevailed."[2] Women's voices were not yet attributed much publicly recognized power.

The restrictions and blocks placed on potential women candidates made it far more difficult for women to become ordained and settled than for men (*ROP* 1936:224). These restrictions were in accordance with traditional gender role expectations: women who were raising children or who were married (or planning to be married) and were of child-bearing age or could not pass a test that showed their "emotional stability" (*ROP* 1948:123-25) were considered ineligible for ordination.[3] Indeed, there was little recognition that women could be ordained, apart from highly exceptional cases.[4] While a report made to the 1948 General Council recommended that "the ministry continue to be open to women," the authors of the report also declared that a woman cannot be ordained if "at the time of her final examination before Presbytery, [she] is unable or unwilling to give herself wholly to the work of the ministry." Accordingly, a woman could not continue to function as an ordained minister if she "becomes a mother" (*ROP* 1948:123ff).

In the 1950s ordained women were expected to pursue different ministries from ordained men. Specifically, they were to focus on children and youth, as this was consistent with women's roles (*ROP* 1954:174). When the roles of women as wife, mother and self-sacrificing caregiver began to be challenged, confusion, fear and struggle resulted. The "new freedoms" women were gaining were to be celebrated, but at the same time were viewed with suspicion—particularly concerning how they would affect the family.

Women's Church Groups

The importance of women to the United Church is evidenced by the concern recorded by the 1928 General Council regarding women workers. This council authorized the formation of the "Inter-Board Committee of Women Workers" in order to "recruit most effectively the number and quality of women workers needed by The United Church in all its departments; and to relate each qualified candidate to that type of work in which she can make her greatest contribution." Furthermore, in 1930 the Women's Missionary Society (WMS) proudly observed that "when more than half a century ago the work for women and children in many lands was delegated to the women of the church, even the most optimistic prophet could scarcely have foreseen the magnitude to which it has attained" (*ROP* 1930:209-10). Clearly, women made a recognized contribution to the life of the Church.

The Depression of the 1930s witnessed an even greater involvement of women in the churches' social service work: "Women are the nervous system of the church; through them all the messages of human pain and joy circulate. And until the establishment of social service agencies, women's organizations were the nervous system of their communities."[5] Churchwomen organized soup lines, and provided necessities such as clothing and fuel for those without.[6] Many United Church women devoted a great deal of their energy responding to this crisis; however, it was the men and children who received the greatest sympathy in the *ROP*s. As the Board of Evangelism and Social Service noted:

> The evils of prolonged unemployment [are numerous]....Children have been made to pay the cost out of their under-nourished bodies and hungry hearts. They were under-fed, were often sent to school hungry, poorly and scantily

clad…[and men] out of work become hard and irritable. Failure, disappointment and the feeling of helplessness make men bitter and moody. (*ROP*
1934:101-102)

This focus on men and children was related to the understanding of appropriate gender roles; the violence of men during the Depression was to some
degree understood and accepted, whereas women were responsible for maintaining a happy family. Men were often left jobless and hence unable to
fulfill their prescribed gender role, whereas women, it was thought, could
always provide care. Furthermore, men authored the great bulk of the ROPs
and, of course, tended to write from their own experience and the accepted
norms of the day.

This separation of the public and private spheres was reinforced by leading contemporary theologians such as Reinhold Niebuhr. Niebuhr wrote
that "sacrificial love is a moral norm relevant to interpersonal relationships
(particularly family relations), and significant for parents (particularly *mothers,* heroes and saints), but scarcely applicable to power relations."[7] Niebuhr's
insistence that the private domain was the only place where sacrificial love
could be more than an "impossible possibility," coupled with his equation
of women and motherhood with the private sphere, reflected and reinforced
the belief that women were responsible for providing love and nurturing where
it might not otherwise exist.

The Dominion Council Woman's Association (WA) was formed on Novem-
ber 19, 1940, with the purpose of advancing the "homebuilding of The
United Church of Canada," by serving as helpers to the (largely male) clergy.[8]
The formation of the WA was greeted with great support from clergy and
other members of the General Council. The Moderator's response to the first
WA report in 1940 included the following words of praise:

> We rejoice in the splendid and sacrificial work of the women of the Domin-
> ion, represented through this organization of our church. Every minister's work
> is sustained and strengthened by the educational, spiritual and especially
> social maintenance of the church life by the local association. Today, they not
> only continue these phases of our work, but have taken on the enormous
> burden of knitting and sewing for war purposes. (*ROP* 1940:380)

On the other hand, the Women's Missionary Society (WMS) indicated
that they were receiving insufficient support.[9] The WA may have received
more support than the WMS for the following reasons. First, the Church
was under serious financial constraints, as was the rest of the country. The
WA devoted itself not only to raising money, but also to giving this money
to the Church. By contrast, the WMS raised most of its own money but also
spent money and asked for financial support from the greater Church. Thus,
while the WA supported the needs of the clergy and the rest of the United
Church, the WMS was a relatively autonomous organization that required
money from the wider Church.

Secondly, as Shelagh Parsons observed, the "organizations reflected two different understandings of women's role in both church and society: the one independent and aggressive in world mission, the other serving, sacrificing and passive on the homefront."[10] The WA conformed more closely to traditional gender role expectations than did the WMS in a time when there were looming threats to the traditional family unit.[11] Largely due to the war, many women had joined the workforce to support their families, and there was a fear that many of these women might not leave their paid positions and return to care properly for their families:

> The Home Mission leaders of our Church everywhere are concerned about what is happening to the womanhood and childhood of our land. Labour shortages, patriotic appeals and the lure of high wages have brought the number of women employed in industry up to probably the highest level at any time in our country's history…and social agencies have been concerned about the breakdown of the home. (ROP 1944:307-308)

There was great concern that the evils of the public realm were threatening the sanctity of the private realm, including both the home and the church.

The home was understood as the place of the de facto good family; to criticize or threaten to change the traditional family, including its gender roles, was tantamount to threatening the nation and the "coming Kingdom of God" (ROP 1940:89). The inviolability of the family made the existence of abuse unthinkable, and therefore silenced much suffering. Through the purity of the family, God would come again. The assumed basic structure of the family had yet to be questioned.

In response to a request from representatives of United Church women's groups to study the "relationship of women's organizations to one another and to the church as a whole" (ROP 1954:213), the 1954 General Council established a committee to study the organizations. The 1956 General Council received a report from this committee and recommended that the two women's organizations be merged into one, to foster unity among the Church women themselves but also within the Church as a whole (ROP 1956:177-78).

The WA and WMS, after long and involved negotiations, joined in 1960 to form the United Church Women (UCW).[12] This new organization came under the direct control of the General Council; changes to the constitution of the UCW could be made only by the General Council (ROP 1962:227). Structurally, the new unified women's organization was not autonomous but directly accountable to the male-dominated General Council. The Council, then, was to more closely define the role of women in the United Church.

"New Freedoms"

A further example of this tension between the recognition of women's autonomy and the desire to maintain traditional gender roles can be seen in
reports regarding marriage and family. A 1946 report by the Commission
on Christian Marriage and the Christian Home arose out of concern for the
purity and preservation of the Christian family: "It is against such a background and in the light of the growth of illegitimacy, desertion, legal separations, social diseases, mixed marriages and divorces, that the Church must
plan her campaign to exalt the standards of 'The Christian Home and Christian Marriage'" (ROP 1946:114).

ROPs, previous to the submission of this report, had highlighted this
growing fear for the well-being of the Christian family. For instance, in
1944 and 1946 it was pointed out that the number of "broken homes" due
to divorce had increased drastically in recent years. Of the nine identified
causes of this looming threat, three were gender specific and identified the
changing role of women as the central factor: "The admission of the right
of women to petition for divorce since 1924, and the new sense of freedom
among women…[the] increase in the number of wage earning women
[and]….Drink among women has increased" (ROP 1944:277). Also, tradition and scripture were understood to support a clear stance against divorce
in the 1946 report (ROP 1946:126). Regarding the increase in the divorce rate,
the authors of the report surmised that "if this trend is unchecked it can
destroy the basis upon which our national life is founded" (125). This concern with divorce was also manifested in a section of this 1946 report which
addressed the difficulties involved in the case of a minister asked to remarry
a divorced person. This report allowed that a minister did not have to
remarry someone if (s)he did not believe that it was morally right. In 1948,
a response to "On Christian Marriage and Christian Home"affirmed the 1946
recommendations regarding the remarriage of a divorced person (ROP
1948:128-29). Although "church people" needed to demonstrate "forgiv-
ing sympathy" to those who fall short and divorce, divorce was to be considered only in extreme circumstances: "The Church must teach her children
that marriage which is instituted of God, blessed by Jesus Christ, and to be
held in honour among all men, must not be lightly and unadvisedly dis-
solved, but rather that every means of reconciliation be employed for the
salvation of the home" (ROP 1946:147). The report called on the church,
home, school and community (142-44) to take an active role in the protection and preservation of the Christian home. The traditional, defacto
good, family unit continued to be glorified as necessary to salvation.

The 1946 report of the Commission on Christian Marriage and the Christian Home addressed a perceived threat to the very fabric of the nation and
to Christianity. The issue was defined as a need to save the nation through
the most basic and essential unit of society: the Christian home. The question was how. The "Christian Home" was defined as:

(a) Two parents who are genuinely interested in the happiness and welfare of all members of the family....

(b) It is a home which provides for its members a feeling of emotional security....

(c) It is a place where all members, including the children, can feel that their friends are welcomed and can have a good time.

(d) In this home personality is the basis of values. Human personality is more important than possessions....

(e) This home provides a planned scheme of discipline [not arbitrary but consistent]....

(f) The Christian home has a set of values which creates the tone of the family life. (ROP 1946:118)

The Christian home was ideally a place where a man and a woman were united by the vows of a Christian marriage, worked together, loved mutually (ROP 1946:108) and produced children who also were treated with love and respect. Although women were considered the emotional caretakers of their families, they too could expect emotional support and nurturing from their husbands (108, 110-13). However, the report also implied that women were expected to set the families' moral standard, which was understood primarily in sexual terms, including the preservation of the chaste, monogamous nature of the marital relationship (see, for example, ROP 1946:112-13 as quoted below).

Although the Church recognized that women were gaining new rights, and that this was to be lauded, there was clearly some unease regarding both the ability of women to handle these new freedoms and the possible implications of this change for traditional moral standards. Another such example found in this 1946 report of the Commission on Christian Marriage and the Christian Home is concern registered about the increase in childless homes; women's right to have some control over their reproductive abilities was recognized even while this right was also seen as problematic:

> The Church's approach to this problem will need to be broadly based and comprehensive: it will be required to consider the individual, as well as the need to continue the life process; a sense of trusteeship of the heritage that the individual owes to the past and the future; and an appreciation for the conquest that womanhood has won concerning the rights of her own body. (ROP 1946:119)

The same report, under the subheading of "The Emancipation of Women," expressed the fear that women would "sink" to the male moral standard:

> Women have won a fairly general acceptance of the single standard of sexual morality, i.e., the realization of the fact that with the understanding of the art of controlling natality, unchastity is as pardonable in the case of the woman as in that of the man. Thus, the single standard achieved is not the high standard of Christian tradition but the low standard of too many males. (ROP 1946:112-13)

Women were placed on a moral pedestal but were also perceived as easily influenced and led astray. Women, pure though they are, were associated with a gullible innocence that had to be protected by male designed, external rules. Apparently, men did not have this same purity but neither did they have the same gullibility; they were, rather, wise to the ways of the world. Order helped to maintain virtue provided by innocent women and, so, provided conditions necessary to communal salvation.

Women were the moral guardians of the family and, hence, the nation (ROP 1942:83). As the Board of Evangelism and Social Service wrote, "As fares the family so fares the nation and her citizens overseas and at home." During wartime it became particularly important to maintain some sense of order and stability (ROP 1944:108). The desire to preserve gender roles resulted in a struggle between honouring women's autonomy and controlling it in order to preserve traditional Christian standards.

The increasing availability of paid employment for women, particularly through the 1940s and 1950s, due to World War II, was another factor that disrupted the traditional role of women. Reports regarding the redemptive homes, for instance, indicated great concern regarding the increase in the number of working single mothers: "The fact that unmarried mothers can quickly find work, has resulted in their stay in our redemptive homes being made all too short, with the result that not a few newly born babies do not receive the love and attention that they should have from their own mothers" (ROP 1944:269).

A mother was to devote her time and attention to her children. Single working mothers were breaking their prescribed gender role in two ways: they were unmarried and they were employed outside the home. These women were not fulfilling their roles as full-time family caregivers;[13] the "mother is the manager of family life....She brings up the children, deals with the neighbours, the school, and other family matters. The father is the wage-earner" (ROP 1950:33). General Council reiterated this claim in 1954 when it declared that family life depended "upon the spiritual resources of the parents and particularly of the mother" and that "there is no substitute for a mother's care for young children" (ROP 1954:232).

An official challenge to this claim came in 1962 when the Commission on the Gainful Employment of Married Women concluded that families do not "suffer when mothers work" (ROP 1962:277). The commission's report claimed that scripture strongly supports the "emancipation of women from any social and religious forms and customs that deny or prejudice her essential dignity as a free and responsible being" (ROP 1962:262). This recognition was not new in the United Church. Once again, women's autonomy was supported insofar as it did not threaten traditional family stability and order.

A further relevant change in the 1960s was the recognition in the ROPs that mutual consent was a necessary part of "sexual union" within marriage (ROP 1960:157). The goodness of sexual union within marriage was no longer assumed. The ROPs continue to value the well-being of community, families and individual women. The shift that was beginning was not the rejection of any of these values but was, rather, the increasing awareness that the marital relationship was not defacto good.

At the same General Council that received this report, the Commission on Ordination stated that "we wish to acknowledge the changed status of women in the modern world" (ROP 1962:393). However, this statement was the preface to recommendations that would continue to limit the women who were eligible for ordination. Women were still considered to be the guardians of their home, children and marriage; therefore, while they were married, ordination was not an option (393-96).[14] However, if a woman married after she was ordained and desired to continue to function as an ordained person with a pastoral charge, there was no official policy to prevent her from doing so. It was not until the next General Council meeting in 1964 that married women became officially eligible for ordination.

This tension between the recognition of the need for women's increased independence and the desire to maintain the status quo continued to shape reports and debates of General Council. On an official level, the United Church struggled with the recognition that the changing role of women *within* the church was to some degree both necessary and desirable.

In 1956, the concern for the preservation of the family was evident in a General Council resolution that a planned booklet regarding the remarriage of divorced persons: "clearly outlin[e] the sacredness of the marriage vows, the sinfulness of the failure to keep the marriage contract, the forgiveness of God for those who acknowledge their sin with humility and repentance, and the strength and guidance of God available for those who would make a new beginning in life" (ROP 1956:90).

Regardless of the reasons for the end of the marriage, divorce was sinful, but with repentance one could remarry. There was a renewed emphasis on the mission of the United Church to help failing marriages work, and thereby to decrease the number of "broken homes."[15] It was assumed that the well-being of all family members was best served by preserving the family unit itself—it was not often recognized that the family itself could be more abusive than salvific.

Also indicative of this desire to preserve the supposedly traditional Christian family was a continued insistence on at least some aspects of traditional gender roles. For instance, the 1960 report of the Commission on Christian Marriage and Divorce, *Toward a Christian Understanding of Sex, Love, Marriage,* "set forth a Christian understanding of sex, love, marriage and family responsibilities" (ROP 1962:135). This understanding reaffirmed traditional gender roles within the marital relationship: "Men are expected to play the roles of lover, husband, and father. Women are expected to accept men as lovers, to be their wives, to conceive, bear, feed, and cherish their [husbands'] children" (ROP 1960:174). Men's roles were active and implied ownership whereas women's roles were passive, receptive and nurturing.

The commission's second report, published under the title *Marriage Breakdown, Divorce, Remarriage: A Christian Understanding*, expanded on the causes of marital discord, including the threat posed by the changing role of women. Authority in the household no longer automatically rested with the husband but was often shared: "This increases the possibilities of tension and conflict....[On the other hand, it] also increases the opportunity and necessity for mutual understanding and co-operation" (ROP 1962:137). This shift was recognized as a source of marital difficulties but it was also understood to hold possibilities for renewed relationship.

The authors of this report maintained that it was sometimes necessary for a marriage to end in divorce.[16] The main reason cited was personal safety: "A woman who has separated from her husband because of cruelty, drunkenness or mental instability may not have adequate protection under the law so long as she is married to him" (ROP 1962:142). The gendered terms of this example may indicate that there was some recognition that most women have greater cause to fear physical violence at the hands of their spouses than do most men. However, reconciliation continued to be valued highly. A divorced person must be repentant and must understand the meaning of marriage as the "intended...life-long and complete union of a husband and wife for their mutual partnership, for the procreation of children, and for the fulfilment of parental responsibility" (160) in order to be remarried in the United Church. Thus, there emerged a more pronounced tension between the recognition that some marriages are damaging and potentially dangerous on the one hand, and the desire to preserve marriage and the traditional family on the other. The needs of family members were beginning to challenge the absolute priority of the preservation of the traditional family.

In 1974, General Council approved a report submitted by the Committee on Theology and Faith that affirmed the "Permanence of Christian Marriage" (ROP 1974:284). This report stressed that couples must enter the marriage relationship with the intention of permanence while recognizing that in spite of all intentions there can arise reasons that necessitate separation or divorce (284). This report arose at least partially in response to the sexually permissive 1960s and countered the suggestion that a marriage could be "*intentionally* temporary."[17] Any couple who was not clear that they fully intended their relationship to be permanent was not to be married by United Church clergy.

Concluding Remarks

Since its formation, The United Church of Canada has struggled with the changing roles of women and a changing understanding of the family. The tension between the recognition of women as autonomous moral agents and the desire to maintain traditional order, and therefore traditional gender roles, is a theme throughout United Church history. Similarly, the tension between the desire to preserve the sacredness of the traditional patriarchal "Christian family" and the growing recognition that within this sacred domain, destructive and even life-threatening behaviour can lurk, gradually increased over the years.

Similar to wider societal trends, throughout the 1930s, 1940s and 1950s, The United Church of Canada focused on the preservation of the traditional family. In the economically depressed 1930s, there was concern that mothers not physically neglect the family. Later, during the second world war, the concern shifted to emotional neglect; women were castigated when they began to seek employment in the public sector and consequently devoted less time to the care of the family. When "family breakdown" was on the rise, much of the responsibility for this threat to national well-being was directed at women and their new freedoms. However, simultaneous with this outcry against women's "increasing freedoms" was a growing recognition that enforced, restrictive gender roles did not nurture women's growth as autonomous subjects. The normative nature of roles combined with an uncritical approach to the family and its internal power distribution, had served to reinforce male dominance and to silence women's suffering.

The work of discerning the meaning of women's autonomy in the context of the overall communal good was challenging. As women more overtly questioned their traditional gender roles, the ROPs indicated increasing confusion or ambivalence regarding the meaning and implications of the Church's commitments to the well-being of community, family and women. The increasing regard for women's autonomy had a very different face than the contemporary notion of autonomy that has become conflated with extreme individualism. Rather, women's autonomy became valued as it intersected with community; upheld was a relational autonomy that valued the subjectivity of all community members and recognized that sometimes these values were competing or conflicting and so must be weighed. Such an approach was understood to be congruent with Christian faith and the social justice that has been understood by the United Church to be mandated by this faith. Also, as more women, post-World War II, decided to remain working outside the home, the ROPs indicated a struggle to discern what if any communal moral good there was in such a change. Later, it became clearer, in the 1960s, that aspects of the wider community were damaged by couples remaining in an abusive marriage, resulting in a shift to the Church's stand on divorce.

As the nuclear family and traditional gender roles were critiqued, and as women protested through voice and action, change unfolded. The 1970s would bring a growing awareness of systemic sexism, as identified by newly formed and mandated United Church committees.

CHAPTER IV

Case Study:
In God's Image...Male and Female

I N AUGUST 1980, amid much controversy, the Task Force on Human Sexuality submitted *In God's Image...Male and Female* to General Council, where it was approved as a study document. This document and the subsequent report on human sexuality, *Gift, Dilemma and Promise* (1984), are central moments in the development of The United Church of Canada's positions on sexuality, gender and the family. The next two chapters will examine these two documents as case studies with attention to the ways in which they assisted or blocked the United Church's recognition of the issue of violence against women.

Process, Methodology and Working Style

The 1980 study was prepared in response to a request from the 1972 General Council:

> Whereas we believe that a variety of common social problems such as adultery, divorce, the need for abortion, etc., are often the result of a confused understanding of human sexuality; and whereas we understand human sexuality to be a beautiful gift of God intended to be used for creative and expressive purposes within the context of responsible human relationships and see it thus as a serious area of church concern; and whereas the Church shares society's alarm at the steadily increasing epidemic of venereal disease, now recognized as a national medical problem; be it resolved that the Executive of General Council appoint a committee to:
>
> (a) Consider the subject of human sexuality using both presently available studies and new resources; and
>
> (b) Communicate its findings through the Executive of the General Council to church members in terms which portray human sexuality as being inter-personal rather than merely technological or physiological.[1]

The issue is defined as a socially "confused understanding of human sexuality" that contributed to increasing social problems such as adultery, divorce, abortion and the rising incidence of venereal disease. At the same time, human sexuality is understood as a "beautiful gift of God." While the Church recognized the goodness of sexuality, fear of its misuse had dominated the Church's officially recorded history. This new emphasis on the beauty of human sexuality was an important step in the development of an embodied theology and sexual ethic. Without the emergence of such an ethic, it would be difficult to recognize the relevance of violence against women to Christian theology; without a celebration and valuing of women's bodies and sexuality, it is impossible to recognize and condemn violence against women.

It was not until six years later, in 1978, that the Working Unit on Sexuality, Marriage and Family of the Division of Mission in Canada established a task force on human sexuality which eventually produced the study document, *In God's Image...Male and Female*. This team defined the issue similarly to the 1972 understanding: "We have not been taught [in our society] to understand and appreciate ourselves as sexual beings. Because of this the power of sex in our lives is often misdirected into repression, anger, exploitation, or avoidance, when it could be liberating and fulfilling" (*In God's Image:* 2). Further, because of this distortion, fear and ignorance, church members "who should know its joy and power and glory as God's gift, are victims of the confusion and have often led the way in puritan repression" (7, 2). Unfortunately, this claim that a confused understanding of sexuality is often at the root of anger and exploitation could imply that male abuse of women is solely a product of this confusion; the relevance of a systemic gender power imbalance was not yet recognized and named.

Over fifteen months, this ten-person task force prepared a study on the theological and ethical implications of human sexuality. The group consisted of "four lay women, two lay men, and four ordained persons," all of whom were very involved in the United Church. Collectively they offered "expertise...[in] biblical studies, theology, education, counselling [and the] social sciences." All of the members contributed to the writing of the document. Members wrote separate chapters and later reviewed each other's work (*In God's Image:* VI).[2] This method resulted in some inconsistencies and a lack of continuity. Most important, this working style limited the amount of critical dialogue with other groups and individuals.

A staff resource person for the Working Unit on Sexuality, Marriage and Family, Dr Robin Smith was a member and paid staff person on the task force. The working unit also appointed the balance of the task force members.[3] As evidenced by remarks in various correspondence, Smith was acquainted with most of the task force members previous to the formation of the group. This link was important since this likely meant that at least some members of the task force shared some experiences and possibly lacked diversity it may have had if the members had been selected by a more diverse committee.[4] The commonality of experiences was relevant to the task force's work since they put a strong emphasis on experience as a source of authority: "Whatever we offer to the church must be solidly based on the realities of our own experience."[5] Our experiences help to shape our beliefs and worldviews. As ethicist Roger Hutchinson contends, experience shapes the formulation of our ethical positions:

> We are probably as in touch with reality when we are telling our stories as when we are attempting to articulate our most basic convictions. The glimpses of reality which guide our actions are sometimes embedded in stories; sometimes expressed as the hard facts of scientific demonstration; and sometimes presented as consequences or rights claims, or as arguments based on our vision of a better world.[6]

The task force members did not discuss their experiences in this study document. Some of these stories probably would have helped the readers to better understand their writings. Although the task force was limited by their connection and commonalities, these factors also made it much easier to complete the document and so to prompt the rest of the Church into discussion.

The task force wrote the study to help members of the Church explore human sexuality in the context of "our individual sexual experience," "Christian faith and biblical experience" and "modern biological, psychological and social sciences" (*In God's Image:* vi).[7] Partially in response to concerns and anger expressed over a perceived attempt by the task force to *replace* the authority of the Bible with science and reason, Smith, as chairperson of the task force, explained that it was necessary to attempt to bring these different sources of authority into dialogue with each other, if the goal was to discern the word of God: "My dream and longing, therefore, is that we will find a way in which we can both draw on the great experience of the church and the living experience of Christians today so that these create a dialectic in which God may more realistically speak to us."[8]

In the following pages, I will clarify the central ethical arguments made in this report concerning:

- What it means to be male *and* female.
- The authority of the Scriptures for moral choices.
- The exploitation of sex.
- Sexism in modern society.
- Fidelity and exclusivity in marriage.[9]

An analysis of these areas will determine how this work on human sexuality assisted or blocked the emergence of violence against women as an issue on the agenda of the United Church. This chapter will show that while *In God's Image* made a significant contribution to the exploration of sexuality, the dominant discourse the task force uncritically used often precluded a recognition of systemic male violence against women. This was in part related to the task force's methodology and in part to the reality that the meanings of systemic oppressions including sexism were only beginning to be recognized by the late 1970s. Although the purpose of this document was not to examine violence against women, its understanding of sexuality influenced the ways in which the Church understood the issue of violence against women. This study was, however, particularly important since it was the first officially received United Church document expressly written to explore human sexuality.

Theological Claims[10]

Theological claims and assumptions regarding human sexuality undergird many of the ethical positions of *In God's Image*. First and foremost, the authors claimed that human sexuality is a gift of God, is an intrinsic and pervasive dimension of our being, and as such encompasses much more than "genital activity" (*In God's Image:* 1).[11] As Nelson affirmed regarding a draft of the report, "The message comes through with extraordinary clarity that sexuality is a basic and God-given dimension of human life, and that it is to be integrated fully into who we are—and who, by God's grace, we are becoming."[12] We are sexual beings made in the image of God (5). The importance and centrality of this claim was connected to the initial definition of the issue: there was a confused and puritanically repressed understanding of sexuality within the church community.

The study uses Genesis 1:27 to support the claim that *each person* contains *both* "maleness and femaleness": "So God created man in his own image, in the image of God he created him; male and female he created them." "Them" refers to one being; each human is male and female.[13] Based on this claim, it was reasoned that "God's intention for human sexuality is that all persons discover the full experience of maleness and femaleness in themselves and each other" (*In God's Image:* 41). While this interpretation recognized that both males and females are created in God's image and pointed to commonality between the sexes, it assumed qualities to be intrinsically masculine or feminine and did not challenge gender stereotypes.

The authors of the study contended that, in and of itself, sexuality was neither "divine [n]or demonic" (*In God's Image:* 27). Depending upon the quality of the relationship, human sexuality can be a mutually fulfilling gift that nurtures wholeness in the recognition that sexuality and spirituality are profoundly interconnected (4), or our sexuality can be used in demonic ways, as "a powerful exploitative tool causing pain and alienation. Rape, incest, sexual assault, prostitution and sado-masochism distort God's intention for human sexual union" (45). When sexuality is "reduced to sexual acts" and not used to nurture wholeness, it is sinful. Generally, North American culture has encouraged reductionist understandings (2) of sexuality that do not nurture wholeness: "sex is expressed in conventional attitudes and stereotyped ways of relating to one another, drawn more from respectability or fear than from love and respect for others. Distorted, it is used for power trips and to exploit rather than to affirm" (2).

Within this argument, the report recognized the limitations and potential destructiveness of gender stereotyping. Consistent with much of the report, this particular argument against gender stereotyping was based on the contention that such stereotyping contributes to a reductionist understanding of the expression of human sexuality. However, while the author may well have recognized that gender stereotyping limits women's subjectivity and compromises women's agency in particular, the emphasis and primary concern was to remain in keeping with the initial definition of the issue by addressing sexual repression.

Sexuality expressed in a manner that does not focus on the quality of the relationship but only on the act of sexual intercourse itself violates right relationship. This is sin—"alienation from our body-selves, from each other, and from God" (*In God's Image:* 84); sin is understood as a violation of right relationship. The ethical argument of the study is that since our social view of sexuality (which tends to be reductionist and, therefore, presents sexuality as a tool to be used to gain or demonstrate power over another) often encourages destructive and sinful behaviour, and since "it is God's intention that sexuality enrich the whole person and the whole society," then we need to rediscover an understanding of sexuality that celebrates mutual wholeness (7).[14]

What makes a relationship mutually whole? The answer to this, asserted the task force, lay in the "great commandment...we are to love God, neighbour, and self."[15] We first experience God's love through the love of others and we are then "able to love ourselves and others [and God] as we discover that we are loved by God" (*In God's Image:* 5, 57). The experience of this love, then, serves as a starting point for the realization of a mutual sexual relationship in which the "'continuing incarnation [of God] is expressed.'"[16] The author did not explore more fully the manifestations of such a relationship. Concrete manifestations of a mutual relationship (as contrasted with one that was not) need to be named for this concept to carry consistent meaning. Without such a discussion, a commitment to mutuality could be professed without an understanding that it means anything other than that determined by one's own particular experience. This is consistent with the casuistic claim that paradigmatic concrete cases are required if ethical norms are to be developed. Since "no rule can be entirely self-interpreting," meaning can be derived only through general agreement of paradigmatic concrete cases.[17] For instance, a woman may experience violence from her partner but her partner may not perceive his acts as violent; in fact, he may see his use of threats and sexual and/or physical violence as loving acts intended for the good of his spouse. The development of a clearer understanding of the norm of mutuality as based on a series of ethical cases, such as the above general case, is necessary to the development of a clearer understanding of what constitutes mutuality and what constitutes sin.

A further difficulty regarding the task force's theological assumptions was a tendency to a dualistic view of human sexuality: sexual expression was defined either as contributing toward the "union and communion with others and with God" *or* as destructive and subversive of "God's intention for human sexual union" (*In God's Image:* 45). The meaning of sexual expression is unclear in many relationships, even to those involved. Also, some sexual expressions are ambivalent; they contain fulfilling elements as well as limiting or potentially destructive elements.

The task force contends that there is always hope for the transformation of those who engage in sinful sexual expressions. Part of God's intention is that we "develop our sexuality" and continue to learn throughout our lives (*In God's Image:* 5). A sense of our accountability "to ourselves, others and God for our sexual behaviour and attitudes" helps to ensure our continued education (58). This ethical claim was built on the assumption that our attitudes are learned and, can therefore be changed even if our context remains unchanged (4). This claim is contentious; for instance, it is questionable that all sexual offenders can be rehabilitated, particularly if our patriarchal cultural context is not also changed.[18] Perhaps some offenders can change in spite of a culture in which many are marginalized. However, education, although necessary, has not yet been sufficient to rid our world of abuse.

The report goes on to say that "it is the renewal that comes from God's acceptance and forgiveness that enables sexual experience to become more and more rich and creative in our lives" (*In God's Image:* 7). However, it neglects to point out that God does not always intervene to stop the suffering and to "enable sexual experience to become more and more rich and creative in our lives."[19]

The identification of sinful sexual expressions as those that are not mutual, including the use of sexuality as a tool for the exertion of power over another, was an important step toward the understanding and identification of abusive sexual behaviour, but needs further explanation. This understanding of sinful sexual behaviour could have been further developed if two assumptions had been recognized and challenged. First, the issue was defined primarily in terms of the ways in which reductionist and repressed views of sexuality contribute to sinful sexual behaviour. Although this approach illuminated the connection between the abuse of power and sexual abuse, it did not point to the relevance of the web of oppressions in society and, most notably for the purposes of this book, the systemic power imbalance between most men and women. Second, this discourse does not seem to have been informed by conscious perspectives of those who had been or were being sexually abused.

Scientific and Experiential Claims

As a study regarding human sexuality, *In God's Image* is applicable and relevant to all people regardless of age, since we all experience the "need to be touched," contends the task force. Moreover, "sexual interest, desire and response, though different from our youth, continue throughout life" (*In*

God's Image: 52). These claims go hand in hand with the proposition that our sexuality develops throughout our lives, and as the authors point out, we explore our developing sexuality in many ways. For instance, one way in which young people develop bodily awareness is through masturbation: "self-stimulation to orgasm gives the young person an experiential awareness of his/her sexual response cycle." As embodied beings, made in the image of God, we are called to know and to love ourselves. Masturbation, reasoned the task force, is one way in which to become comfortable with our own sexualities, through greater self-knowledge (52).

The claim that bodily pleasure through masturbation is a moral good is helpful to the discernment of violence against women. Women have long been associated with the body and the carnal; the mutable, the sexual and the feminine have been grouped together and negated. The claim that our sexual embodiment is good—a gift of God—was radical in that it challenged this traditional dualistic assumption.

The report identifies sexual fantasy as another "common" and important facet of human sexuality. Sexual fantasy, it says, can be very helpful since it can "enrich a sexual relationship," "provide a sexual outlet denied to us by our situations," "tell us about ourselves," "be useful for rehearsing responsible sexual behaviour," and does not need to diminish in any way—in fact, it can "enrich"—faithfulness and fidelity (*In God's Image:* 53).

However, some ethicists caution that fantasy is not always good; human beings are much more complex than the report acknowledged:

> Even if fantasy is not turned into action, it may yet be harmful….Fantasy can become all-consuming. It can distract from necessary choices. It can distort judgment….While a good fantasy can make me alive, energetic, creative, and ready to deal with reality, a warped one does exactly the opposite. It drains energy, turns me inward, and ultimately makes me less able to deal with reality….Fantasies can even become addictive.[20]

Further, the influence of our sexist culture needs to be taken into account when evaluating fantasy for ethical merit: "We should…acknowledge the possibility that fantasy will affect the person about whom we fantasize….Even when men think they are just having a 'healthy fantasy,' they may be objectifying women in their thoughts."[21] As *In God's Image* states, we are a relational people and affect those with whom we are in relation. Even if objectification does not occur, fantasies can affect others negatively. We need to be aware of this possibility and instead of simply accepting sexual fantasy as a good, also be critically self-aware.

Perhaps in a desire to encourage the growth of comfort with and valuing of our embodiedness, the report neglected the complexity of the issue of fantasy, and focused on endorsement rather than a critical ethical approach that carefully explored both its giftedness and possible dangers. Again, the issue was defined in terms of whether or not expressions of human sexuality were repressed or liberated; repressed was bad, liberated was good.

Unfortunately, the well-being of others, particularly women, became secondary to the freedom to develop one's sexuality through sexual fantasy.[22] Having said that, this dualistic approach, while limited, was still radical for the time in which it was written. Probably, it was a necessary step along the evolutionary way to a more just way of thinking.

Biblical Authority and Hermeneutics

The author of the second chapter of *In God's Image*, "Sexuality and the Bible," began by proposing and describing six principles interpreting scripture. The first was that all "consciousness and understanding is historically conditioned" (*In God's Image:* 14). As an example of the shaping influence of context, the writer emphasized the influence of the "rise of the women's movement" in creating a "shift of consciousness." This influence had been very positive, according to him, as its proponents had worked for the recognition of women's moral agency (15).[23]

The second principle was that we need to give the Bible "distance" from us in order to let it "have its own integrity" (*In God's Image:* 14). He recognized the potentially explosive nature of the topic of human sexuality and the church. It follows that "matters of sexual conduct have…[the] capacity to disrupt not only personal but also social and national life" (10). A similar claim has been made since early in the life of The United Church of Canada; the moral fabric and well-being of the nation have been understood to be directly tied to the well-being of the family and, by extension, to the expression of sexuality.

So, in the face of such strong beliefs of the power and pervasiveness of human sexuality, how can the Bible be allowed sufficient "distance" in order that it might speak about human sexuality instead of simply confirming predetermined, possibly distorted, interpretations? As an example of distortion, the author discussed the churches' inheritance of a Hellenistic repudiation of the body (*In God's Image:* 21). On the one hand, this is an important point since this Hellenistic repudiation continues to be a dangerous tendency and clearly affects biblical interpretation. On the other hand, the author provided no example to demonstrate the possibility of using the Bible to justify sexual permissiveness. This was part of an overall bias on the part of the writers of the study to emphasize the goodness of sexuality and the body at the expense of a recognition of the limitations and potential dangers of the expression of human sexuality. The task force's initial definition of the issue—as the need to address the confusion regarding sexuality and the church's tendency to "puritanical repression"—strongly shaped the authors' approaches.

The third principle was that "scripture builds upon, reinterprets, and even corrects scripture." The writer pointed out that Jesus himself did so "with astonishing frequency." One must take the entire Bible into account when interpreting scripture. Moreover, this biblical tradition of self-critique and reinterpretation opens the door for contemporary critique and reinterpretation.

The fourth hermeneutical principle was that the Bible must be set "free to find its vital point of contact with our lives and illumine the present." The author neglected to address what this means and what we should do with scripture that is inconsistent with central norms, that we may draw from the Bible and our experience.[24]

The fifth principle was that we must be "vulnerable" when reading the Bible—let it critique us as we critique it. Again, it is not clear how he envisioned this process. Nor is it clear how he applied this to his ensuing discussion of the Bible and human sexuality. It seems that a necessary precursor to this vulnerability is the principle regarding distance; if we do not interpret the Bible based on predetermined conclusions, we can begin to be vulnerable to the message in the Bible and allow it to critique our attitudes and behaviour.

The final interpretive principle was that "Jesus is for us the central norm by which scripture is to be judged" (*In God's Image:* 14). The author argued that we can only understand Jesus's messages if we are also open to other sources of authority: "If we are to be responsible to his living Word speaking to us now, we must also take account of all that the natural and social sciences can teach us about the world and ourselves" (35). Consistent with the rest of the study, the writer drew his norms from scripture, tradition, science (reason) and contemporary personal experience. He contended that all four of these sources of authority are indispensable but each could be dangerous if it became "dogma" (12). To avoid this reification, it was necessary to maintain a dialectic among all four sources so that each might challenge, critique or support claims drawn from the other.

He claimed that from a biblical perspective human sexuality in and of itself was neither "divine nor demonic"; how it was motivated, intended and experienced was what made it good or evil. The author acknowledged the biblical ambivalence toward human sexuality. Some passages celebrate human sexuality (for example, the author of the *Song of Songs* delights in the body and "even sexist dualism is strangely banished from this lover's garden"). Other passages focus on the temptations of sexuality and the evils of the body. However, even passages in the latter category do not deny the expression of human sexuality; "Asceticism in sexual life is foreign to biblical thought" (*In God's Image:* 18). Further, the writer stated that there "is no thought in Jesus's teaching that the ascetic way is better, higher or more holy" (26).

Jesus's healing acts are identified as evidence that he "was unequivocally on the side of physical health and wholeness" (*In God's Image:* 30). Further, Jesus frequently broke taboos of his time by his associations with women. The author appealed to a series of biblical passages from the synoptic gospels and argued that: (1) "if God is a father she/he is also a woman"

(32), and (2) Jesus was comfortable with his own sexuality. To summarize, "Jesus's personal acceptance of sexuality was strikingly manifest in his close associations with women...especially with women looked down upon by others as sexually unclean and sinful" (36).

There were a number of responses to the claims in this chapter. Maxine Hancock, representative of the United Church Renewal Fellowship (UCRF), an unofficial conservative group in the Church, wrote at least two critiques of *In God's Image*. Hancock strongly disagreed with the author's claims regarding Jesus's sexuality: "[He] attempts to attribute sexual passion to Jesus and goes so far as to broadly hint that there is reason to think he may have had sexual relations, perhaps was even married....[Jesus] stands in utter judgment of this report which attempts to besmirch his own purity as an excuse for shoddy morality for ourselves."[25] Hancock defined the issue as an attack on fundamental Christian values and an attempt by the task force to undermine the United Church's faithfulness to Christian values.

The UCRF assumed that an emphasis on purity and control of our sexuality was a necessary starting point for any discussion regarding human sexuality. On the other hand, the task force assumed that they needed to release people from puritanical repression regarding sexuality and to encourage our liberation through the joyous, creative and mutual expression of our sexuality. The two definitions of the issue were radically different; the agendas were opposed in that one sought continued if not greater sexual control and discipline whereas the other was committed to moving away from what was perceived as a pervasive reductionist and repressed approach to sexuality.[26]

Ethical Decision Making

The central issue addressed in the fourth chapter of *In God's Image*, "Expressing Our Sexuality," was the confusing complexity of what it means to be sexual and faithful Christians: "At the heart of the sexual question lies the ethical question. The Christian asks how, in today's confused, confusing world of sexual change, is it possible to act lovingly, responsibly, joyfully, freely as a sexual person. There is more than one way to answer that question honestly" (*In God's Image*: 60). This chapter proposes a model for ethical decision making regarding sexuality.

As the report stresses throughout, the commandments to love God with all our heart, mind and soul and to love our neighbour as ourselves are the "starting points" of a Christian ethic: "In response to God's action we discover the meaning of covenant and agape. This becomes the basis for ethical action in faithfulness to God, to others, to oneself" (*In God's Image*: 61).[27]

The next step is an exercise in self-awareness: to clarify one's own story/identity and experience, and how this affects one's understanding of the issue.

Next, one applies four norms presented in the study. First, is the sexual relationship in question "creative and liberating?" Does it challenge confining stereotypes or does it succumb to social prescriptions? Part of this norm— part of the meaning of liberation—as defined by the author, is that we must learn to "love ourselves as we are, others for what they are, and God." However, this criterion needs clarification in order to account for the complexities of the interaction between ethics, society and the individual. Although it is important that our sexual behaviour be shaped by love and not simply "programmed," it is also important to recognize that not all of what "society" says is necessarily either liberating or confining. Also, it sometimes may not be appropriate to "love ourselves as we are [or] others for what they are." If justice and mutuality are accepted as Christian norms, are we to love ourselves or others *as we or they are* if we or they are living in violation of those norms? (*In God's Image*: 69-70).

Second, "Is it [the sexual relationship] mutually supportive?" The focus in this section is on those immediately involved in the sexual relationship. However, it is essential to acknowledge that others are often affected by the relationship and to ask whether this criterion applies to them as well. What about the situation in which someone will be hurt, regardless of the decision made? It is important to acknowledge this dilemma as an ethical issue in itself (*In God's Image*: 70-71).

There are relationships in our society that are not mutual; instead, they are "exploitive, attempting to use the other for some desired end" (*In God's Image*: 70). When generally mutual relationships begin to experience destructive moments, the author contended that "the vicious cycle thus set up can only be broken when someone is willing to forgive, reconcile, heal....The paradox is that it is in being willing to lose ourselves for love's sake that we find ourselves" (70-71). True as this claim may be for some couples, the author failed to acknowledge the potential danger of this argument, especially for women. Women have been told that self-sacrifice as an end in itself is a laudable virtue. Ethicist Carol Robb summarizes the ethical difficulty involved in the understanding of self-sacrifice:

> Feminists challenge self-sacrifice as a norm uncritically accepted by women. In most ethical theory, when people are asked to be self-sacrificing, a wide range of turf called "prudence" is assumed to exist on which they may stand to demur or to weigh conflicting claims. However, since a central part of what is understood to be "feminine" is to be nurturant and other-regarding to the extent of self-sacrifice, women are exempted from the option of prudence.[28]

Self-sacrifice, as a virtue and end in itself, is not redemptive.[29] In losing themselves "for love's sake" and for the sake of patriarchal theological and cultural norms, women have often lost their subjectivity to others; they have not often "found themselves." The relevance of sexism must be accounted for when assessing the viability of this argument as a normative claim.

Further, with the benefit of analysis written *after* the completion of this report, I would argue that the cycle "can only be broken" when the one responsible repents, acknowledges the action, makes restitution and takes steps to ensure that it does not happen again. Wider socio-cultural systems and structures also must be attended to if cycles of violence are to be effectively addressed. If a relationship is to be mutually supportive, it is necessary to recognize and take into account the wider socio-cultural context as well as the subjectivity and accountability of the people involved. This norm could have been more adequately expressed as, "Is it mutually supportive, *does it honour the moral agency of both sexes, and does it demand accountability?*" and must be understood as a contextual question.

The third norm asks whether the sexual expression is "socially responsible." Because we are contextual and relational, we must be critically aware of both ourselves and our context to make responsible decisions. As in the first criterion, this one stresses the need to take a critical view of social stereotypes, particularly gender stereotypes: "One urgent necessity is to challenge the sexual assumptions of western culture and the ways they are expressed in the language, organization, systems and structures, and the controlling myths of our time" (*In God's Image*: 71). While this analysis was necessary and important, it would have been more complete had it acknowledged that some of these "sexual assumptions" and rules may have had redemptive components.[30] A hermeneutic of suspicion is appropriate as we consider the societal structures and attitudes that affect our understandings of human sexuality.

The fourth and last norm was that the sexual expression in question should be "joyous"; it is important to have fun and to enjoy sexual play: "There seems to be a conspiracy everywhere to pretend that it's wrong to have fun, that pleasure is wicked and that the erotic exists only to lure us into temptation" (*In God's Image*: 72).

These norms emphasized sexual liberation and happiness—but, probably unintentionally, at the expense of a recognition of some of the complexities of both people and society. The emphasis was on the need to experience play, engage in mutuality, be liberated from socially constructed stereotypes, and avoid the cultural assumptions and constricting "myths." This was likely a corrective to a past prohibitive theology and its prohibitive norms. If so, then the author of this section may not have been familiar with the social ethical history of the United Church. This would be understandable because this history previously has not been explored in regard to sexual ethics. As concluded in chapter 2, the Church was moving gradually toward a more relational sexual ethic that recognized the complexity of human sexuality. Instead of identifying and appealing to this ethical shift as part of the United Church's identity, a "new" method for ethical decision making was proposed. This method included norms stressing sexual liberation and celebration.[31] Because of this emphasis on the need to celebrate our unequivocally important embodiedness this study neglected the need for ethical rules that are primarily prohibitive and/or limiting. Norms that acknowledge our brokenness, as well as norms that celebrate and nurture our sexual growth, are necessary to an adequate sexual ethic.

The task force's definition of the problem and initial response centred on the need for liberation from a prevailing repressive view of sexuality. This focus contributed to one of the most frequently levelled charges at the writers of the report: they threw out rules and principles in favour of an individualist situational ethic. One article, in the *Toronto Star*, claimed that the report "says sex outside marriage can be acceptable if practised in 'a responsible and joyous way.'"[32] Another claimed that "all this previously taboo stuff is all right as long as it's done in good taste."[33] Yet another said that "individual love" was the only criterion.[34] Without a clearer understanding of concrete situations that were deemed unacceptable, the manner in which the norms (which did indeed centre on certain principles as discussed above) were presented may unintentionally have opened the door to distorted interpretations and more angry reactions.

In God's Image concludes that, although the model presents guidelines and a method for ethical decision making, "The model seeks to represent the fact that there are many factors, personal, interpersonal, societal and faith, that have to be considered, but that the final decision is made by each person, hopefully with an informed conscience" (*In God's Image*: 74). Perhaps it is also important to flesh out the meaning of "informed conscience" through references to each individual's *accountability* to God, self and community.[35]

Intimacy and Sexual Exclusivity

The issue of this chapter is: "The prevailing view in our society is that fidelity is equivalent to sexual exclusivity" and "in an age when all traditional stances are being re-evaluated, the notion of sexual exclusivity as a necessary component of marriage is…being challenged" (*In God's Image*: 65-66). The author argued that sexual exclusivity could be given freely as a part of fidelity if the couple concerned desired it. Further, although "Christians are called to an honest and loving intention to faithfulness" in marriage,[36] sexual exclusivity may be neither sufficient nor necessary to faithfulness (67).

Understanding sexual exclusivity as the "basic test of marriage" has distorted the meanings of both marriage and intimacy, claimed the author; such an understanding reduces marriage to sexual acts and negates the importance of the quality of relationship. Moreover, the demand for sexual exclusivity within marriage in the Judeo-Christian tradition, the author surmised, is probably related to "an attitude of ownership": historically, women had been regarded as possessions and were valuable because they could potentially "produce male heirs" (*In God's Image:* 61-66). Early in its history the United Church had named this concern—"The Christian husband will readily repudiate every assertion of claim resting on a tradition of proprietary rights in his wife" (*ROP* 1932:280)—but did not understand it to be connected to the marital requirement of monogamy.

The material for *In God's Image* in the study regarding fidelity was largely taken from another United Church study document, *Marriage Today.*[37] Written in 1978, this document was not an official statement of the United Church but a resource meant to generate discussion. According to this document, fidelity included intimacy and the "intention to faithfulness."

The task force also claimed that the criterion for Christian marriage ought to be the "intention to faithfulness" (*In God's Image:* 67). Faithfulness "to oneself, to God, to others" is necessary to intimacy, and we are able to be faithful because "God is faithful."[38] Besides mutuality, intimacy also requires vulnerability and risk-taking. However, permanence does not ensure intimacy, and intimate relationships are not limited to marriage and do not necessarily include genital intimacy but, by the same token, do not necessarily exclude it. Also, just as permanence does not ensure relational intimacy, genital intimacy does not ensure relational intimacy: "Intimacy includes far more than genital sex" (65).

The task force reiterated Nelson's claim that sexual exclusivity should not be the basic test of marriage since it forces many people to choose between sexual exclusivity and permanence (*In God's Image:* 67). Furthermore, since permanence has a higher value than exclusivity (for the teleological reason that "support and friendship" are part of an intimate and permanent relationship), therefore, one should not terminate a marriage if one's partner is sexually intimate with another, if the marital relationship is otherwise growing in intimacy: "Logically it is not the act of sexual intercourse with a non-spouse but the quality of the relationship that would seem to pose a threat to a marriage" (66).

On the other hand, one could reason that if permanence is the higher value, then one should choose sexual exclusivity in order to preserve the higher ethical good of permanence. The author(s) did not agree that a person should have to choose.

Furthermore, some couples may choose not to have sexual exclusivity as part of their marital relationship, knowing the significant attendant risk that the secondary relationship may become primary: "It is too easy to rationalize what we desire," and "there is much possibility of hurt to oneself and others." However, the text is clear that genital exclusivity ought not be a *prescription* of Christian marriage: "Nelson's final sentence, and some Christians would confirm the possibility, reads, 'it [fidelity] includes openness to secondary relationships of emotional intimacy and *potential genital expression, but* with commitment to the primacy of the marriage.' (italics added)" (*In God's Image:* 67).[39]

While the author warned of the dangers to couples who *choose together* to reject the requirement of sexual exclusivity, the dangers of sexual intimacy outside the marriage relationship when this is *not agreed on by both* marriage partners were not clearly stated. Instead, the focus was, probably unintentionally, on the *justification* of one partner's participation in such a relationship.[40]

The stated aim of Chapter 4 of *In God's Image* was to encourage people to think more about *why* they may insist on sexual exclusivity in marriage instead of simply accepting it as a deontological rule without reflecting on what it means; the aim was "to challenge the church to a deeper understanding of the gospel so that genital exclusivity will not be a mere legalism but that genuine and authentic commitment to and hard work for mutuality and faithfulness will become more and more the mark of Christian marriages."[41] Although the chapter dealt with this aim, it also functioned to justify physical sexual intimacy with a "non-spouse." The author's motivations were not clear.

Sexism

A subgroup of the Task Force on the Changing Roles of Women and Men in Church and Society (TFWM; see chapter 6), released a response to and strong critique of this chapter in November 1981. While both task forces agreed that sexism is sinful and contrary to the will of God (*In God's Image*: 3, 84), they defined and explained sexism differently.

The sexuality task force stated that: "the Christian church until recently has been a powerfully legitimizing force for the support of sexism" (*In God's Image*: 81). Many, including myself, would agree that the Christian church has participated in the perpetuation of sexism but would dispute the claim that the church had moved beyond "legitimizing" sexism. The TFWM also disputed this claim. If the sexuality task force had indicated that the church, or at least segments of the church, had begun to address gender issues and that this gave cause for hope, this claim probably would have met some agreement. The authors discuss the issue in relation to the teachings of Jesus: "For almost 2000 years we have had the written accounts of Jesus' radical treatment of women available to us but have not recognized what he was saying about the equality of men and women." Though Jesus demonstrated through his life and work that women and men are equal, we in the Christian church have persisted, "until recently" in legitimizing "discrimination or superiority on the bases of sex (gender)" (81).

As it was, although the TFWM agreed that sexism is sinful and contrary to the will of God, they argued that the sexuality task force's definition of sexism was limited and "inadequate."[42] The TFWM defined sexism as "a way of perceiving reality, an all-pervasive worldview which not only affects and informs roles and status, but cultural and economic systems and institutions as well" (TFWM: 1). They argued that the 1980 study, for the most part, did not consider societal factors but limited the understanding of sexism to the individual.[43]

The sexuality task force argued that sexism is a problem for both men and women, and that both men and women experience its ill effects. The TFWM took issue with this claim and posited that sexism has been "practiced" by men—"It is...not basically a women's problem"[44]—and women suffer most of the ill effects of sexism. Regarding the effects of sexism on men, the 1980 report claims that men "are realizing that sexism has limited their lives leading to stereotyped roles and emotional strait-jackets" (*In God's Image*: 83). The TFWM minutes state that "it is inaccurate that men have realized that sexism limits their roles."[45] However, the argument in *In God's Image* did not claim that men "have realized" this, rather that they are in process.

A central concern of the TFWM was the 1980 study's delineation of "three different viewpoints" of the women's movement. The author presents as fact Gayle Graham Yates's understanding of the women's movement, and espouses Yates's goal of androgyny as the most desirable response to sexism. The three viewpoints Yates presented are described as follows:

> *The Feminist view* is simplistically women becoming equal to men by learning to be like them. *The Women's Liberation* position is, again simplistically, so pro-female that it is anti-male....The Androgynous position is women and men equal with each other—the characteristics and values of neither traditional sex role are assumed to be superior to the other, either implicitly or explicitly. (*In God's Image*: 83)

The TFWM found these distinctions "misleading": "Feminism and woman's liberation [and "women's movement"] are terms used by most people interchangeably. This is particularly true in the Canadian context" (TFWM: 4). They also critique this approach because it was based on the understanding of one author: "For this report to rely so heavily on one author's perceptions of the women's movement is unbalanced" (5). They also expressed disagreement with the definitions.

First, the TFWM claimed that Yates described "women only in their relation to men....She speaks of women against men, women equal to men by learning to be like them, and women and men equal with each other—never *women* defining *women*" (TFWM: 5). Necessary to subjectivity is the opportunity and ability to speak for oneself; as full moral agents, women must have their own voice to articulate and define their own experiences.[46] Furthermore, they claimed that the concept of androgyny is "inadequate and even dangerous to the cause of women" (6).

The TFWM argued that the sexuality task force moved too quickly to wholeness and reconciliation and that more time must first be devoted to dealing with sexism. Otherwise, we will not be able to move to wholeness in community: "Before we begin that search for a common co-humanity we must first seek an acknowledgement of participation in sexism (confession) and a sign of the intention to change (repentance)." The TFWM pointed to the claim that: "through dialogue, reflection and co-operation we can rediscover our wholeness and common humanity" (*In God's Image*: 84), and suggested that it would be appropriate to edit this claim and add the provision that "confession" and "repentance" are also necessary (TFWM: 2).[47]

The remaining ethical argument of the TFWM concerned androgyny. Although they attributed good motives to the writers of *In God's Image*— "Androgyny, or male and female, masculine and feminine in one person, has emerged partially as an attempt to eradicate the negative affects of sex-role stereotyping" (TFWM: 5)—the TFWM identified some potential dangers and limits of this concept. First, androgyny assumes that gender differences are limiting (6). However, the TFWM argued that it is not the gender *differences* per se that are limiting but gender *stereotyping:* "Many feminists began to realize that it was not their gender that was the main source of their inequality, but the imposed, alienating restricting negative stereotypes ascribed to that gender and the misogynist attitudes towards those differences" (7). Therefore, it is not androgyny that will dispel sexism but radical changes in attitudes and structures.

Chapter 5 of *In God's Image* also argues against the use of stereotyping, particularly gender stereotyping. Since the sexuality task force understood sin as broken relationship, "alienation from our body-selves, from each other, and from God" (*In God's Image*: 84), stereotypes were defined as sinful since they foster predetermined assumptions. These assumptions are often based on and serve to perpetuate fear and hate. When the task force examined gender stereotypes in this light, they concluded that all stereotypes and expectations based on gender were sinful since they inhibited growth, relationship and love. One woman reflected on the pain and alienation wrought by this type of stereotyping: "When these indicators [i.e. gender behaviour] do not match the expectations my culture (mostly male and patriarchal) deems acceptable for 'women,' I am seen as different, sometimes labelled aberrant or deviant, and I become confused, unhappy, and lonely for acceptance" (*In God's Image*: 40). Although the report states that stereotyping ought to end, it did not make a connection between gender stereotyping and androgyny.

The authors of *In God's Image* claimed that Genesis 1:27 meant that there are male and female qualities in each person: "It seems reasonable to understand the use of 'them' at the end of the quotation to include the extent to which there is maleness and femaleness in each person." This interpretation was then used to support the concept of androgyny (*In God's Image*: 41). The TFWM argued that this factual claim is wrong, and used the exegetical work of biblical scholar Phyllis Trible to support their claim that the biblical verse refers to two distinct beings—"one male and one female"— not one androgynous person (TFWM: 8).

A further assumption underlying a claim of androgyny is that all our gender traits are learned and none are "in some way shaped by our biology" (TFWM: 9). The TFWM argue that this factual claim has not been and probably never will be empirically proved.

Ironically, by "continually assessing in terms of 'masculine' and 'feminine' we serve to perpetuate sex-role distinctions." Furthermore, since androgyny assumes that male and female traits are mixed and contained within each person, our maleness or femaleness is reduced to "biological or to reproductive functioning only." The TFWM argued that this "come[s] perilously close to lending support to that body/mind split and dualism we seek to overcome" (TFWM: 10-11).

An important ethical question concerns the level of informedness in chapter 5. It does not appear to draw on or acknowledge the work of the TFWM, and did not even list the task force among the United Church groups that were working on the concerns raised by the women's movement and feminism (*In God's Image*: 82-83). A further example that may indicate insufficient knowledge is the boxed statement: "We thank the Lord, that we in the United Church are not like other denominations....We have been ordaining single women since 1936 and married women since a later date. In fact, in 1979, 9 percent of the faculty of the Toronto School of Theology [TST] and 28 percent of the student body were female" (81). There are a few problems with this statement. First, was this an attempt at humour? Further, an implication that the Toronto School of Theology was limited to The United Church of Canada was and is not true. The TFWM, too, were confused about the meaning of this statement: "Was it intended as sarcasm or as a serious statement? Either way we felt it to be inappropriate and offensive" (TFWM: 2). The context in which this statement was written seems to indicate seriousness; the preceding sentence reads: "The Christian church until recently has been a powerfully legitimizing force for the support of sexism."

The TFWM perceived the intent of the sexuality task force was to encourage the eradication of sexism but argued that they were unsuccessful primarily due to a lack of information: "The intent was to illuminate, but the effect is to distort, confuse and mislead" (TFWM: 4). Chapter 5 of the report was, at best, incomplete.

Concluding Remarks

General Council received *In God's Image... Male and Female* as a study document and requested that a preamble be attached to the study which clearly stated that it was a study document, "NOT a policy statement" but intentionally an "unfinished document" that would aid in the process of producing a "comprehensive draft statement on human sexuality for discussion at General Council no later than its 30th Session" (ROP 1980:911, 962-63).

The assertion that sexuality is neither divine nor demonic in and of itself was the starting point for much of the study's discussion. This claim was very significant in that it emphasized the United Church's increasing attention to and valuing of the quality of relationship as a morally relevant factor in assessing the goodness of sexual expressions. However, the potential *goodness* that could be experienced through expressions of human sexuality was emphasized while the potential *destructiveness* of sexuality was minimized. The theological analysis was also weighted in this direction. This bias was connected to the task force's definition of the issue and initial response: they understood human sexuality to be a source of confusion, and particularly within the church community, generally approached with unhealthy "puritanical repression." This repressed attitude has led to continued confusion and often a reductionist understanding of sexually intimate relationships. Unfortunately, the writers emphasized joy in the giftedness of our sexuality at the expense of a recognition of the potential for sinful sexual expression. At least partially due to this slanted approach, many readers perceived the writers to have promoted a permissive sexual ethic.

A common critique of this study pertained to ethical methodology; did the authors discard ethical rules in favour of a permissive sexual ethic? Did the task force build their report on an individualistic liberal ethic? Some members of the Alberta Conference Division of Mission in Canada Caucus, when asked for feedback on the study, stated that they "saw it as overreacting to the sexual rigidity of a past time," and consequently, as rejecting rules that benefited the community.[48] The task force had repeatedly cautioned against an over-reliance on rules: "We have to think through, and rethink, our attitude to rules, rather than taking them as simple, easily applied standards for behaviour" (*In God's Image*: 73). The staff person expanded on the task force's approach to the use of rules: "We are not trying to take away rules: we are saying rules have a place, but we downplay that place somewhat because in the Christian society rules are made too much of. We have become legalists, and Jesus was no legalist. What we need instead is to recognize the value of the rule, not contradict it, but go beyond it to the deeper way of expressing love."[49] However, this ethical reasoning was used at least once in the study to justify ethical conclusions which probably were not based exclusively on an attempt to avoid reified legalisms.[50]

The authors set up a somewhat dichotomous view of ethical methodology: "[There are two] contrasting styles of ethical decision-making....One emphasizes rules and treats some rules as absolute....The other style is contextual and recognizes that there are many other elements, personal, physical, social, and so on, as well as rules, in a decision making situation....Rules ...are valuable, but of limited value" (*In God's Image*: 74). This explanation oversimplified modes of ethical decision making. In particular, no distinction is drawn between absolute rules (which must be followed regardless of context) and binding rules (which generally are to be upheld unless they come into conflict with another such rule, in which case the two must be weighed and a judgment call made). The task force's perceived need to get away from an absolutist approach resulted in a skepticism of binding rules as well as absolute rules. Rules have a limited role in the practical discipline of ethics but not a limited "value."[51] Furthermore, the task force came dangerously close at times to favouring relativism.[52] The task force's understanding of ethical methodology contributed to a distortion of some concrete issues; any position perceived to limit sexual expression was rejected in favour of a more flexible approach in which allowances or justification could be made for a variety of behaviours. The intent behind this seems to have been twofold: to avoid a legalistic approach to complex matters, and also to create the means to justify falling short of the intentions that are part of a committed relationship.

The lack of concrete statements regarding, in particular, the potential dangers in the expression of human sexuality created a block to the recognition of violence against women as a pervasive issue relevant to any discussion regarding human sexuality. Further, the relevance of systemic power imbalances, including sexism, was not consistently applied to the ethical reflections.[53]

Another factor contributing to the perception that this document advocated a permissive sexual ethic is the lack of conscious continuity with past related United Church documents. Without a recognition of the United Church's ethical shifts over time, it is difficult to argue where it is going or needs to go. While one's personal experience is relevant to an assessment of what is needed in the construction of a sexual ethic, it is not sufficient—the Church's history also needs to be considered as a source of authority. As relayed in chapter 2 of this book, the United Church had rejected sexual acts outside marriage on the basis of a belief that such behaviour countered the biblical message and threatened the well-being of both the family and the nation. The report neither reflected nor directly addressed this history.

The document also lacked continuity *within* its pages. Since different authors wrote the chapters, the ethical analyses varied. For example, although the chapters regarding the Bible and sexism took the influence of sexism seriously, it was not recognized to the same degree in other chapters. The working style of the Task Force on Human Sexuality contributed to this lack of continuity, sacrificing as it did an interactive working style to expediency. Therefore, the task force did not have the benefit of much critique while they wrote the study. Given that eight years had passed between the request from the 1972 General Council and the completed study, the focus on expediency can be justified. Clearly, it was important that such a study be produced in as timely a fashion as possible.

The leadership of the task force was also problematic. By assuming a great deal of responsibility for the study either through perceived necessity or choice—by serving as staff person and being involved in the selection of task force members—Smith had a great deal of power and influence in defining and ethically analyzing the issues. Moreover, he took on most of the responsibility of responding to correspondence to the task force regarding the study. In short, responsibility and accountability were not evenly distributed. The structure of the task force as it was implemented by General Council Executive allowed for the services of only one paid staff person, so he may well have felt obligated to assume this responsibility. However, the contemporary TFWM was similarly structured, and through critical attention to this issue of working style, they worked at a model of shared power. Having said that, let me also be clear that Smith and the other task force members deserve much appreciation and recognition for the courage to express their views so publicly. Also, each dedicated much time to the composition of their respective chapters and/or sections. All members, as evidenced by the piles of letters in the United Church archives, received much abuse for expressing views that generated impassioned, emotional responses across and outside of the Church. There can be no justification for such abuse; much of the correspondence was appalling and my heart goes out to all who had to endure such a sad reflection of part of the Church's membership.

This study contributed significantly to breaking the Church's silence around sexuality, and to upholding sexuality as part of God's good creation. It would have provided even better ground for an adequate sexual ethic had the following points been addressed. To begin, the writers' standpoints and worldviews ought to have been declared. Also, the study emphasized the goodness and potential for liberation within sexual expression but downplayed the potential for destruction. In addition, the task force did not indicate an awareness of The United Church of Canada's roots, or the relevance of these roots to a study regarding human sexuality. Further, dialogue and critique with other United Church groups were not pursued. Finally, though several important points were made regarding the complexity and importance of human sexuality, an adequate foundation was not established for the recognition of violence against women as a relevant systemic socio-cultural issue.[54]

CHAPTER V

Case Study:
Gift, Dilemma and Promise

*A*FTER THE UNITED CHURCH General Council received the study document, *In God's Image...Male and Female,* feedback to the study was gathered and collated. The three most contentious subjects, according to this feedback, were "biblical interpretation, fidelity and...homosexuality."[1] The General Council Executive posited two reasons for this, based on an assessment of the collated data. First, there was a significant amount of disagreement over the interpretation of Christian authority: from where does it come and how is it derived? This factor pertained to the task force's use of "personal experience, scientific insights and biblical/faith knowledge" as sources for the discernment of God's message and will. The disagreement was not so much over the validity of the four sources as how these sources were interpreted and used.

The second reason for the dissension, as perceived by the Council Executive, was the "emotional nature of sexuality."[2] Of those respondents who addressed "at least three of the five 'issue' areas, none were found whose 'direction of attitude'...contained both 'favourable' and 'unfavourable' responses. All were either solidly 'favourable' or solidly 'unfavourable.'"[3] The respondents were consistent and, possibly, had difficulty in discerning the ambiguities that are usually connected with such a complex topic as human sexuality. These consistently unambiguous responses may reflect unexamined reactions more than thoughtful and self-aware responses.

Interestingly, fewer respondents addressed the issue of the nature of sexuality, (*Gift:* 83-88) than that responded to the topics of authority, fidelity and homosexuality. Of those who responded, "two-thirds affirmed the stance of the study (90).[4] As discussed in the previous chapter, sexuality has been discussed since the formation of the United Church. Further, the goodness of our sexuality (which often was equated with sexual intercourse) and of sexual pleasure, when expressed in the context of marriage, has been affirmed from the beginning. As shown in chapter 2 above, the United Church had been moving toward a sexual ethic centred more in the quality of relationship, but also formed around certain deontological norms. These norms, historically, have included the intention to faithfulness and sexual exclusivity within a marriage relationship, mutuality—including mutual consent to sexual expression—and rejection of expressions of genital sexual intimacy apart from the marital relationship. The latter norm was being increasingly questioned as some couples opted not to marry and same-sex couples could not marry. One particularly contentious point brought into sharp relief by the study was the question of what constitutes a faithful, covenantal relationship; many indicated that marriage was the only appropriate context for sex. Many of the respondents who expressed disagreement with the study were consistent with the historically held United Church view that sexual pleasure is good only when it is consensual and in the context of a marital relationship. Although by the early 1980s the United Church had moved closer to a primarily relational sexual ethic, a primarily act-centred sexual ethic has continued to influence much of the Church's membership.

The purpose of gathering responses to the 1980 study document was not to allow them to dictate the United Church's position, but to foster dialogue. However, there seems to have been little effort to understand the preponderance of unfavourable and sometimes hostile feedback. It was acknowledged that, in spite of the negative feedback, "the documents were valuable. They contained much wisdom and reflected the hopes, fears, joys, pain of many people in the church" (*Gift:* 5). However, there was no further exploration of what was behind these often very emotional responses. The March 1981 minutes of the Working Unit on Sexuality, Marriage and Family state, "The important thing…is the process of dialogue going on towards the developing of perspectives….There is a major concern both to help the church form its mind and not to take a merely mathematical approach to decision-making which would lead to a lowest common denominator rather than a prophetic stance."[5] Given the need for clear decisions, and given the nature of the responses, this would have been a very difficult task indeed. The temptation to dismiss the critical and especially hostile responses as reactionary and puritanical would have been tempting. A further point should be made: all of us who are church members also have a responsibility to attempt to dialogue in faithful but caring ways whether we like the subject at hand or it is something that causes us great fear or anger.

Process, Methodology and Working Style

The process of constructing the 1984 report, *Gift, Dilemma and Promise,* was more complex than the process behind the 1980 study. Three official bodies—the Executive of General Council, the Executive of the Division of Mission in Canada and the Working Unit on Sexuality, Marriage and Family—were each asked to choose two "electors." These six electors, then, would choose the members of the writing team. This team was established by September 1982, and was directed to gather feedback from across the Church regarding *In God's Image,* and people's perspectives on the issue of human sexuality in general.

To advise the writing team, the Division of Mission in Canada directed each Conference to choose a "key person." This person's role was to "coordinate a team which would provide support, leadership training, and assist in the feedback process of the Study in Human Sexuality."[6] These people were chosen based on their "background in sexuality...knowledge of family education and...Christian perspective."[7] Each Conference and key person, in consultation with the unit, chose participants for four pre-writing workshops." Included among the participants were representatives from "interested groups" including the Task Force on the Changing Roles of Women and Men (TFWM) and the Theological Perspectives Unit (TPU).[8] Regional representation and the participation of people with "specific biblical, theological or ethical skills or perspectives, as related to sexuality" were also important criteria for the selection of participants.[9] The recorded purpose of these workshops was "to provide a time for interchange of views, quiet reflection, clarification and clear presentation of attitudes so that these persons might offer their best insights to the church" (*Gift:* 6). The inclusion of representatives from other United Church groups with related concerns indicated a growing awareness of the importance of dialogue. This was a step toward a communicative ethic; interested parties with a variety of viewpoints were invited into dialogue in order that mutual challenge and growth might occur as truths were sought.[10]

The manuscript process was also very involved. The draft went twice to the Sexuality, Marriage and Family Unit before this Unit approved it with changes. Then it went to the DMC Executive, followed by presentation for review to Conference DMC caucuses. The unit emphasized the need for this careful review process: "*Such testing is important for a shared decision-making process.*"[11] Furthermore, as "each 'superior' body enters the arena, makes changes and *accepts responsibility* for the Report, *ownership broadens*" (emphasis mine).[12] According to the minutes from which this statement was taken, it was, not surprisingly, Smith who articulated these thoughts. Based on his previous experience, including the many outrageous attacks he had endured, shared responsibility and ownership of this new report were very important.

At the DMC Executive meeting, it was agreed that "*this Executive concur with the way in which the Writing Team is moving, encouraging the team to complete its task, so that copies of the report can be mailed to the members of the Division in preparation for the DMC General Meeting in January of 1984.*"[13] In January 1984, the DMC "accepted the draft statement in principle and directed that it be presented to General Council" (*Gift:* 6). Subsequently, the 1984 General Council approved *Gift, Dilemma and Promise— A Report and Affirmations on Human Sexuality* and adopted its thirty-one affirmations.

The main purpose behind both this and the the previous study was to seek clarification of the meaning of human sexuality, as experienced within the context of the United Church faith tradition and contemporary Canadian culture, bearing in mind that "a variety of common social problems...are often the result of a confused understanding of human sexuality" (*Gift*: 2). *Gift, Dilemma and Promise* did not point to the need to address the church's "repressed" approach to sexuality. Furthermore, unlike the 1980 study document, this report acknowledged a variety of viewpoints and reflected on them. The affirmations at the end of each chapter were not intended to equally represent these diverse views; they were more in keeping with the historically established and developing United Church identity than were the conclusions expressed in the 1980 study, and were less controversial than those expressed in the earlier document. A writer for *The Observer* described the report's reception:

> A reincarnation of the *In God's Image* report that fed headlines and tempers at the Halifax General Council four years ago slid smoothly through this year's Council. The new human sexuality report...benefitted from its own less radical conclusions and a Council more at ease with the topic of sexuality. The only prolonged debate was around its section on sexual orientation.[14]

Was this report prophetic, or were those responsible more interested in keeping a low profile and avoiding an outcry similar to that of 1980?

The authors define the issue similarly to the way it was defined in 1980, but without any reference to repressed or puritanical attitudes: because our sexuality is so pervasive—"Our spiritual, moral, social, family life is influenced by our sexuality, and the opposite is also true"—we are called by God to persist with the task of understanding and wrestling with human sexuality that we may "in God's grace...try to meet the issues that threaten to overwhelm human life" (*Gift*: 1). Further, "As a church we are called to face and to struggle with the issue of sexuality. To do otherwise is to renege on our commitment as Christians to apply the truth of the gospel to every area of life" (10). Although the report contains some similarities to the 1980 document, the authors are careful to state that it is neither "a rewriting of the 1980 documents" nor the result of the responses to the 1980 study (iii, 5). However, at a meeting of the writing team it was acknowledged that "in very broad general terms the philosophy of this Report is similar to that of the first one."[15]

As with the previous study, the sources of authority the writing team appealed to were scripture, theology, experience and reason (*Gift*: 5). However, this 1984 report held that the hermeneutical starting point is in *both* theory and experience, unlike the 1980 study in which experience was claimed as the starting point.[16]

Part of the writing team's aim was to make the report accessible to a wide range of people. It used simpler language and each chapter contained a description of the "present situation" based on data and other claims derived from science and theology, "stories from life," "questions for study and discussion," "insight from the scriptures" and "acknowledgments and affirmations." The purpose of the stories was to "put [a] human face on descriptions of issues"[17] and to employ experience as a credible authority. Acknowledgments were "intended as descriptions of the social and personal reality in which Christians, like others, live," and affirmations were offered as "general guidelines for use in The United Church of Canada" (7).

The working style and writing process used in the creation of this report were different from those of the 1980 report. More people were involved and much time and energy was dedicated to the design of the 1984 report regarding format, style and content. Further, feedback and discussion regarding human sexuality was a high priority; dialogue was an important part of the research process. The feedback received through responses to the 1980 study and particularly through the pre-writing workshops, was used extensively in the report (*Gift:* 1). The report was written using a consensus model, and the views it expresses are consistent from one chapter to another. If not for the previous study, it seems unlikely that this report would have been written with such care and investment. Did these differences in style and process help to establish conditions and a type of discourse that were more conducive to the recognition and understanding of issues that concerned the well-being of all people, particularly the marginalized, such as the issue of violence against women? This question will be explored through a brief ethical analysis of each chapter.

Sexuality and Selfhood

This chapter explores why the church should be studying human sexuality, beginning with the assertion that sexuality pervades all aspects of human life through a variety of expressions (*Gift:* 10). For instance, some of us are heterosexual, some homosexual and others bisexual. (The writers did not include transgendered people or others not named here. In the United Church as elsewhere, these people began to gain recognition after 1984.) Other examples include the expression of sexuality within a monogamous relationship through masturbation or within "freely chosen celibacy." For this reason, the writers argued that we should refer to "human sexualities": "The plural is important—it not only encourages us to acknowledge that our experiences are many and varied, but also discourages us from making glib or restrictive judgments about what is acceptable or normative behaviour" (11). No one experience is normative; to assume that one can speak for others is to dominate by claiming one's particular experience as normative. This approach from the viewpoint that there are multiple sexualities avoids the problem of generalizing the particular and further enforcing the very dominant heterosexual norm.

Sexuality, the writers wrote, begins at "the moment of birth, if not before." Since this development continues throughout our lifespans, the writers argued that "the value of sensitive, informed and ongoing education in the area of sexuality cannot be overemphasized." The church has a particular responsibility to contribute to this education and, since our attitudes to gender differences are shaped by our context, education is necessary in order to deconstruct gender stereotypes and role limitations: "When it comes to roles and tasks...gender is [at least] as much shaped by life as it is God-given" (*Gift:* 13, 14). This is a significant claim particularly when considered in the light of male violence against women. If gender roles are learned, then male violence against women is not inevitable. What aspects of life must be reshaped in order to teach behaviour that is life-giving and not limiting or exploitative? Although education within our current context is necessary, it is not sufficient. The authors of *Gift, Dilemma and Promise* stopped short of the claim that our patriarchal and capitalist culture must be radically overhauled as part of any sexual conversion away from violence toward wholeness and mutuality. They argue, instead, that our culture needs to be "redeemed" and "transformed" (67).

Human sexuality, the report affirmed, is a gift of God. Sexuality is also dilemma and promise. The creation stories demonstrates that sexuality is gift. Moreover, Genesis 2:18 affirms that humans are meant, by God, to live in community: "Human beings are to provide support and companionship for one another" (*Gift:* 17).

The Bible also affirms sexuality as gift through the doctrine of the incarnation. The report's writers state: "Early Christianity affirmed the primacy of the body both in God's self-revelation in Christ and in human existence." As well, Christian tradition supports the claim that Jesus was fully human and fully divine, which is interpreted to assert the goodness of the body (*Gift:* 18).

Material recorded at some of the pre-writing workshops expounded on the theological links between the body and the Divine. Those at the Naramata workshop discussed the relationship between "spirituality and sexuality." They argued for the healing of the body/spirit dualism: "The more we separate Body and Spirit in our understandings and attitudes, the more we separate ourselves from self, others and God; [and conversely] the more I accept and embrace and grow with my sexuality [through the grace of God], which is both gift and dilemma, the more I accept, embrace and grow with the God who is with us."[18] This is part of the giftedness of our sexuality; as we integrate body and spirit, we move closer to God.

The dilemma of our sexuality began with the Fall: "Life (of which sexuality...is an integral part) is not exclusively 'good'" (*Gift:* 18). The writers acknowledged that human sexuality is "affected and distorted by human sinfulness" but they neglected to discuss the theological and ethical question of the meaning of sin: "To deny or ignore the contamination of human sexuality by *sin (whatever we may mean by that)* is to fly in the face of reality" (20, 18, respectively; emphasis mine). An understanding of sin was necessary to this discussion. It is not sufficient to claim the presence of sin in the expression of human sexuality without defining what this means, particularly since common agreement on this cannot be assumed.[19]

The report's discussion of the scriptural presentation of the dilemma of human sexuality was limited to the influence of "sin." However, perplexity is also present when we are healthy and loving; it is grounded in the dialectics between individuality and relatedness, freedom and order, openness and commitment. The 1980 report made the same oversimplification: the writers often contended that human sexuality is either expressed in "good" ways or exploitative and sinful ways. The struggle and complexity of the expression of human sexuality was neglected in parts of both reports. Although the 1984 report did not deny the complexity of the dilemma, neither did it not adequately discuss the dilemmas involved in day-to-day, healthy and loving expressions of human sexuality.

The promise of our sexuality, contended the writers, lies in our Christian faith: "Faith does not leave us in the dilemma, without hope of recourse. Rather, it offers the promise of transformation. By faith, we are increasingly freed **from** 'the power of sin' (Romans 3:9) and **for** a new and deeper experience of our sexuality" (*Gift:* 19). The power of the Spirit leads us toward the gift of sexuality; through Christ, in the Spirit, we can redeem human sexuality. Again, what is not clear is exactly what we are redeeming sexuality from; what is sin? The ethical claim is that we must work toward the redemption of human sexuality, through God's grace, because this is what God intends and because this will lead to mutual communion (17). The implication is that sin distorts communion and God's intended gifts. Dilemmas, not resulting exclusively from sin but from the complexities of the human condition, are not discussed.

The writers followed up this discussion with strong statements against "exploitive sexual behaviour and other destructive expressions of sexuality." They affirmed that the church is called "to reduce the incidence of such destructive expressions, and to improve our ministry to all who are harmed by such behaviour"; to "initiate and support research and educational programs to increase our understanding of the causes" of this type of behaviour; "to speak out concerning the abuse of human sexuality in individual lives, in the community and in the structures of society" and "to a ministry of prophetic witness in the face of evil" (*Gift:* 21). As laudable as these claims are, the meaning of exploitative sexual behaviour is unclear. Most would agree that exploitative sexual behaviour is wrong; however, generally speaking there is confusion and disagreement about what constitutes such behaviour.[21] Also, no connection was made between sexism as a systemic power imbalance and exploitative sexual behaviour.

In the "midst of the ambiguity" of human sexuality, the writers pointed out, is the need to make responsible decisions. As the writers claimed, this task is complex and difficult but necessary: "Even in the midst of ambiguity, we are called upon to make responsible decisions with regard to the expression of our sexuality and to cope with the consequences" (*Gift:* 20). The sources for this decision making are "common sense, scientific knowledge, personal and social values, advice from others, and, especially…the context of the Christian community." How these elements are to be used and what they all mean or include is not clear. Ultimately, the writers claimed, "each person is responsible for his or her own decisions" (14). Similar to the 1980 study, accountability is discussed only insofar as we have to live with the consequences of our decisions. Smith asked the writing team an important question: "Is our focus too much on ultimate personal responsibility for decision-making (which is real) and not enough on social responsibility (which is also real)?"[22] The 1980 report had the same difficulty: individual responsibility was stressed sometimes at the expense of both social responsibility and social accountability, although it must be pointed out that one of the norms named regarding decision making was that decisions ought to be socially responsible. The report's focus on the individual's responsibility arguably could have been broadened by more attention to social responsibility.[23]

The dilemma of our sexuality is present in day-to-day living. Two factors involved in decision making are cited: one, the duty "to love one another" and the other, the need to balance rules with God's grace (*Gift:* 19). This approach to ethical decision making acknowledges that while rules can become legalistic (as was expressed in the 1980 study), rules also serve good purposes.[24]

Sexual Morality

▶ MARRIAGE

The writer observed that "there is a widespread desire in our church to take a strong affirmative stand in defence of marriage" (*Gift:* 22). Furthermore, "a deep pastoral need is expressed, by some who have grown up in a sexually permissive era, for the church to state clearly what it believes to be right over against what is merely popular by today's standards" (23). What was popular in this case? The assumption was that the popular stance was a permissive one. While this may or may not have been the case in wider Canadian society, the loudest voice—at least as indicated by the feedback to the 1980 study—within the United Church was the one calling for a "strong affirmative stand in defence of marriage." Whether or not a stand in support of sexual exclusivity in marriage was prophetic, the feedback to the 1980 study indicated that such a stand, at that time in the United Church, would *not* have been an unpopular one.[25]

The report notes that "approximately 40 percent of the people who marry **this** year [1984] will have their marriages end in divorce" and that there is an increasing demand for social "services to the battered and emotionally abused, the single parent, and the children of divorce" (*Gift:* 22). Apart from the increase in need for services for the abused, these were similar concerns to those named in the 1960 and 1962 reports. Both lamented the increasing divorce rate and pointed to the need for support for the single parent and to the damage often done to the family and the neighbourhood particularly when a marriage dissolves but does not end. However, neither *Gift, Dilemma and Promise* nor the 1980 report cited these previous reports.

What was the Church to do in the face of these escalating social concerns and the increasing power of the "contemporary idols of permissiveness" (*Gift:* 22)? The authors described the widespread belief that the Church must take a strong role in response to these problems: "Against this tide of threatening influences, there is an understandable desire to have our church launch a salvage operation" (*Gift:* 22). Furthermore, in the "Acknowledgments and Affirmations" section at the end of this chapter, the writers stated that "marriage as an institution can undergird each relationship and provide stability for society" (36). This language and claims are reminiscent of arguments made in the 1940s to describe the role of the Church regarding the social problems/evils that were threatening marriage, family and the nation: in the 1946 report of the Commission on Christian Marriage and the Christian Home, it was declared that "in the light of the growth of illegitimacy, desertion, legal separations, social diseases, mixed marriages and divorces...the Church must plan her campaign to exalt the standards of 'The Christian Home and Christian Marriage'" (ROP 1946:114). The language of both reports suggests the perception that the defence of marriage would require a fight essential to the well-being of the country.

In response to this concern, the writing team proposed a renewed understanding of and commitment to the biblical concept of covenant; "Covenant is that unique and mutually agreed-upon relationship with our God experienced by all who are claimed and possessed by God's promise" (*Gift:* 24). The first criterion for a covenantal relationship is that it must be mutual— both parties are "equal partners." The United Church's commitment to the norm of mutuality, in principle, was longstanding. Further, the writers claim that God desires a mutual relationship with us, in which we "act together in the mutual plan of salvation." Therefore, in Christian marriage, a covenant is made between two people—one male and one female—who are able to love mutually because "we are first loved by God." Also, in spite of the sexist nature of our culture, and in spite of the social tendency to permissiveness, "in a true Covenant marriage partners will continually work to disown secular values that reduce either partner to second-class status" (24, 25). The heterosexist assumption of marriage was not critiqued.

Although this report did not make specific reference to the contentions of the 1980 study, it was clear that according to the 1984 writers, a choice did not have to be made between genital exclusivity and permanence. The 1980 study contended that this choice was often necessary whereas *Gift, Dilemma and Promise* did not describe genital exclusivity and permanence as sometimes conflicting options. Rather, the report described the commitment to marriage in the Christian tradition as a covenantal choosing of mutual partnership with the ongoing intention of a lifelong commitment, through the grace of God (*Gift:* 28, 29).[26] This writing team posited that marriage partners could and should choose to work at the relationship and uphold both permanence and genital exclusivity. To support this ethical argument, the writer appealed to the scriptural story of God's covenant with Israel. Based on this account of covenant, the writer concluded that the "Covenant relationship then involves an exclusive choosing" (26).[27]

Following through on this understanding of covenant chosenness, the writer claimed that, on the negative side, the requirement of "Sexual exclusivity...can...lead to a...growing resentment...[and] the stored anger may become expressed in harassment and put-downs, or explode into acts of physical and sexual violence...but if the choice is freely made and renewed in meaningful ways over time, it can lead to the positive kind of commitment...that...enriches us" (*Gift:* 26).

Abuse is now commonly recognized, as many people also understood in 1984, to be rooted in patterns of power and control, not primarily in uncontrollable outbursts of anger. Most abuse is *ongoing;* it is not contained in *moments* of explosive anger. The fear and implicit threats that the abused partner, usually the woman, has to live with, control her life and distort her worldview. The meaning of "free choice" therefore also needs to be more fully explored. Such choice is not readily accessible to many who are abused; freedom becomes distorted as do self-esteem and empowerment; one's moral agency is compromised.[28] A woman may be so terrified that the choice seems to be between living—by remaining in the abusive relationship—or dying. What is meant by a "meaningful" renewal of commitment? An abused woman's experience of a meaningful renewal may mean an apology and a gift. The nature of an acceptable expression of commitment needed clear definition in recognition of the variety of experiences of those in the United Church who would read such documents.

Further, the writers claimed that although we may experience "unhappiness, pain or loss" in a covenant marriage, God is always with us "through whatever we must face." This can sound like a dangerous platitude, particularly since the church has told abused women that their suffering is somehow redemptive (*Gift:* 28).[29] This claim is often not credible for a woman in an abusive relationship since the abuse is not something that she should have to "face."[30] A further danger is that if the church does not recognize the experiences of various groups of people, then it becomes irrelevant to them; the church has nothing liberating to say. It must be stated that God is with us but God does not want us to stay in this relationship and continue to be hurt; abuse destroys the covenant.[31] This type of discourse needs to be clear and intentional. In this report, the experiences of those who are abused are not taken into account; a dominant discourse is maintained at the expense of a more liberating discourse that attempts to take into account experiences of marginalized people.

The writers argue that sexual intercourse *should* remain exclusively within the marriage relationship since the intentions of Christian marriage are most "fully achieved and symbolized when sexual intercourse in marriage is exclusive." These intentions include: nurturing each other's gifts, "putting the other before one's own interests in a lifelong commitment which is spiritual, emotional and physical," and risking and being vulnerable in the relationship" (*Gift*: 37).

The traditional theological assumption that all humans possess an inclination to pride, excessive self-love and undue self-assertion must be questioned in the light of the self-abnegation of many women. The claim that one should elevate another's interests over one's own neither recognizes the feminist claim of the need to value one's self-worth nor God's commandment to love our neighbour as ourself. While the nurturing of each other's gifts can contribute to a mutual love, the intention to put the other's interests above one's own creates the potential for both partners to lose their subjectivity. However, since we live in a sexist culture, a woman partner is at greater risk. The last listed intention—to be vulnerable—is certainly a necessary and intrinsic part of our sexuality in relationship. However, what it means to be vulnerable needs clarification within the context of mutuality.[32] In particular, it ought to be stated that power must be shared and power imbalances recognized and addressed, since this clarification would help to guard against the dangers of the unqualified assertion that one must elevate one's partner's interests over one's own.

The act of sexual intercourse in marriage, as expressed in the report, was understood to be "intended" as:

- a profound expression of the whole person;
- a yearning for total union with the other; and
- a creative and holy expression of fulfilment in the other person.
  (*Gift*: 37)

Gone was the emphasis of the 1980 report on fun and liberation. This report affirmed the lifelong intention of Christian marriage and took a strong stand against any claims that could be perceived to include permissiveness (37).

The authors of this report re-examined the meaning of covenant in relation to the Bible and attempted to be inclusive and faithful. However, it was not always possible to be critically aware of the partiality of their perspectives. At points, the author(s) unintentionally neglected the perspectives of many women, particularly those women with a conscious feminist experience.[33] Theology written from the perspectives of the powerful became normative over thousands of years and we have had to work hard to introduce the variety of experiences and lenses through which people experience the Holy, the self and the world. Feminist theologies, for instance, have developed from and helped many women to look critically at their experiences of suffering, pride and self-sacrifice. As discussed earlier, many women have been encouraged more toward a denial of self and a giving-up-of-power than to a will-to-power. As a result, much of traditional theology does not apply to the experiences of many women. This chapter on marriage needed to attend more to the perspectives of the marginalized and, in particular, to those who are critically aware of their experiences of systemic marginalization. We must critique the messages that normative male theology sends to women; as Legge states, "We must ask *whose* culture and *whose* experience are shaping theological ethics."[34] Necessary to this critique is an understanding of the relevance of sexism to theology.[35] Without such a critique, violence against women cannot be fully exposed. An adequate theology of marriage must take into account the experience of women in abusive relationships if such theology is to be relevant to and respectful of their experiences and lives.

▶ INTIMACY

The report defines intimacy in terms of societal confusion and resulting problems: "Ours is a society of vast confusion when it comes to questions of intimacy....Some seek intimacy in promiscuity" (*Gift:* 39). The Church, then, has a responsibility to give direction on this matter: "Some people in the church are in great pain over what they perceive as a lack of clarity" (40).

The need "to clear up some of the confusion that was apparent at the last General Council as to what was meant by the word intimacy"[37] may have been the underlying issue prompting the attention of a full chapter. This pressure, confusion and the reaction against *In God's Image* was expressed in Petition 25 which was referred by the 1982 General Council. The petition directed the DMC "in its draft statement on human sexuality at 30th General Council, to affirm that fidelity does require sexual exclusivity and that marriage should not include 'secondary relationships of emotional intimacy and potential genital expression.'"[37] The first part of this petition, regarding the necessity of sexual exclusivity to fidelity, is discussed in the foregoing section on marriage; this section will deal with the question of intimacy.

Petition 25 generated much concern and discussion. Authors of the 1980 study argued that if we are sexual, embodied beings, then it follows that any intimate relationship necessarily includes the *potential* for genital expression.[38] Most of us have more than one intimate relationship. For example, a minister's counseling relationship with a parishioner is an intimate one; should this relationship be refused because it is intimate?[39] An article in *The Observer* explained that in its intent on requiring sexual exclusivity in marriage, the petition "also appears to have denied married people intimate relationships with others." This article reported that "many Commissioners indicated that they did not intend this."[40]

Participants in the writing of the report also experienced this difficulty regarding the construction and application of ethical rules as they apply to sexual exclusivity and intimacy. For instance, the participants in the Cedar Glen pre-writing workshop, when discussing sexual morality, reflected (as had Smith) that the "church is still receiving appeals for specific guidelines rather than generalizations. We are caught between generalized moralizing and the specific demands of each situation. The church['s]…real task may be to share the spirit of Christ and let people make their own decisions."[41] As has been shown, this was a misplaced debate; both principles and context are morally relevant factors.

The real issue may have been a difference in underlying orientations to the question of sexual exclusivity, not a disagreement over ethical method. Perhaps the responses from the Church indicated a desire to reaffirm the traditionally accepted norm of genital exclusivity within marriage, not to reinforce a legalistic acceptance of a rule; perhaps for many it was both, combined with a fear of change.[42] For instance, some of the same people who expressed a desire to reaffirm this norm may not have condemned someone who has strayed had that person become repentant. The danger the writers of this report expressed was similar to that perceived by the writers of the 1980 report: in this quest for clear rules around Christian marriage, would a legalistic approach be embraced rather than "the spirit of the law" (*Gift:* 23)? This was not a new concern. The writers of the 1960 report *Toward a Christian Understanding of Sex, Love, Marriage* made a similar point in a different way. They claimed, in different terms, that the binding rule of genital exclusivity in marriage did not preclude the possibility of forgiveness and repentance if a spouse breaks that rule.

The Initiating Unit of the DMC, in consultation with Smith, "passed on the input from the working groups" in the DMC regarding the meaning of Petition 25. For example, one working group recommended that "Petition #25 be interpreted to re-affirm the unacceptability of adultery, but in no way to preclude the development of close personal friendship." Further, the Initiating Unit encouraged the Working Unit to interpret Petition 25 according to a paper distributed by Smith which stated that the final report "should take seriously the Petition's statement on fidelity but also discuss the realism or feasibility of the second part in seeking to remove the potential for genital intimacy if persons are to be allowed the values of intimate friendships beyond marriage."[43]

The issue was not so much the potential for genital expression in intimate relationships as what we do with that potential. The other issue concerned the 1980 study—why was the potential for such expression emphasized? Further, why was the need for limits on that expression not discussed apart from the claim that "secondary relationships" can be dangerous? Smith stated:

> I would reiterate, with some surprise that it should be questioned that the United Church is fully committed to marriage as an institution ordained by God and the Report continues to affirm our traditional support for sexual exclusivity in marriage. If anything, this Report, as indeed its predecessor study document, seeks to deepen the understanding of sexual exclusivity so that it is in no way token but the basis of a deep, mutual and fully mature relationship. That is our unceasing goal.[44]

Although the 1980 study challenged the meaning of sexual exclusivity as the basis for marriage and sought to develop a deeper understanding of the meaning of marriage, it also stated that sexual exclusivity was not *necessarily* a part of marriage. The study document stated that some couples may decide that sexual exclusivity is not a desirable norm for their relationship. Further, it was explained in the document that sexual intercourse with a non-spouse did not necessarily mean that anything was wrong in the primary marriage relationship. However, the writing team was clear that they valued committed, mutual marriage relationships; the intent of much of the discussion regarding marital exclusivity seemed to be that all efforts be made to preserve and nurture marital relationships in which there was love and respect.

Intimacy must be defined before any claims regarding the requirements of intimacy are made. The authors of *Gift, Dilemma and Promise* define intimacy as more than genital expression. Further, intimacy may but does not have to include genital expression (*Gift:* 38). Intimacy is a "hunger" experienced by everyone for closeness with another person and God. Accordingly, God intends us to need each other and to therefore "live in community" (53).

Intimacy necessarily includes mutual vulnerability, patience and risk (*Gift:* 46). By being vulnerable, we open ourselves to risk, and that includes the risk of being hurt, just as it includes the possibility of joy. Without mutual vulnerability in a relationship, then exploitation and abuse can occur (54): "It is important to recognize that our intimate relationships with humans may have a potential *dark* side. We live in a fallen world" (47, emphasis mine).[45]

The writers of the report argued that because of our fallenness, mutuality requires setting limits on some intimate relationships. This responds to the concern regarding the potential for genital expression in any intimate relationship: "Limits must be set to the physical expression of intimacy when it is outside the marriage relationship" (*Gift:* 47). Our fallenness, I submit, is not the only reason for the need to set limits. The complexity of human relationships as well as the difficulty in seeing oneself clearly contribute to the need for limits. As Lebacqz and Barton reflect, "Marriage covenants, as important as they are, are not a sufficient guarantee against improper sexual relations."[46] This necessary setting of limits is not only to be done out of respect for one's marriage commitment but is also necessary in order to respect the integrity of self and others (*Gift:* 54).

In this regard, the writer could have discussed the danger of physical intimacy in any relationship in which there is a power imbalance, such as the minister-parishioner relationship.[47] The issue of consent, as a requirement of mutuality, needed to be pursued. In 1960, mutual consent was identified as an issue regarding "sexual union." Consent, the 1960 report argued, is necessary to the "integrity of both [marriage] partners" (ROP 1960:157). Consent is relevant to questions of intimacy and its expression. Further, an analysis of sexism and power needs to be applied to any discussion regarding consent.

The next topic addressed in *Gift, Dilemma and Promise* regarding intimacy was sexual intimacy and single people. According to the Church, how can single people appropriately express their sexual desires? The writers acknowledged that the Church's position has been to deny genital expression to single people. However, in reality, it has been more acceptable for single men to be sexually active than for women. The writers argued that this has been due to a sexist, proprietary view of women. Traditionally women have been viewed as either "fallen or on a pedestal. Neither was particularly human. The situation today is different" (*Gift*: 48). This last factual claim is highly debatable. Most feminist critiques hold that contemporary society continues, albeit not so pervasively, to see women through a dualistic lens; the Mary/Eve split continues to define the way in which women are viewed.[48] While it is true that by 1984, social changes favourable to a recognition of women's subjectivity had occurred, it is also true that more change is necessary to eradicate the view that women are either "fallen or on a pedestal." Having said that, it is important to note that the relevance of sexism was identified and applied to this discussion of sexual activity and singleness.

The writer stated that single people need to follow the same standards for the expression of intimacy as do married people: mutuality and vulnerability are essential parts of intimacy. However, there is no conclusive statement as to whether or not the Church supports genital intimacy in committed but non-marital relationships. Instead, the writer concludes that "what is necessary is that the church take seriously its need to help single people in this kind of decision making." Furthermore, the report claims, "the church has, in many ways, fallen short in its treatment of single people. It needs to repent of that failure. It has not helped single persons, celibate or not, to experience deep sexual feelings" (*Gift*: 48-49). One manifestation of this failure pointed out in the report is the "enshrine[ment of] the nuclear family" (52).[49] Clearly, the unmarried adult does not fit into this normative conception and is, therefore, often alienated by the church.

Clearly, the issue of intimacy is a complex and difficult one, as acknowledged by the writer.[50] Although this chapter of the report begins to look at important questions of embodiment including what it means to be intimate and why limits are necessary, this discussion could have gone further by examining the implications of power and sexism for intimate relationships. Such a discussion would have helped to clarify the meaning of mutuality. However, the discussion provides a carefully thought out response to a contentious and important issue.

Sexism

The understanding of the issue of sexism in this report is similar to that put forward in the TFWM critique of *In God's Image*. The 1984 report defines the issue as follows: "Sexism is discrimination on the basis of gender....But it is also a product of inherent, inherited social, political, economic structures." Sexism also involves a gender power imbalance: "The powerless are both culturally and historically female, and the powerful are male. However, like all prejudice it demeans both the victim and the oppressor" (*Gift:* 55). Domination is systemic; all oppression is inextricably linked and self-perpetuating. Further, participants at the PCTC pre-writing workshop claimed, "Liberation of the oppressed brings about liberation for the oppressor."[51] Sexism is experienced, in our culture, on both a personal and systemic basis (56).

There was an underlying issue involved in the writing of this chapter of the report. The author was concerned that the approach not be too "radical" for fear that it would further alienate people of the United Church and prevent members from understanding and embracing the issue. The recent uproar over inclusive language validated and strengthened this concern. The team had to decide whether they should "take a radical justice approach, emphasizing both systemic and personal issues, or...take a more muted approach, for pastoral reasons, in order to increase the likelihood of being heard in the church?"[52] This debate was part of an ongoing dialogue with the Theological Perspectives Unit (TPU) regarding the content of this chapter.

A question arises out of this discussion about the meaning of "pastoral." To what degree and under what circumstances if any is it ethically justifiable to protect others and oneself from possible conflict in the hope that this approach will improve the possibility of conversion to one's point of view? Eventually, "it was agreed that to make systemic sexism almost the exclusive issue would be wrong" but the reasons behind this decision are not explained.[53] The TPU felt strongly that the "truth must be stated, and followed through in pastoral dialogue."[54] In a similar vein, a participant at the PCTC pre-writing workshop reflected that "we cannot be prophetic without also being pastoral nor pastoral without also being prophetic. Recent emphasis has been on the pastoral and on the avoidance of confrontation."[55]

The author observed that the issue of sexism evoked a variety of responses, which she suggested could be identified as "apathy, anxiety, antagonism and action." An option that is not identified is the possibility that some people's responses could be characterized by more than one of these terms. Apathy was explained as the response of people "who claim they just don't understand the problem"; there is no problem according to the ways in which they perceive their personal experience. However, believing that you have not experienced sexism, is insufficient reason for rejecting it as a problem that affects many others. The difficulty with this perspective is "one of levels of awareness and education." The author claimed that education and increased awareness would be sufficient to convince apathetic people that sexism is a problem (*Gift:* 56).

"Anxious" describes those people who are concerned regarding "the changes that the elimination of sexism would bring to our society." This group is unsure of what to think of the issue: "They are…at this stage unsettled and upset by the changes the issue has brought and might still bring to their lives" (*Gift:* 57).

The third category comprises those who are antagonistic toward "the **changes** necessary to eliminate sexism" (*Gift:* 57). These people are characterized as enjoying the current traditional social order—they often benefitting from it "both economically and socially"—and they see "feminism as a cause of the breakdown of the family." The author stated that the "established order" is constructed on the "principle of subordination, God–Man–Woman." She also expressed hope that change can occur and is occurring in the Church: "in the last few years there is greater awareness [within the United Church] of the…present effect [of sexist attitudes]" (*Gift:* 60). Importantly, the author used material gathered by the TFWM to support this claim. Unlike the 1980 study, the work of the TFWM was validated by being used as a resource for the writing of the report.[56]

The last group of people is made up of those "who are active in their battle against sexism."[57] They help to raise consciousness regarding the "horrible truth" that sexism undergirds much behaviour that is "destructive" to women: the high incidence of rape against women in Canada; gender-skewed poverty statistics; the high incidence of wife beating; the fact that pornography is a growth industry, and more—all these factual claims are supported with data from Statistics Canada (*Gift:* 58).

Sexism, as demonstrated by even this limited description of responses, is "difficult and confusing" and "means different things to us." Although each of the above reactions is understandable to some extent, the church must work toward *eradicating* sexism since "not to work for this goal is to thwart God's will" (*Gift:* 60). Theologically, the author claimed that in order to be faithful to the Christian prophetic tradition, the church must name sexism

> Structurally as social evil and as a sin. We have to recognize and acknowledge it, in ourselves and our world, repent of it, and endeavour through the grace of God to eradicate it….We cannot agree that it would be faithful to the gospel to condone resistance to necessary change. We believe that we are called to struggle against sexism as a destructive force and work for our wholeness as children of God. (*Gift:* 60)

Because sexism is economically, psychologically and physically destructive to women and because such destructiveness is contrary to God's will, we are therefore called as individuals and as communities to work for the end of all sexism. Sexism not only limits our roles and our "potential," it also limits God "by defining and imaging our Creator in only masculine terms and forms," contrary to biblical teachings (*Gift:* 60).[58] Although no further theological analysis was offered, almost all of the theological reflection as quoted above was the result of feedback from the TPU. Also, at least partially due to their critique, the chapter's overall stance against sexism was clarified and strengthened.[59] Through the incorporation of critical feedback from the TPU, the author was able to expand her theological analysis of sexism. Dialogue with other interested United Church groups such as the TPU and the TFWM challenged the author and helped to enlarge her moral vision in this area.

The writer claimed ambivalent biblical support to end sexism. However, the bottom line was that we are all "children" of God regardless of our sex or gender. This point is illustrated through reference to Jesus's interactions with women and Paul's statement that we are all one in Christ (*Gift:* 64-65). The Bible, in this chapter, was used to evoke the memory of God's love for humanity, particularly the marginalized. The Bible's ambivalence toward women was also acknowledged.

Sexism is sinful since it is "destructive to human dignity and opposed to the will of God" (*Gift:* 67). The emphasis in this chapter was on the reality and power of sexism and our call, as people of God, to eradicate all forms of it. Further to this, the writers claimed that the contemporary patriarchal organization of society could be "redeemed": "We affirm that the traditional patriarchal structuring of society can be redeemed and eventually transformed through the grace of God and the struggles of those willing to face the contradictions of sexism" (67). Some readers of the draft report disputed this theological and ethical claim. One reader from DMC asked if it meant that we will "go from a bad patriarchy to a good patriarchy?"[60] To be redeemed implies to become good in God's eyes. How can patriarchal structuring become good unless it becomes something other than patriarchal? In fact, the final recommendations to the writing team from the DMC included the suggestion that the term "redeemed" not be used in this context; patriarchal society can be transformed into something new but it cannot be redeemed while it is still patriarchal. The writing team disagreed with this understanding. They seemed to believe that people's attitudes could be changed through education, and society could maintain its basic shape but somehow not be sexist (56). The reasoning behind this claim is not clear, particularly given the feedback from other sources.

Concluding Remarks

The purpose of both *In God's Image…Male and Female* and *Gift, Dilemma and Promise* was to clarify the meaning of human sexuality in troubling times. Did these two reports succeed, and in so doing, help to establish a sexual ethic that could provide a foundation from which the collective United Church could begin to name and address related issues such as violence against women? The foregoing analysis demonstrates that these two human sexuality reports succeeded in some significant ways, and also failed in other ways to establish an adequate sexual ethic. Factors contributing to this limited success were the groups' working styles, the lack of awareness regarding the United Church's past as it relates to issues of sexuality and gender and a failure to establish the overall relevance of sexism.

❱ Working Style

As previously discussed, the *In God's Image* task force was more goal than process oriented. One manifestation of this was the impatience that sometimes was recorded regarding feedback. The pre-writing workshops discounted as reactionary many responses to the 1980 study.

The writing team for *Gift, Dilemma and Promise* was more concerned with process than was the previous team. They devoted much time to collecting critical feedback and discussion through four pre-writing workshops and communication with other United Church groups with related interests. For instance, both the TFWM and the TPU were consulted regarding the writing of the chapter on sexism. This approach fostered dialogue among United Church members regarding human sexuality and this dialogue influenced the report.[61] Dialogue and connectedness among United Church members and between various United Church task groups were important parts of the research process.

❱ History

To understand the conflicting responses to *In God's Image*, a self-conscious awareness of the United Church's story and identity is important. Through a critical awareness and analysis of past documents and past concerns, we become better able to understand the areas where we need more discussion before other issues can be adequately addressed. The potential for building and realizing the transformative effects of memory can be cut short by a compartmentalized approach to history. History is process; the past shapes our identities in an ongoing way. We must recognize this, and choose what to challenge and on what to build.

The writers of both *In God's Image* and *Gift, Dilemma and Promise* could have benefitted from a greater awareness of some of the United Church's relevant history. The Church has long struggled to recognize women's agency and subjectivity in the face of a desire to maintain an order dependent upon the preservation of traditional gender roles. Connected to this dilemma has been the developing awareness that the "enshrinement" of the traditional nuclear family as a part of the United Church's historical and ongoing identity has been alienating and even dangerous. Further, self-critique regarding the Church's approaches to the family and sexuality was a relatively new development; traditionally the Church had been accustomed to the role of the nation's conscience (particularly in these areas), not to self-critique as much as to other-critique. Sexuality had always been valued in the United Church as a gift from God, but historically it had also been treated with suspicion; within the context of marriage the expression of sexuality was good, but outside marriage it was seen as dangerous to self, family and country. Over time, the United Church, at an official level, became concerned with the quality of the relationship within which sexuality was expressed. For instance, by the early 1960s consent was not assumed in every act of marital sexual expression. Around the same time, divorce was recognized as sometimes necessary to the physical well-being of the members of the family. It is not coincidental that these changes occurred in concert. If these struggles and changes had been examined and included as part of the reports, it would have become clearer, although possibly not easier, what issues needed to be dealt with before others could be discussed more effectively.

The most contentious subjects addressed in the 1980 study were fidelity, the interpretation of the Bible and homosexuality. Upon an examination of the United Church's history, this is not surprising. Before these topics could be approached in a productive manner, other topics needed to be more fully discussed. For instance, the assumption that the nuclear family is a God-given institution upon which the country is built needed to be further challenged and alternative paradigms discussed before many people could begin to consider the possible acceptability of same-sex couples. This is not to say that one should wait indefinitely for some fabled sure moment in which to address controversial issues. Jesus certainly did not. It does mean that committment to lasting change necessitates laying the foundation as well as possible while not avoiding strategic risk-taking.[62] Clearly this requires discernment and it is easy for any of us to make mistakes, just as it is difficult to assess our mistakes.

Connected to an emerging critique of the heretofore sanctified family was the movement from a primarily act-centred to a primarily relational-centred sexual ethic. As the United Church became increasingly concerned with the quality of the marital relationship, issues such as consent (1962) began to arise. With this change, the purpose of sexual intimacy began to be seen as including more than procreation and union; the giving of self in sexual expression was also a celebration of the goodness of creation and of mutual love. As a result, the traditional understanding of marital sexual intimacy as always good was no longer accepted. Following from this, the question of the acceptability and appropriateness of sexual intimacy expressed in relationships other than marriage began to arise.

It would be easy to forget that all this was quite a new development and that the struggle with the meaning of the family and marriage had just began. Moreover, even the understanding of gender roles within marriage continued to be debated. These issues of family, marriage, the purpose of sexual intimacy and gender roles were ongoing and needed to be further explored in terms of emerging questions such as the meaning and place of fidelity and sexual orientation.

Neither task force explored this ongoing history. Had this occurred these issues probably would have been identified. The failure to establish connections to the past and to the United Church's ongoing history caused some relevant ethical issues to go unrecognized.

Connected to storytelling is the question of what and whose discourse we use when presenting ethical issues. Our standpoints inform our ethical convictions and worldviews. My standpoint, as a privileged white middle-class woman living in Canada, who has experienced forms of male violence as well as life-giving relationships with men, has contributed to the type of feminist discourse out of which I write. This partiality means that I cannot claim to speak for those with different experiences and that I am subject to their critique.

The authors of *Gift, Dilemma and Promise*, as with those of *In God's Image*, did not clarify their standpoints and did not state what type of discourse they would be using. To be fair, when they wrote the value of this was not recognized widely and the authors simply may not have thought of it. A large part of the documents' discourse was a dominant one; significant parts (not all) of the documents were informed by the normative white male perspective of traditional Euro-American theology. For instance, included in the chapter on marriage (in *Gift*) is the claim that the marital requirement of sexual exclusivity can lead to acts of physical and sexual violence. As explained earlier, this theory did not take into account the experiences of many abused women.[63]

▶ Content Methodology[64]

Both reports relied on scripture, tradition, experience and reason/science as sources of authority. Both emphasized experience as particularly authoritative. However, upon careful examination, it becomes clear that the larger parts of both documents were not written from a perspective of "women's feminist experience." As feminist theologian Pamela Dickey Young explains, "women's feminist experience" involves a conscious awareness of and response to the ways in which women have suffered or been limited in a patriarchal culture: "Women's feminist experience is the experience of questioning all that we have been told about being women. It is the experience of refusing to take at face value anyone's definition of what it means to be a woman. It is the experience of redefining what 'woman' means by redefining whose experience counts as valuable."[65] Young goes on to note the critical factor that "women's feminist experience exposes a patriarchal theology for what it is, half a theology, and judges it accordingly."[66] Without an application of women's feminist experience, theology fails to adequately address women's lives, especially women's experiences of suffering. Although *In God's Image* and *Gift, Dilemma and Promise* both include an entire chapter on sexism, this material was applied only to some other topics in the reports. A participant at the PCTC pre-writing workshop contended that "it will be important [in the report] to make connections between issues where these are clear, for example, between sexism and sexual orientation, not handling them in separate chapters. Someone else affirmed that what was called for here is not a sequence but an interweaving."[67] Such interweaving occurred either inconsistently or not at all; as a result the documents provided an inadequate base for recognition of and response to women's experiences.

In God's Image offered a limited understanding of sexism. This was due, at least partially, to a lack of communication with the TFWM. Further, only the chapter on the Bible attempted a consistent gender analysis. The chapter on sexism in *Gift, Dilemma and Promise* was more comprehensively researched but the application of sexism to the other chapters needed work. In a patriarchal context women are generally less socially powerful than men. An adequate sexual ethic must take this systemic power imbalance into consideration and apply an awareness of sexism to any analysis of related topics.[68] However, both reports failed to do this at points. For instance, the 1984 report reflected theologically on marriage without naming the experiences of abused women (including physical, sexual, spiritual, emotional or verbal abuse); the report encouraged mutual self-sacrifice without any gender analysis; the danger of and temptation to the glorification of suffering was not discussed; and pride was assumed to be one of our greatest temptations.[69] At the beginning of the chapter on marriage it was stated that there was an increased demand for social "services to the battered and emotionally abused," but there was no gender analysis; the recognition of abuse as an issue was not connected to the recognition of sexism as a socio-cultural system. Further, when marital "physical and sexual violence" was mentioned, there was no accompanying analysis of sexism and power dynamics.

Although the reports named both heterosexism and the "enshrinement of the nuclear family," they critiqued neither in the discussion on marriage. For instance, although the increasing divorce rate was named as an issue, neither marriage itself as a patriarchal institution nor the desirability of preserving this institution in its current form was critiqued. Although both *Gift, Dilemma and Promise* and *In God's Image* began to critique some long-held social concepts such as gender relations, gender roles and heterosexism, it proved much more difficult for the writers to consistently apply these ideas to long-held United Church theology and beliefs.[70]

The writers' neglect to name, consistently, systemic power imbalances and their relevance to discussions regarding human sexuality was also evident in discussions of mutuality and exploitation. Although both documents cited mutuality as a norm, for any sexually intimate relationship, the meaning of mutuality remained unclear. Mutuality, it was noted, includes reciprocity, equal care and commitment to each other. However, this understanding was not adequate; mutuality must be defined with explicit reference to systemic social power imbalances. Without this recognition, the issue of violence against women, for instance, cannot be identified as a socio-cultural pattern.[71]

We need both to be attentive to women's frequent experiences of marginalization and to seek justice. This is not to say that a mutual relationship between a man and a woman in the Canadian context is impossible; rather, it is to demand awareness of the greater vulnerability of many women to men within relationships as well as on the world in general. An appropriate mutuality must be defined in the light of the vulnerability involved in intimate sexual expressions and the recognition of structured social oppression.

Such an understanding of power is necessary to the recognition of "exploitative sexual behaviour." *Gift, Dilemma and Promise* made no explicit connection between sexism and exploitative sexual behaviour. The meaning of exploitative sexual behaviour, apart from the understanding that such behaviour is morally wrong, was unclear. This needs to be clarified and concretized. The systemic gender power imbalance of a patriarchal culture coupled with traditional Christian understandings of body, sexuality and women as lowly and dangerous, make women vulnerable to sexual exploitation. Furthermore, sexual abuse of women is frequently perceived as normative. For example, "no means yes" is not an uncommon assumption, and the list goes on.[72] If this confusion between sexuality and violence is to be addressed, an understanding of the relevance of sexism to heterosexual sexual behaviour must be reached, otherwise an adequate understanding of exploitative sexual behaviour remains out of reach.

To understand the relationship between sexism and exploitative sexual behaviour, one also must understand the feminist contention that the personal is political. Sexuality is very personal but it also has social and political implications. The United Church, historically, has been well aware of a connection between the family, the marital relationship and the well-being of the country. However, the recognition that the personal is political involves more than drawing a connection between the so-called public and private spheres; it also presupposes a recognition of the forces that function to negate people. As ethicist Marilyn Legge explains (well after the writing of both documents),

> The feminist insight that the personal is political captures the insight that there is indeed a direct relation, however complexly mediated, between the social order and subjectivity, between language and consciousness, between institutions and individuals. For the personal to be political involves placing personhood and peoplehood at the centre of our ethics, valuing the human in relations informed by self-responsibility and love, and resisting all that concretely negates people.[73]

One force that negates people is sexism. The recognition of this systemic gender power imbalance and its interconnection with other forms of oppression including racism and heterosexism, is necessary to an adequate understanding of the relationship between the personal and political. For instance, as Legge alludes, the contention that ethical decision making is ultimately up to the individual is true in one sense but it neglects an analysis of the power of institutionalized systems of domination over the individual. The position expressed in the 1984 report, that the individual is ultimately responsible, underestimates the force of socio-cultural patterns and prejudices. Such a contention underlines the culpability of the individual in choosing exploitative sexual behaviour; it individualizes exploitative behaviour rather than illuminates the socio-cultural dimension of sexual exploitation. Certainly every individual must take responsibility, but if we are to address the roots of the problem, we must recognize that exploitative sexual behaviour is more than an individual problem; it is rooted in a patriarchal culture and inextricably tied to other systems of domination. In short, ethical decision making is the responsibility of both the individual and the community.

Both human sexuality reports exhibited weaknesses in awareness of relevant history, working style and content. These weaknesses contributed to a failure to provide a sexual ethic adequate to a recognition and understanding of systemic male violence against women. The Church community as a whole must accept some responsibility for this failing as it is we, collectively, who decide and direct the allocation of resources, and of course, the Church's history is part of each of our stories and vice versa. The writing teams must also accept responsibility but, on the other hand, they are the ones who committed their time and efforts to this important work for the Church, and this must be recognized and gratefully honoured. Also, it must be acknowledged that part of the limitations were the result of context; there was not much written on the subject of sexual exploitation and theology, for instance, by the early 1980s.

Both documents began with an understanding of human sexuality as a gift of God with the potential for growth, joy, confusion and destruction. As theologian Chung Hyun Kyung illustrates through the telling of her own story, we are often less connected to and comfortable with our sexuality than we could be:

> "Mom, stop it!" I screamed at her, but she did not look at me. She continued her dance, moving nearly naked in the forest. I felt ashamed of her; I wished she were not my mother. There was nothing to hide the scene before me. There was a deathly silence around us, except for Mother's singing and the sound of the river....She looked like a person who did not belong to this world. I saw real happiness in her face while she was singing and dancing. I could see her breasts, the lines of her body—large, like a whale's—through her wet underwear. I did not want anybody in the world to see that shape, my mother's body that had worked and lived.[74]

An embodied theology must begin with bodily experience; an embodied theology presupposes an appreciation of our bodies. The importance of this was upheld by both reports. Both began with the assertion that our bodies and our sexualities are gifts of God. They bring joy, dilemma and sometimes deep pain.

Although much in these two documents must be critiqued, the fact that human sexuality and gender were addressed by United Church members who were willing to devote time, energy, passion and risk to these important subjects is a witness of hope. While I am committed to a critique of their work so that we may learn and continue with the work of justice, I am also in awe of their willingness to engage in this risky business and of the passion that must have inspired their dedication.

CHAPTER VI

Case Study:
The Task Force on the Changing Roles of Women and Men in Church and Society

*J*HIS CHAPTER WILL EXAMINE the development and work of the Task Force on the Changing Roles of Women and Men in Church and Society (TFWM). The sources used for this examination are, as in other chapters, parts of the official record. Archived minutes of meetings, letters, memoranda, *The Observer* and the ROPs are the primary sources. As with the rest of this book, this window into The United Church of Canada's history is meant as just that, a window. This is a partial history that will help with further exploration into the United Church's work, particularly concerning gender issues and sexism as part of our North American culture's system of oppressions.

During the 1970s, a shift occurred regarding the degree of concern the United Church expressed for the status of women. In 1970, the Steering Committee on Concerns submitted to General Council a list of priorities dividing the concerns of the United Church into three categories—high, medium and low priority status. Of the forty-two items, five were given low priority status. "Status of women" was one of these five (*ROP* 1970:120). However, this was soon to change. Notably, in 1974, the Toronto Conference recommended that General Council establish a task force on the status of women employed in the Church.[1]

In June 1974, the Task Force of the Division of Mission in Canada on Women and Partnership Between Men and Women in Church and Society met for the first time, chaired by Dr Harriet Christie. Fourteen women and four men composed this group at its first meeting.[2] The purpose of this task force was to study women's roles, primarily within the United Church, and to work for equal treatment of women and men within existing Church structures.

The initial recommendations from the Division of Mission in Canada regarding the functions of the task force were:

1. To develop a philosophy and desirable goals for the Division of Mission in Canada regarding the role of women.
2. To examine the present situation in The United Church of Canada re:
   i. The involvement of women in decision making bodies in the Church.

ii. The attitudes which prevent growing partnerships between men
and women.

iii. The involvement of women in professional work in the Church.

3. To be informed regarding issues in society which arise because of discrimination, on the grounds of sex or marital status and, where considered wise, recommend action or take action on behalf of the
Division of Mission in Canada to seek to remove the cause of discrimination.

4. To seek to bring the concern of the Church for freedom, equality and
partnership for all people to bear upon the movements in the country working for a change in laws, business practices and attitudes
towards women.[3]

The task force decided that their emphasis should, at least initially, be on
the role of women in the United Church. Later, the issue of partnership
between men and women would be discussed.[4] The name of the task force
did not reflect this priority. The power of naming and who was to name this
group was to be an ongoing issue. Historically, women have not had the
power of public voice and, therefore, the power to name their experiences
and the power to shape society's responses to issues that affect women.[5] As
women in the United Church began to gain the voice with which to express
their experiences, many of them worked to self-name.

With these articulated goals and functions, the task force began a liberal
feminist examination of women within the United Church. By this I mean
that their focus was on structural equity reform; they were concerned primarily with such issues as employment equity, equal pay legislation and
balanced gender representation on committees. A critique of the United
Church structure, supported by empirical data, was an important step
toward understanding some of the ways in which sexism functions. An
examination and critique of the nature of the Church's structure itself would
come later.

By their fourth meeting, the group had discovered data indicating that
men were receiving more financial support from the United Church for education than women.[6] A related subject concerned the number of women
employed in the head office of the national Church or serving on Church
committees.[7] There was a disproportionately high number of women in the
clerical positions and, similarly, of men in executive positions. The task
force recommended that the Staffing and Personnel Committee attend to the
principle of "equal pay for work of equal value…as a means of bridging the
gap between executive and clerical categories."[8]

The task force also commissioned research regarding the number of
women on United Church committees. The results were quite detailed; to
summarize—27 percent of committee members at the National level (Divisions) were women, 30 percent in Conference committees, 32 percent in
Presbytery committees and 38 percent in pastoral charge committees—
women comprised approximately one-third of the committee membership
at all Church levels.[9]

The task force also looked at attitudes: how did stereotyping and language reinforce the "disadvantaged" condition of women? How could these attitudes be changed?[10] To address these concerns, the task force monitored the official United Church magazine, *The Observer*.[11] An initial survey of five issues of *The Observer* revealed that of all the references to and pictures of "male/female, clergy, laity," 824 references or pictures involved men, 193 concerned women.[12] In response to this observation, staff of *The Observer* agreed to publish "an item on women and the church in the March [1975] issue." The task force supported this and encouraged the writing of more articles by and about women.[13] This was a step toward raising the visibility of women's experiences—as defined by women.

The task force also examined the language used by the writers and editors of *The Observer*: "[we] consulted with editors and drew attention to McGraw-Hill guidelines for non-sexist language."[14] This led to a request in 1976, for "someone in [the] national church to get resources to compile guidelines for non-sexist writing and editing for church publications."[15] Later that year, Kay Bentley and the task force, in conjunction with DMC, produced "Guidelines for Equal Treatment of the Sexes in Resource Materials."

This awareness that language reflects and enforces thought patterns extended to a critique of liturgical language. The theological criterion for using language inclusive of both genders was that "our work and actions in worship [need to] reflect the fact that liturgy is the work of the whole people of God—not simply that of the men of God. Hence, the hymns we sing, the prayers spoken, the scripture read and other actions in worship should express this fundamental principle."[16] Since men, women and children are equally made in God's image, all elements of worship should represent both male and female.

Education and networking were two additional foci. In order to foster a connection with the wider women's movements, the United Church regularly appointed a representative to the National Action Committee on the Status of Women (NAC).[17] The task force also took a great interest in International Women's Year (IWY), 1975, and recommended to General Council Executive that IWY be observed on March 9, which was approved, and continues today as Internatonal Women's Day. Subsequently the task force sent a letter to all pastoral charges suggesting that they reflect on the role of women during corporate worship on 9 March 1975.[18] These new networking efforts with wider Canadian women's movements generated greater awareness within the Church and laid further ground work for the development of critique and self-critique. A dialectic between the United Church and parts of the Canadian women's movement was begun by the task force's success in establishing communication.

Contrary to its original mandate, and although networking, education and the raising of awareness were significant concerns, the task force's main focus remained on institutional reform: "The task force has examined the present situation re involvement of women in decision making bodies of the church; in professional work in the church, but we have not focussed on the area of attitudes which prevent growing partnership between men and women. If we intend to take seriously the second part of our title we must tackle this matter."[19]

The task force began to question their original mandate and to ask some critical questions, which the DMC Executive then reviewed. The two original foci assigned to them were reexamined:

1. related to women—discovering the need for change in the church and working through all possible channels to bring about this change; and being alert to [the] women's movement in Canada.
2. related to partnership between men and women in Church and society—working with mixed groups to better understanding of "partnership," support groups for men and women bewildered by change, etc.

The task force concluded that its work thus far had not adequately addressed these particular foci: "We are aware that we have not made any secure links with the Women's movement and their concerns, and we have not yet been successful in communicating our concerns to many of the UCW [United Church Women] groups. We are also aware that we have done nothing directly related to 2 above (although we recognize that the implications of all our work is obviously related)."[20] The group knew that the Church needed its work, and since this work had only begun, they requested that their mandate "continue for at least another year, with a broader membership."[21] While their emphasis on process and exploration of the issues was a more time-consuming process than a consensus model which required one story and position, it nurtured mutual critique and the participation of a variety of voices.[22]

Upon review of the task force, the DMC Executive decided not to renew the task force's mandate, since a "Task Force on Women" was "token and ineffective" in addressing a problem that they understood to be much larger and deeply rooted: "It became clear to us in discussion that this is an area of work which involves attitudinal change, which has implications for our developmental approach to children and youth, which relates to the need of men to find a new identity, and which includes the need for changes in our Church language and imagery."[23]

To explore the best possible ways with which this problem could be dealt, the DMC created a working group "mandated to follow up on two tasks: '(a) clarify the concern regarding women: their new awareness, struggles for justice, changing roles and their relationship with men; [and] (b) to formulate some directions for the Church's response'" (ROP 1977:279). While both the task force and the Executive agreed that the current mandate was neither appropriate nor adequate, the Executive chose not to ask the task force to engage in the follow-up work. Instead, a new group was created that retained only a few members of the task force.

Seven women and three men attended the first meeting of this working group, to be called the "Committee to Clarify the Concerns Regarding Women." Shelley Finson, past chair of the task force, also chaired this committee. Neither the name of the group nor their minutes indicated a radical departure from the past agenda of the defunct task force. Other identified issue areas, aside from "institutional functioning," were classified under the titles "personal," "societal," and "relationships/family." The committee identified human sexuality primarily as a "personal" issue and did not include it as a societal or familial concern. Regarding the family, the committee cited "assumptions" and "new forms of 'family'" as concerns; the traditional form of the family was not assumed to be normative.[24]

This group named some theological principles as guidelines for its work. The committee noted that although "both male and female are created in God's image" and as such are equally "precious" to God, men are believed to be "superior" to women in society. Further, though men and women were created as distinct beings and "God saw that this was good," it has been argued that biological differences require that "females be submissive to males" in order to reproduce.[25] Problematic, according to the committee, was a dualistic approach to gender that assumed the separation of the sexes and the domination of men over women.

Such domination is an abuse of power, resulting in broken relationship; this is sin. What is more, the committee claimed, domination is systemic and breeds further domination and alienation: "Sin (lusting for God's power) leads to alienation from the earth, each other, and God. This alienation manifests itself between male/female in systemic patterns of domination (subjugation, hierarchy, separateness and competition)."[26]

In spite of this grim reality, the committee wrote that there was hope in the midst of this brokenness: "Jesus Christ enters the situation of alienation to incarnate salvation and liberation. This brings the possibility of re-establishment of one-ness." Jesus lived in solidarity with the marginalized and "calls us to become one with those who suffer oppression and injustice (solidarity)." The committee did not define further its understanding of solidarity, except to maintain that a critique of power was necessary to dismantle oppression.[27]

Based on these theological and sociological claims, the working group agreed on a set of "operational principles." First, we "are called...to live within th[e] uncertainty" of the "differences and similarities" between males and females, aside from the more obvious physical differences. Further, because of this uncertainty, the working group reasoned that assigned sex roles limit the realization of our "gifts, talents and callings."

Further, it was claimed that "the" male perspective and experience is normative across the world and this "shapes our impression of reality." Unfortunately, the working group failed to acknowledge the diversity of male experiences and also the possibility of the existence of non-androcentric cultures.[28] Broad generalizations can function to trivialize and silence those who do not fall within the norm, and therefore, even when critiquing dominant norms, our human complexities need to be kept before us.

Connected to these claims was an argument for a widespread attitudinal change:

> We continue to suffer as Christians from living with a past and a tradition which is patriarchal and hierarchical in nature, and which is deeply embedded in our scripture, out theology, our language, in the structure of our institutions, and in our understanding of God and of each other. [Further, patriarchy and androcentrism]...pervade every area of life...[and] point to the need for a radical change in attitude, both conscious and unconscious, and constant vigilance and deep searching of our roots.[29]

The working group was predominantly concerned with changing attitudes and exploring the roots of sexism. As Rosemary Radford Ruether argued a few years after the writing of these minutes, this exploration was essential to the discovery of one's subjectivity and identity: "One cannot correctly pose the question of the meaning of the Christian identity today until one is willing to tell the story of Christian origins truthfully. Or, to put it another way, people who have to lie about their history cannot clarify their identity."[30] The working group functioned primarily at the stage of telling their stories and identifying issues. At this point, the group was inclined to make some broad generalizations as they began to find their voice.

The working group identified specific tasks as important to its mandate, relating to the following areas: worship—inclusive language, images of God and stories of women "in our heritage" needed to be developed as indispensable elements of worship services; models of ministry based on "partnership and equality rather than patriarchy and dependence" were advocated; and concern was expressed regarding "equal pay and opportunity for advancement of women in professional ministry." The importance of including women's experience in theological reflection, the interrelatedness of theology, sexuality and gender relationships as well as the influence of our patriarchal context on our theology were named also as issues. The need for Christian education for people of all ages, "which incorporates the new awareness re attitudes, roles, values" was listed as another important task. The working group also called for changes to traditional understandings of marriage and family and for "new patterns of relating" within these institutions. Lastly, the group identified two needs regarding "women in the church": to reconstruct women's history and to build supportive "structures...[and] atmosphere" for women in the Church.[31]

The 1977 General Council received the working group's progress report, which affirmed the dignity and subjectivity of all people and confessed the patriarchal and androcentric nature of "every area of life" (ROP 1977:270-80).[32] The working group identified various present and historical examples of the church's oppression of women: the exclusion of women from the written history of the church, the androcentric nature of dominant theology, the almost exclusively male leadership in the church, and the pain many women experienced from the almost exclusive use of male language in worship and elsewhere (ROP 1977:279).[33] The authors of the report generated this goal:

> To raise the awareness of the institutional Church—its bodies, Church leaders and individuals, to the issues which the changed consciousness of and about women has brought before society and our Church. (ROP 1977:281)

The 27th General Council endorsed this goal (ROP 1977:302).

The DMC's Working Unit with Adults took over when the working group disbanded. This unit proposed that a national, ad hoc task force on women's concerns be set up for one year with the purpose of "communicating, animating and educating, advocating for action and supporting."[34] An ad hoc group was formed and met twice.[35]

In the 1970s, women with feminist experiences had begun to make themselves heard in The United Church of Canada. Previously, women by and large had rarely had the voice to get the Church's agenda to include the issue of male violence against women. By this time lack of voice was no longer a significant block to naming and addressing women's experiences of male violence and other concerns.

Mandate and Purpose

In March 1980, the DMC asked that the General Council Executive establish an interdivisional task force on the "role of women and the changing roles and relationships of men and women in society." The Executive approved the formation of the "Interdivisional Task Force on the Changing Roles of Women and Men in Church and Society," (ROP 1982:399) responding to the DMC's claim that the "church which once played a prophetic role in justice issues now lags behind the state in many of these areas" (ROP 1980:155).[36]

The TFWM was to be "action-oriented" and to work to fulfil the following mandate:

> 1. To raise the awareness of the institutional church…to the issues which the changed consciousness of and about women, and the changing roles and relationships of women and men have brought before society and the church [as endorsed by the 27th General Council, and]
> 2. To effect necessary changes in our theology, language, attitudes and practices that will bring about new understandings of the equal worth of all people—particularly the equal worth of women and men. (ROP 1982:399)

These functions, as put forward by the DMC, included: to act as educator for the rest of the United Church regarding "the inequities that exist in male-female relationships," to "exercise a prophetic role in the justice issues related to women in our church and in society," to "initiate" projects and further research on gender issues, to develop policy and theological statements, to examine and share with the rest of the United Church the value of liberation theology (including feminist theology), to work on the dismantling of sex-rolism and to research the "hidden history of women in the church."[37]

The TFWM defined sexism as a systemic and structural power imbalance between men and women (ROP 1982:403-404).[38] The task of the group was large. The insidious nature of sexism, the TFWM discovered, was such that even the efforts of this task force would be subverted, both intentionally and unintentionally.

Membership

Initially, the working unit had recommended that there be one full-time, paid staff person nominated by the task force members and that 75 percent of the members be women, "all of whom are able to affirm the mandate provided by the 27th General Council and the underlying theological convictions."[39] However, the General Council Executive changed the above criteria in two ways: the staff person was to be named by the DMC Executive and there were to be "not less than 60 percent and not more than 75 percent women."[40]

The implications of these changes were twofold: first, the DMC Executive would have more power over the TFWM by virtue of selecting the staff person, and the TFWM would have less autonomy and be more accountable to the DMC Executive. Second, it became possible to have a lesser percentage of women on the TFWM. Although the Executive did not insist that the recommended percentage of women be dropped, they did decide that the percentage could be dropped and still be appropriate. Notably, neither group specified from where or what backgrounds the members should come other than the requirement that they "are able to affirm the mandate provided by the 27th General Council and the underlying theological convictions."

There continued to be concern about the TFWM's membership. One of the task force's first acts was to make a motion to add two members who had both been involved on earlier task groups regarding women, Shelley Finson and Daphne Anderson:

> Whereas Shelley Finson and Daphne Anderson have been involved in the growth, development and leadership of the women's movement in the church; and Whereas the Task Force requires their knowledge and expertise, Therefore we strongly recommend to the sub-Executive of General Council that Shelley Finson and Daphne Anderson be added to the membership of the Task Force immediately.[41]

In response, Anderson was appointed to the committee, with Finson as an alternate. The TFWM was unsatisfied and recorded some questions regarding the exclusion of Finson: "What is the justice issue here? Can the church tolerate strong women?... How, when did Shelley's name get dropped? Do we need to ask why people are so cautious of us?"[42]

The TFWM pursued the matter through a letter to the then moderator, Lois Wilson. They expressed their will that Finson be a member:

> A *noticeable* pattern throughout history is that people who begin this process of asking fundamental questions, become ostracized at the point when their concerns are being acknowledged by the community. The effect is that the cutting edge of the movement is dulled and irreversible divisions occur. Those who are asked by the community to "raise our awareness" often flounder because they are cut off from those who have prepared the way. We are asking that Shelley be appointed as an integral part of the task force, so that this will not happen to us.[43]

The group saw Finson's exclusion, whether conscious or not, as an attempt to silence a strong critical voice and to break the continuity of the TFWM's work.

Certainly, there is a long history of the persecution of nonconformists. Critique has the potential to explode the illusions and self-deceptions of society; it has the potential to reveal where unjust power lies and thus to challenge this power. Hence, critique can be a very powerful and threatening tool. Ruether points out some of the extreme measures that have been taken to subdue attempts to thwart the status quo. Jesus, the Jews and the women labelled as witches all provide examples of the high price that has been exacted from perceived dissenters of the existing social order. Jesus was crucified for his subversiveness, the Jews were slaughtered for their differentness, and women were murdered because they refused to conform.[44] As Ruether notes, the "persecuted group is seen as breaking down the established authority of the social consensus."[45] Whether Finson was excluded because of her non-conformity is a matter of conjecture; it is a possibility.

Sexism Is the Issue: Naming

In March 1982, the TFWM observed a significant shift in its understanding of the issue: "Our Task Force has realized, through our past year's work, that there is an important distinction between the condition of the changing roles of women and men and the underlying structural dimension of sexism."[46] Thus, similar to the previous Task Force on the Partnership of Women and Men, this task force believed that their current name—"The Task Force on the Changing Roles of Women and Men in Church and Society"— did not reflect the nature of their work. The issue went much further than simply changing gender roles;[47] the group considered themselves "a task force on sexism," understanding sexism to mean "any attitude, action or structure which discriminates against people on the basis of gender" (*ROP* 1982:172). They identified manifestations of sexism:

> Men have been authorities...decision-makers, rational, in control and 'public,' [and] women have been servants, supporters, followers, passive and submissive, confined to the 'private' sphere. Church teachings, attitudes and practices have blessed this dominant/subordinate pattern as God's 'natural order.' This pattern of domination/subordination is pervasive in church and society.[48]

The church's complicity in sexism is a sin that requires confession, repentance and conversion before resurrection can be experienced.

Theologically, the TFWM stated, sexism is a corporate and personal evil. Further, sexism is inextricably tied to all other forms of systemic oppression:

> We believe sexism is a demonic force that mitigates against vision—[there is a] connection [between]...oppressed [groups]—[there is a] necessity to confess/repent the institutionalizing of privilege at the expense of others; privilege is the power to control decisions to marginalize, to ordain groups, discuss the insights and abilities of others, [and the] power to decide not to damage.[49]

The TFWM defined sexism as pervasive, interconnected with other forms of oppression, and characterized by a systemic gender power imbalance in favour of men over women, with the clear potential for the abuse of that power.[50]

By 1981, the TFWM had identified the systemic nature of sexism; they had made connections between the oppression of women and the oppression of other groups such as "Indian women," and more generally between sexism and violence against women, racism and classism.[51] By 1982 there was an emphasis in the TFWM's minutes on "Native people." In April 1982, the task force discussed native people in relation to its membership policy. Some members argued that people of different racial backgrounds, particular aboriginal peoples, should be required in the membership. However, the group could not reach a consensus on this issue and decided to "inform the Nominating Committee that our mandate, as we understand it, now includes a strong emphasis on the links with racism and classism, and our need is for new members who would have a strong awareness of this and can affirm it."[52]

This process is characteristic of other decisions of the TFWM; consensus within the group was not usually a predominant value. Rather, the emphasis was on the expression and discussion of different points of view. This process allowed for conflicting points of view, mutual critique and, subsequently, a development of sometimes competing ideas; the task force's process was consistent with their values.

When the task force outlined its goals later that same year, the third goal was to "act in solidarity with marginalized people, in order to enable the church to be faithful to the justice call of the Gospel."[53] Heterosexism and "our solidarity with lesbian and gay people" emerged as particular areas of concern,[54] and the group identified links between sexism, racism and heterosexism. As a group that does not conform to societal norms, the "gay community [is]...a threat to patriarchy" and, as such, is vulnerable to various "punishments" ranging from the denial of spousal benefits to murder, similar to nonconforming women.[55]

The TFWM decided that to stand in solidarity with those who have a homosexual orientation, they needed to hear more from gay and lesbian people, particularly regarding their experiences of heterosexism. One way in which they did this was to invite representatives of AFFIRM—a United Church group that functions to support gay and lesbian people in the church and their families, friends and advocates—to attend a meeting in September 1983 and share some of their experiences and insights.[56] The taskforce worked to develop such an understanding of solidarity, as did the subsequent Standing Committee on Sexism. As the TFWM explored the interconnectedness of oppressions and reflected on the meaning of solidarity, the need to rename the task force became more pressing.

Sociologist Gillian Walker describes the struggle of women's groups to get the issue of violence against women named and on the agenda of the government of Ontario. Walker concludes that once the issue was on the government's agenda, it became appropriated by various professional bodies, notably the Department of Health and Welfare and the courts. Through this appropriation, the issue became renamed and redefined so that it could better fit into already existing mechanisms. For example, wife abuse became family violence or domestic disturbance, effectively removing any overt recognition of women's systemic oppression. The issue became separated from women's experience of suffering and distorted by its absorption into these existing structures. Walker describes this process as one of "seeking recognition and a struggle for control of the 'issue'; for control, that is, of how it should be defined, understood, and acted upon."[57] The issue of naming is critical to the understanding of an issue and, consequently, to the concrete responses. The TFWM thought that the title "The Task Force on Sexism" would better reflect its "'interpretation of the mandate the Church gave us, [as well as help to raise the consciousness of the rest of the United Church regarding sexism].'"[58]

The TFWM noted that its name had been changed often by General Council, the Council Executive or the DMC since 1974. The members claimed that this constant name-changing and membership upheaval served to undermine and sabotage their efforts. They took this concern a step further at the 1982 General Council and charged those with power over the task forces of attempting to co-opt and silence their voices of dissent:

> One of the ways as a society that we keep individuals and groups of people from gaining power/identity is by: 1) Setting up new groups; 2) Keeping the group separated from those people who have provided significant leadership in the past and have a history in the work; 3) Continually changing the name or the identity of the group or task; 4) Discouraging networking between

groups involved in the same issue; 5) Playing groups off against each other.
It is destructive to continually: 1) Ignore those who have offered keen insight
and leadership; 2) Change the membership of a group so that the group continually needs to start over again.

This is what happened to the National Task Force on Changing Roles of
Women and Men in Church and Society. It may have been unconscious
because it is the pattern of our society. We chose to challenge that process
and as a result one of our initial actions was a request to General Council
Executive that two of the women who had been identified with this issue
and given strong leadership be added to the Task Force. (ROP 1982:405-406)

The reason behind this frequent name changing may or may not have been
a deliberate adherence to a social pattern committed to the preservation of
the status quo; it may simply have resulted from the growing pains accompanying the creation of a new group established to study and act on a newly
articulated and defined issue. The reason notwithstanding, Walker's study
demonstrates the difficulty and paradox of raising issues that arise from
the experiences of marginalized groups within established social structures.

Feminism and Theological Method

The TFWM's first goal was to reflect theologically about gender issues and,
in so doing, to develop a feminist theological method: "[Our goal is to
draw] especially from the experiences of women to rethink our traditional
theological assumptions, images and methods and to formulate, through
conversation new theological approaches in which we keep moving towards
clearer understandings of the justice demands for a faithful people."[59]
Accordingly, their objectives were: to engage in the process of "theological
reflection/research/study as a group," to develop a theological method based
on experience and feminism and to educate the United Church regarding feminist theology.

The specific tasks that followed from these objectives included the development of new images (e.g., the dance or circle), the engagement of the
leadership of women who were familiar with feminist theological models,
the development of "theologies emerging from male experience as it relates
to participation in sexism" (the men's subgroup took on this task), to continue to work on the issue of inclusive language and to develop ways to
engage in "story telling/reflection."[60] The following paragraphs will explore
the TFWM's understanding of storytelling as feminist Christian theological
method, and the exploration of their image of the dance.[61]

Experience was identified as the hermeneutical starting point for doing
theology: "Theologizing...begins with *our* experience and then seeks illu-
mination from collective wisdom and witness of the scriptures and the
Christian tradition" (ROP 1982:557). The task force explained that the
value of experience and storytelling is historically grounded; this method-

ology is not new; it is part of a long Christian tradition and scripture: "The oral tradition was crucial to the history of the people of Israel. As they told stories of their common experience as a conscious political act in order to define themselves over and against a dominant culture, their understanding of God and how God acted through these experiences was deepened" (ROP 1982:557).[62] Storytelling can be a way to retrieve dangerous memories that provide an alternative to the dominant understanding of the way things are; as with the ancient people of Israel, memory and storytelling can help to lead a people closer to justice as long as the memories and stories of one particular group are not perceived to contain *the* only truth.

The factual claims underlying the TFWM's understanding of storytelling as it applies to women, were: 1) all women share a "common experience"; 2) the personal is political; 3) storytelling is particularly important for a marginalized people; and 4) storytelling illuminates a people's understanding of and faith in God. Feminists have vigorously debated the first assumption. Although no one person's experience is identical to another's, those who experience a shared context such as that created by sexism, share some commonalities.

The second assumption the TFWM made was that storytelling is a political act. Through the retrieval and retelling of stories of past hopes and suffering, a marginalized community can be empowered to challenge the dominant paradigm. Storytelling, then, is particularly important to the disadvantaged, which is the third claim made by the TFWM. For example, storytelling and theologizing by women in a patriarchal culture is a radical act: "Because in the past, theology has been predominantly a task performed by men, the uniqueness of women's perspective [as informed by "our bodies, our work and play, our emotional and intellectual life"] has either been ignored or misinterpreted...in feminist theology the particular life stories of women are essential" (ROP 1982:557).[63]

Feminist theology is concerned with women's experiences and affirming "woman's wholeness and value as part of a process of self-liberation in community with others" (ROP 1982:558). This storytelling process is one that continues indefinitely—there is no one end point; there is no one truth. As the TFWM stated, this theological method is an "ongoing dialogue" (557).

The TFWM believed in the importance of applying these theological insights to themselves: "We...know that the way we *live*—as women and men in community—is as important as life itself" (ROP 1982:560). For the TFWM, this involved theological reflection on their *experience* as a group. Through this reflection process, the members found that they learned new things about themselves and each other regarding the pervasiveness and "subtlety" of sexism. By actively engaging in this self-critical action/reflection model, they found themselves changing and moving; they "imaged" themselves "as dancers learning a new dance." The TFWM invited the rest of the United Church to join in this dance (560).

This image of a dance emerged regularly in discussions of the group's self-understanding. Reflection on group process occurred at most meetings and consumed much time. It was valued as necessary to a collegial rather than hierarchical dynamic. The group did not consciously give more power to any one individual; each member used her/his particular gifts and experiences in the group dance.[64]

Institutional Reform

One of the TFWM's goals was to "discern and develop strategies for creating awareness of sexism and effecting change in our institutional structures and systems, theolog[ies], policies, programs, language [and images], attitudes and practices as we live out our theology [as a faithful people]."[65] The objectives were to critique the "existing structures of the United Church," facilitate the self-critique of the United Church regarding sexism and related "blocks," "come to clear understandings of misogyny as women and men of the task force" and continue to work on the issue of inclusive language and "theological implications." An overarching objective was to "analyze power where its use perpetuates sexism."[66]

▶ "STRUCTURES AND SYSTEMS"

Critique and education regarding sexism in the institutional United Church was a concern for the TFWM as it had been for its predecessors. The group requested in 1981, that all divisions and departments in the Church National Office "take at least half an hour at staff meetings in October, January and March to discuss the issue of sexism as it relates" to individual workers and their "department[s]." The goals were to "raise awareness among staff about the issue of sexism, and to encourage each division, department and unit to relate the issue of sexism to its area of work."[67] Apparently, there was very little awareness of a gender power imbalance at Head Office; there was "little or no acknowledgment of the United Church as an unjust employer." As an attempt at further education, the "differences between mutual, empowering working relationships and hierarchical, exploitative conditions were also discussed." However, there was little or no perception of need for affirmative action regarding the employment of women at United Church House.

The task force also surveyed the Church regarding relevant policies and practices: "[We intend to] assess the current status of all women at Church House and the Conference Offices and, based upon the results, to recommend to the General Council Executive the most effective ways to remedy any injustices in our policies, practices and attitudes respecting employment, promotion and opportunities for women employees."[68] The TFWM believed that the United Church was committed, in principle, to the "just treatment of women and men in its employment policies, practices and attitudes" but people may have differed in their understanding of what constituted discrimination.[69] The audit also was intended to illuminate patterns of discrimination: "Discrimination is itself more thorough and systematic than is often first realized. A comprehensive approach is needed to avoid ad hoc or piece-meal responses to isolated issues." The TFWM hoped that the United Church would take ownership of this self-critical audit.[70]

Facts gathered through the audit showed that a far greater number of females than males were employed in Church House support staff positions: 21 males (10 percent) and 185 females (90 percent). Also, there was a significant gender disparity in the "higher" positions of power: 13 males (72.2 percent) and 5 females (27.8 percent).[71] Furthermore, most responses to the survey suggested that there had been no work on sexism prior to the survey (*ROP* 1984:498).[72]

In their report to the 1984 General Council, based on the audit and other research, the TFWM noted manifestations of sexism:

> Our church is not free of sexism, either. It can be seen in the following examples:
> - The assumption that women will perform similar functions in the church to those they do at home;
> - the predominant use of male imagery and language for God;
> - the reluctance of local congregations to call an ordained woman to be their minister;[73]
> - the inability of many committees to see that family responsibilities and livelihood need to be shared by both men and women;
> - insufficient provisions of childcare;
> - the fact that a research report of the United Church about women in ministry indicated that 1/3 of the respondents had experienced sexual harassment as theological students and/or church employees.
> - [the fact that there is a difference in incomes between the genders]. (*ROP* 1984:490)

The task force called on the Church to end this sexism.[73]

Naming and acting on the existence of sexism in the United Church not only broke the silence but also challenged the myth of the good family—in this case the Church family. Viewed as a good family and guardian of moral virtue, the Church had been lifted above much-needed critique: "Many of us have been taught that the church is different from other institutions, in the way that it is structured and in the way that it functions. We believe that it is important to de-mystify and de-idealize the notion that the church as an institution is unique and therefore better and sinless" (*ROP* 1984:499).

The TFWM believed it was silenced when it threatened this understanding of the United Church as a good family; harmony and maintenance of the status quo were valued above conflict and above justice for women: the "institutional church has ignored, trivialized and marginalized those working to raise the awareness of the church" (*ROP* 1984:500).

A common thread through the TFWM's work toward institutional reform was their experience of resistance (*ROP* 1984:484-85). The task force understood that power rested with those who defined the norm, that is "white, upper and middle-class, heterosexual males" (489). They noted that this was characteristic of patriarchy: "Patriarchy can be understood as a social system with a norm and value structure that grants men partial or total control over female existence. The institutional church has been shaped by patriarchy" (495), and it can be threatening when the balance of power threatens to shift.

Until this point, the task force and its predecessors had focused much of their energies, time and commitment on structural critique. However, by October 1984, a shift in the TFWM's focus was becoming evident: in a discussion regarding finished and unfinished work, the group decided that the next phase might involve greater "focus...on education, reaching out, [and] perhaps less focus on structural change."[74] Earlier, in 1983, a task force member had observed that "we regard ourselves to have the primary task of education, not of being primarily change agents by ourselves."[75] However, the group found it difficult to facilitate change rather than make changes themselves; they valued empowerment and collective change but understandably found it difficult to move at the slow, patient pace required to move *with* and not ahead of others in the United Church. This shift—focusing more on education than on structural reform within the Church—was to be a gradual one.

▶ INCLUSIVE LANGUAGE AND IMAGERY

Language was one component of the TFWM's goal regarding both institutional and attitudinal change. The issue of inclusive language and the experience of "exclusion and pain [some women felt] when confronted by the predominantly male language structure" (*ROP* 1977:279) was named at the 1977 General Council in the TFWM's report. By 1980, General Council resolved to:

> Commit itself to the discipline of opening our language in the following ways:
>   1. That materials presently in use be studied with a view to identifying exclusive language....
>   2. That changes be recommended that would avoid such language.
>   3. That these changes be implemented in new editions and publications.
>   4. That such changes be made available to our constituency even before new editions are available. (*ROP* 1980:943)

Further, the TFWM was asked to compose a set of guidelines regarding inclusive language, which the General Council Executive approved in November 1981. At the next General Council, the TFWM explained the connection between inclusive language and the eradication of "racism, sexism and systematic oppression":

Since language is connected to power it is a justice issue and it's important to connect it to other justice issues. People's response to the issue of language illustrates our response to women's place in society and in the church. Language perpetuates and reinforces the structures which, on a world-wide basis, place women in a secondary and dominated role. Language is one of those issues which must be addressed if we hope to change our society with all its patterns of oppression to a society based on justice. (ROP 1982:157)[76]

The use of exclusively male language for God has far reaching implications. As the TFWM recorded, this language functions to justify and perpetuate the patriarchal gender power imbalance, including systems and structures that operate to reinforce not only this particular power imbalance but also the systemic marginalization of many groups. Furthermore, the use of exclusively male God language contributes to a mind-set that can justify violence against women.[77] A belief that only male mages can adequately represent God supports the belief that men are somehow closer to God than are women. Although the TFWM did not explicitly name violence against women as one reason for addressing exclusive language, they stated clearly that exclusive language functions to "perpetuate and reinforce the structures which, on a world-wide basis, place women in a secondary and dominated role" (ROP 1982:157).

The advent of inclusive language was uncomfortable and threatening for many. As the TFWM pointed out, "We are touching nerve endings, changing some beliefs, and people are (rightly) nervous. Symbols are changing."[78] The records of proceedings of 1982 and 1984 continued to exhibit numerous memorials regarding inclusive language. As the TFWM observed in 1982, "There's more support and more opposition than we'd realized."[79]

Pornography and Other Forms of Male Violence against Women

In 1984, as part of their work toward raising consciousness regarding violence against women, the TFWM provided education about pornography. This work largely dealt with the film *Killing Us Softly*. The TFWM recommended this film to the Adult Working Unit as a "resource for youth groups, women's groups and men's groups" that would function "as a means of consciousness-raising through examination of an area that affects all of our lives. The film identifies ways that women are exploited through advertising and also identifies the power and influence of the advertising world."[80] To facilitate and direct critical discussion, the TFWM prepared a study guide for both men and women to accompany the film.

The aim of the film and study guide was to educate women and men about the objectification of women in the media. The first step the guide indicated was to develop critical awareness regarding the exploitative effect of advertising in our culture on women: "Advertising's image of women is unreal and therefore also unjust and unloving."[81]

The guide invited women to examine how advertising presents "the difference between women's and men's roles, sexuality, [and] control of our lives" (ROP 1982:555), in order to empower women through a critical recognition of the "untruth" told in advertising about women's lives and experiences. The men's discussion focused on taking responsibility for "perpetuating this injustice" and looking for ways in which men could work to stop the objectification of women in the media. Part of this responsibility involved examining their own relationships with women to discover how their popular image of the ideal woman "promote[s] or hinder[s] satisfying and significant relationships with women" (ROP 1982:555).

After listening to several women's stories, the TFWM concluded that "men's experience of sexism differs in crucial and fundamental ways from that of women....Men begin from a position of privilege and dominance in which men's experience is taken as normative." Men must acknowledge their complicity in sexism, be it intentional or simply an acceptance of the status quo, and analyse what power means for them (ROP 1982:555-56).[82]

Hermeneutically, the task force stated that one must start with the experiences of women. Men as the dominant social group then must engage in self-critique:

> Our Task Force sees lots of evidence that our society values men's roles, men's opinions, and men's experiences differently and more highly than it values those of women. The men on the Task Force are beginning to see that until men themselves begin to question the power we have simply because we are male, we are contributing to women's oppression....We think it's important to notice how often our opinions and decisions and directions are accepted simply because we're male.[83]

Accordingly, the group began work in 1981 to "establish a network of men to raise awareness about their involvement—as men—in the issue of sexism."[84] They emphasized the importance of a self-critical process grounded in dialogue.

The 1982 General Council called the task force to give further attention to "violence: battered and abused women, pornography, poverty, family 'breakdown' and divorce."[85] Pornography was the first of many subjects the TFWM related to violence against women. This request indicated that the time had come for more such work.

By 1983, the TFWM were exploring the issue of sexual harassment,[86] noting that the offenders often receive more protection in these cases than do their victims: "Concern is that the woman [victim] is often not supported, sometimes attacked. But nothing is done about the man."[87] The traditional Christian view of sexuality contributes to this dynamic of blaming the victim: "Traditionally, Christian doctrine de-emphasizes the importance of the body and focuses on the sexual act itself and the female body as the bearer of the worst sin."[88]

At the next General Council meeting, in 1984, the TFWM led a "workshop on domestic violence."[89] While the task force understood this violence as a product of sexism, the issue was named in non-gendered terms: "domestic violence." It is not clear why this was the case, but it may be that the TFWM saw this name as less volatile than "male violence against women."

Networking

The TFWM worked at developing a support and resource network[90] in three areas: within itself, within the wider United Church and within the general "movement against sexism."[91]

An "informal network of women against sexism for support, advocacy and resource sharing" was set up, largely through a letter writing campaign. The letter the task force sent out named one further purpose behind the establishment of the network: "We are not sure we will be in existence after the end of this year and are therefore desirous of facilitating people across the church being in touch with one another."[92] Believing that through such a grass roots movement the United Church could work toward eradicating sexism and interconnected forms of oppression, the TFWM created the network to: "i) know what other areas of the country are doing; ii) know who is working on the same issues as you are; [and] iii) share resources, ideas, concerns."[93]

1984 General Council and "Sacred Space"

The TFWM's report to the 1984 General Council reviewed their mandate and outlined some changes in their goals resulting from the members' "changing consciousness and...learning" (ROP 1984:484). The group had grown more convinced that a position statement was less necessary than a methodology for doing theology (e.g., dance and storytelling). Part of this exploration of theological methodology manifested in the TFWM presented at General Council: "Our presence at General Council could be in the form of a tent, that we take commissioners through, which establishes an atmosphere of what we believe, rather than read a document....This would be open to many other groups as well, for the opportunity of expressing in alternative forms their beliefs."[94] As this idea took shape, it became clear that an alternate space was desirable to other marginalized groups would also benefit from alternate space.[95]

The purpose of setting up this space was threefold: first, the "solid endorse[ment]" as opposed to "an arms length approval" by the Agenda Planning Committee of General Council would indicate a "covenant of support" which would be very important to the TFWM's morale.[96] Second, the tent would give an opportunity to develop solidarity among the marginalized groups who gathered. Third, it was hoped that the tent would serve as a "space for dialogue and sharing,"[97] to foster recognition and understanding of the links among sexism, racism and heterosexism. However, in 1990, the subsequent Committee on Sexism would reject this space, calling it the "tent of unpopular causes," in favour of a "display space in a thoroughfare."[98] This transition from perceiving the tent as a nurturing and empowering space to seeing it as alienating and isolating suggests that in 1984, building strength and nurturing took priority. Later, the Committee on Sexism was at a point in which sufficient strength and solidarity had been garnered in order to shift to a focus on outreach and education.

The aim of the TFWM's presentation and resolution at this General Council was "to inspire people to examine their own experience,"[99] particularly regarding their own complicity in sexism. Furthermore, the group wanted Council to "experience and acknowledge its own sexism in a supportive context."[100] Accordingly, Council passed a resolution confessing the "church's complicity in sexism" (ROP 1984:90). Later, among themselves, the task force members expressed concern over the rapidity and ease with which this resolution was passed: "The recommendation on the church confessing its complicity in sexism, and committing itself to address sexism in all spheres of the church's life, was passed with very little discussion....[The] church has confessed its complicity but we don't think we know what that means."[101] The resolution did not stimulate the discussion, engagement and commitment that the TFWM had hoped for. Further, it was noted in *The Observer* that although "Council did approve a confession of the church's complicity in sexism and committed itself to addressing its own sexism...it didn't follow through with many concrete measures."[102] However, this confession is significant because it is through naming that the process of change is often begun.[103] The succeeding Committee on Sexism would note in 1988 that this confession may have been a starting point but the confession did not bring nearly so much action as was hoped: "In spite of the 1984 church confession of complicity with sexism requesting to 'declare and confess the church's complicity in sexism, commit itself to address sexism in all spheres of the church's life, and stand in solidarity with those in society and within the church who confront sexism,' each time the Committee on Sexism meets we hear stories of women we know who have been discounted or ignored. We hear our own stories of sexism as we have experienced it in the workplace and/or in the church."[104]

General Council authorized the preparation of a "study pack" on the TFWM report "in order that the Church may be educated about sexism" (ROP 1984:90). This study pack—*The Changing Roles of Women and Men* and its accompanying study guide, *Sexism in the Church*—were published and released in 1984 and 1985, respectively. *The Changing Roles of Women and Men* served as the task force's report to Council, and the study guide outlined possible workshops for congregations directed toward consciousness raising.

This was the TFWM's final report; its mandate, after being extended for two years, was over, and the task force was disbanded in December 1984. Originally, its term was to have been for the time between the 28th and 29th General Councils but in March 1982 the General Council Executive extended the mandate to December 1984. In November 1984, the Executive established the Standing Committee on Sexism, with the mandate to continue the TFWM's work (*ROP* 1986:248). Meanwhile, women continued to struggle for recognition of their issues and experiences in The United Church of Canada.[105]

Concluding Remarks

When the first groups were mandated to address gender issues, their focus was on a structural critique of the United Church and on group process. From an emphasis on such issues as equal pay for equal work and the number of men as compared to women working in certain positions, the concern gradually shifted to a more radical feminist critique of the *nature* of the United Church structure and processes, as well as its relationship to the rest of society. For example, in 1988, the Committee on Sexism reflected on the nature of the Church structure:

> As a committee we identify our task to be one of engaging ourselves and the whole church in analysis that brings an awareness of the oppressive nature of both our bureaucracy and our Christian tradition. We are particularly concerned with our systemic oppression of women and of children in the courts of the church. Static structures are of necessity hierarchical and are therefore oppressive and alienating for many.[106]

From the inception of the first such task force in 1974 the focus was, through a liberating discourse, on work toward the realization of justice for marginalized people, especially women. The question was how best to express and act upon such a discourse. Initially, equality within the existing structures was most important. As that focus expanded and changed, so too did other aspects of the work.

Storytelling became increasingly important to the TFWM and contributed to its changing approach to gender issues. For instance, networking took on greater importance. As the links between different forms of oppression became clearer, the task force wanted to hear more stories about the lived experiences of other oppressed groups such as AFFIRM. The nurturing of these connections not only created a more effective, broader base for justice work but also contributed to the TFWM's ability to engage in self-critique and to recognize the complexity of the issues with which it dealt.

By 1984, the TFWM emphasis was shifting from structural reform to attitudinal change and empowerment. Though sometimes frustrated, the task force members recognized that moving at a slow pace was necessary if the United Church was to take ownership of and responsibility for issues related to sexism.[107] This change combined with a shift in the TFWM's approach to theology; the group decided that a theology per se was less needed than a *method* for doing theology. As the task force recognized the changing nature and context of issues, it redefined the issues and appropriate responses to them.

A second reason behind this shift in focus also was connected to storytelling. As women with conscious feminist experiences in the United Church gained voice, anger was a common and inspiring initial response to the stories of marginalization. Likewise, as the task force gathered strength and its anger abated, its focus shifted from internal to external. By 1984 they decided that it was time to work more on education, outreach and the empowerment of others. One example of this transition was the decision of the Committee on Sexism to have a display in the main thoroughfare at General Council rather than to continue to meet in "the tent"; the focus had shifted from a need to build internal strength and solidarity to outreach and education.

One further factor in the TFWM's shift in focus was the changing responses of the United Church hierarchy to the task force's work. Although the TFWM and its successor had been viewed with suspicion, by 1984 there were signs that its work was being recognized and valued at General Council.[108] A more self-critical and confessional response from the United Church hierarchy challenged and deconstructed the illusion of the Church as a blissful family. This change, as history indicates, has been and continues to be resisted in some quarters; the preservation of order, of which the traditional nuclear family has been considered a cornerstone, has traditionally been valued over change and upheaval in North American culture. However, when the family members began to break the silence and expose the family as not always just and caring, change began. In short, as it gradually engaged in more internal critique, the United Church began to shed the misconception that the institution was somehow beyond reproach.

These changes and developments in the work of the TFWM contributed to the United Church's recognition of violence against women. The task force and related group's have pushed the Church to realize its complicity in sexism and the damage that sexism inflicts on members of the Church family. Also, the group's working style, with its emphasis on process and internal theological reflection, encouraged the recognition of connections among all groups of marginalized peoples. This working style facilitated different groups working together to address such forms of violence against women as pornography and harassment. Moreover, this dialectical working style was connected to the development of self-critique. As stories were told, processes were reworked and issues redefined.

This partial history of the TFWM shows the importance and relevance of their work to the issue of violence against women. Other United Church groups, as pointed out, also contributed in no small way. However, for the purposes of this book, this particular case study demonstrates some of the transitions and challenges that contributed to a growing recognition of power dynamics and of violence against women.

CHAPTER VII

Taking Stock: A Contextual, Retrospective Look at Sexuality, Gender, Violence and The United Church of Canada

*T*HE UNITED CHURCH'S APPROACH to issues related to gender and sexuality have contributed to our understandings of, and therefore responses to, violence against women.[1] As I wrote at the beginning of this book, if one is to understand the United Church's contemporary approach to violence against women, one first must understand something of past approaches to gender and sexuality. By uncovering some of these causal dynamics, this book adds another piece to the larger discourse regarding violence. In this last chapter of the book, I will draw together some of the threads and locate the United Church's work in the Canadian context.

A Summary of Some Emerging Policies and Protocols, 1982-93

The 1980s were groundbreaking, regarding the perception of the family and the respective roles of family members. In 1982, the TFWM identified the root of the problem of gender stereotyping as a power imbalance between men and women (ROP 1982:403-4). By the early 1980s, the issues of gender stereotyping and exclusive language were identified as manifestations of the greater issue of sexism. In 1984, the Task Force on Pornography drew direct links between gender stereotyping and pornography; stereotypes prescribe certain roles for both men and women that lend themselves to the violence of pornography:

> Society encourages men to express anger and aggression through sexual violence. Pornography sets up women as scapegoats for male anger with its obsession with rape, bondage, snuff films, mutilation, dissection of female anatomy; its fascination with humiliating, conquering, penetrating, sodomizing and objectifying women....Pornography lies about men in that it says they can only be violent, angry and hateful. Pornography also promotes the lie that women get sexual pleasure from pain. (ROP 1984:315)

The authors of this report argued that stereotyping is the primary cause of male sexual violence against women. Also at the 1984 General Council, the TFWM called for the demystification of the family (499). Furthermore,

---

the task force reported its conviction that the United Church was a sexist institution (440).[2]

With the advent of the 1980s came new concerns regarding the family. This new focus began with a renewed interest in the role and well-being of children.[3] This paved the way for a new-found awareness at an official level regarding various types of child abuse, particularly child sexual abuse. In the latter part of the 1980s, General Council began to receive petitions pertaining to child and youth abuse. Previous to these years, I found only one petition that was in any way related to sexual abuse (258), a resolution submitted to General Council regarding "sex offenders" and referred to the Department of Evangelism and Social Service. In 1986, General Council received a petition from Winnipeg Presbytery that requested that the church study the report of the Badgely Commission (a nationally represented committee appointed by the federal Department of Justice and Department of Health and Welfare to study and report on the sexual offenses committed against children and youth), urge the federal government to implement the main recommendation, and that "the DMC present recommendations to the 1988 General Council to guide the thinking and action of the church on the issue of child sexual victimization" (ROP 1986:645). The 32nd General Council, in response to this petition, reported that the DMC had established a programme unit, "Children, Adults and Family Ministries," to "coordinate work in the areas of pornography, prostitution, and family violence." More specifically, this unit corresponded with the federal Minister of National Health and Welfare regarding "violence in the family" (ROP 1988:513).

The 1988 General Council received two further petitions, both from the same two people, regarding "sexual molestation." One requested that the United Church urge the government to create legislation that would ensure that victims of "intrafamilial and/or incestuous sexual molestation" be given the right to bring charges against their abusers "without time limit" (ROP 1988:113). This petition recognized that, for various reasons, a "victim" may not be able or willing to come forward for many years after the abuse began. The second petition was directed primarily at the need to educate and train people in the United Church to become more aware of the dynamics of "sexual molestation" and better equip them to provide pastoral care for those in their midst who had been or were being sexually molested (114). The recommendations of both petitions were carried.

The 33rd General Council received further petitions concerned with the "abuse and exploitation of children" in "underdeveloped countries," the availability of child abuse counselling resources, and the issue of confidentiality and reporting of child abuse (ROP 1990:182-83, 187).

As awareness of child abuse increased, the need to respond became increasingly clear. This new awareness arose from a changing understanding of the family: as the notion of the traditional family slowly began to erode over the years, and related gender stereotypes were challenged, a crack appeared in the myth of the good family—a crack just big enough to allow us to see more clearly the extent to which family dynamics are complex and can be destructive as well as nurturing.[4]

Another abuse issue which gained attention at Council in the latter part of the 1980s, was wife abuse. Previous reports had acknowledged that physical violence sometimes occurred within marriage, but these observations had not been gender specific.[5] In the early 1980s, reports submitted by the Task Force on Pornography and the TFWM addressed wife abuse. Both task forces noted its existence and called for the eradication of such violence, and both reports identified sexism as the underlying issue. The 1984 human sexuality report, *Gift, Dilemma and Promise*, also referred to spousal abuse, in the context of marital fidelity. As discussed in chapter 5 above, the report noted that the sexual exclusivity of the marital relationship can lead to abusive episodes (*Gift:* 26). This theory is non-gender specific and implies that this violence is the manifestation of internalized, built-up anger that is eventually uncontrollable; sexism was not identified as a relevant factor to spousal abuse.

The DMC has since done more work in the area of wife abuse and continues to address this issue. In 1985, a training event was held for Church leaders and, in 1987, a video entitled *One in Ten* was produced which dealt with "the reality of wife abuse, community response and the role of the church" (ROP 1990:502). The DMC also published a series of pamphlets addressing various forms of violence in families.

The United Church of Canada Located in the Wider Canadian Context: Prophetic or Followers?

Growing awareness of child and wife abuse led The United Church of Canada to look more critically at its understanding of itself as a prophetic community:

> The church which once played a prophetic role in justice issues now lags behind the state in many of these areas. The church as a whole has taken some positive steps in relation to the justice issues as they concern women....If the United Church is to give leadership in women's concerns it must continue to work on two fronts: within its own courts and inner life, and as a goad and example to society as a whole. (ROP 1980:155)

Are there any parallels between the developments in the Church in this area and the rest of Canadian society? Has the United Church taken a prophetic role in solidarity with disadvantaged women? As will become evident, the answer is twofold and complex: in some areas the United Church has acted as a goad and prophet to parts of society but in others, different segments of the wider society and marginalized segments of the United Church, particularly women's groups,[6] have prodded the dominant Church to further self-examination and action. I understand the dominant Church to mean that part of the United Church that has had the power and authority to make policy decisions. Not all groups within the Church have had equal voice and therefore equal power to name and define the Church's concerns and direction.

Canadian women's groups emerging with the second wave of feminism, beginning in the late 1960s, raised issues related to sexuality, particularly contraception and abortion.[7] The 1960s closed with the legalization of the advertising and selling of contraceptives.[8] The same legislation made abortions legal when approved by a therapeutic abortion committee (TAC). This was far from satisfactory for many feminists and a call for equal access to abortion for all women gained force throughout the land by 1970.[9]

The United Church was clearly ahead of the Canadian government regarding its positions in these areas. As previously discussed, in 1936, General Council supported the use and availability of contraceptives, albeit with motivation that was not rooted primarily in a belief in women's moral agency. In 1971, General Council received and approved a report on abortion and contraception that argued that abortion was an issue of "personal conscience" and "should be a private matter between a woman and her doctor" (ROP 1971:157, 160). The 1980 report on abortion affirmed this controversial position and was approved by Council.[10] Similar wording had expressed the Church's stand regarding contraception in 1936; in both cases the issue was described as a personal and private matter. On 28 January 1988, the Supreme Court of Canada took a position similar to that of the United Church when it struck down Section 251 of the *Criminal Code*, and TACs were no longer legislated. The court had decided that abortion was a "'[woman's] personal and private decision.'"[11]

During the 1970s, women's organizations—both grass-roots and institutional—proliferated, and the number of issues addressed multiplied.[12] In 1973, the first Canadian rape crisis centre was opened, in Vancouver, British Columbia.[13] Two years later, the Canadian Association of Sexual Assault Centres (CASAC) was formed and by 1978 included twenty-one crisis centres; by 1982, the number had increased to forty-eight.[14] The mid-to-late 1970s were years when feminist groups began to pay particular attention to the widespread nature of physical and sexual violence against women, and the need to respond to it collectively—and on a practical level. It is important that as early as 1932 the United Church recognized, (although this was not reiterated or more closely examined until 1962) that violence did exist in marital relationships and agreed that divorce was necessary in these instances to protect family members and the neighbourhood.[15] Although an example recorded in the ROPs to illustrate this type of situation depicted the husband as violent towards his wife, the official statement did not yet identify a connection between spousal violence and sexism. Prodded and supported by the wider women's movement, task forces concerned with women's issues began to emerge in the United Church in the mid-1970s.

By the late 1970s, pornography had become a serious concern for many feminists.[16] The link between pornography and violence against women and children has been a concern and a hotly debated topic in Canada ever since, drawing lines of division within the feminist movement as well as in society as a whole.[17] Legislation regarding pornography was established in 1959 and is in the *Criminal Code*, Section 163, under the heading "Offenses Tending to Corrupt Morals." It was not until 27 February 1992, however, that the Supreme Court of Canada recognized a link between "hard-core pornography…[and] violence against women."[18] Similar to the United Church, in the past Canadian law had been primarily concerned with the corruption of act-centred sexual morals rather than the abuse of women and children, although undoubtedly the two were seen as connected. Sooner than the court system, but clearly after some other Canadian women's groups, by 1977 the ROPs showed a recognition of this link between violence and pornography.

The late 1970s to mid-1980s witnessed a new focus on racism[19] and heterosexism as issues intertwined with sexism. From this time on, "moving beyond a white middle-class viewpoint" has been a concern and goal of many of the Canadian women's movements.[20] Working toward this goal has involved forming alliances and networking with various organizations—both within and outside women's movements—which have been important in challenging and supporting these movements. The importance of solidarity among those working for systemic change became increasingly clear. In their 1982 report to Council, the TFWM stated: "We believe that to understand and deal with sexism we need to examine the areas of racism and classism because they are all linked; they are different aspects of the same thing: power relationships" (ROP 1982:404).

Government, the courts and women's groups addressed sexual assault and family violence in the 1980s. In 1980, a Supreme Court decision in the case of *Pappajohn* v. *R.*, stated that the appellant could "be excused from criminal responsibility if he had honestly, albeit mistakenly, believed that the complainant was a willing partner."[21] The court defined the accused's perspective as normative. Given that it is not uncommon for violence to be confused with sexual expression, and given that very few perpetrators are willing to accept their guilt, accountability and consequences, this decision effectively sanctioned sexual assault. The United Church first addressed the issue of consent at an official level in 1960; it was recognized, albeit in an abstract and non-gender-specific way, as necessary to marital sexual expression. However, rape within marriage was not considered a crime in Canada until 1983.[22]

I will mention two other relevant changes made to the law in the early 1990s. In 1991 the Supreme Court of Canada struck down the rape-shield law that protected women from having their past sexual lives used as evidence to discredit them as victims of sexual assault. Bill C-49, passed on 15 August 1992, was in part an attempt to compensate for the removal of the rape-shield law: this bill defined consent as "the voluntary agreement of the complainant to engage in the sexual activity in question."[23] Hence, the experience of the abused person gained greater credibility; the accused's perspective was no longer normative in law.

In 1993, the federal government's Canadian Panel on Violence Against Women submitted its final report. The goal stated in this $10,000,000 report was zero tolerance of violence against women in Canada by the year 2000. Clearly, this has not happened. The method used to achieve this goal was to be education, enforced by law where necessary. However, once again this approach assumed that violence against women could be eradicated without radical upheaval of the economic, legal or government structure.[24]

Although it is important that existing structures, particularly government and legal systems, recognize violence against women and related issues, there have been significant difficulties regarding the *ways* in which those structures have defined these issues. In a detailed Canadian study, Gillian Walker observes what she terms a "process of appropriation and absorption" by these existing structures of the issue of violence against women.[25] That violence does occur within the family was not disputed.[26] The difficulties arose in determining how to define and, therefore, how to address the problem. As both the federal Department of Health and Welfare and the justice system appropriated and absorbed the issue, it was increasingly removed from women's experiences of male violence. As a concern of Health and Welfare, violence against women became defined in terms of the family. An uncritical glorification of the nuclear family, and a tendency to medicalize this violence, have contributed to a failure to recognize this violence as a systemic social problem.[27] The men and women involved become individualized as they are reduced to "victims and assailants or perpetrators."[28] In summary, Walker concluded that "when assault as a category was merged with family violence as a subset of deviant behaviour...the [resulting] definition pathologized certain aspects of gender relations and made them amenable to various treatment strategies without attacking the structures that determine them."[29] Without challenging the nature of these structures, violence against women will continue to be defined by the same existing structures that participate in and perpetuate the conditions underlying violence.

Walker's critique also applies to the United Church: the Church failed to name violence against women more clearly and to get it on the agenda sooner because it too was a social structure not free from systemic oppression. Just as the federal Department of Health and Welfare remained within a limiting framework and the justice system reduced violence against women to the type of problem it could solve, the United Church operated within a limiting framework and set of presuppositions. Part of this limiting framework, for example, has been a tendency to sanctify the nuclear family and the Church family.

In summary, at an official level, the United Church has often adhered to a dominant framework and has responded slowly to the prodding of parts of the wider society and more marginalized parts of the Church itself, particularly feminist groups. The United Church, as represented by the *Records of Proceedings,* has historically assumed a leadership role in matters related to the marital relationship and sexuality. However, in matters related to a conscious recognition of a systemic power imbalance between the sexes, the Church has been more responsive than prophetic. For instance, and as outlined earlier in this book, the United Church approved the use of contraceptives in 1936 and named mutual consent regarding marital sexual relations as an issue as early as 1960. The Church recognized divorce as necessary in some marriages to protect vulnerable family members from a violent spouse or parent in 1962. However, this leadership did not necessarily mean that the United Church had been prophetic in these areas.

These moments in which the Church led the way all grew out of established beliefs. These beliefs belied the accepted order which demonized some views and social roles and sacralized others.[30] A clear recognition of the existence and relevance of a systemic gender power imbalance—of sexism—had yet to occur in the 1960s. The common good model the Church assumed led to an assumption that consensus was the best approach to ethical questions. Not until emerging marginalized voices, such as those of the TFWM, began to challenge this model on the basis that it excluded the voices of those who were less powerful or not normative, did the United Church begin to move toward a solidarity model in which differing and dissenting voices were sought out and the complexity of issues and variety of experiences began to be acknowledged and valued.

Areas in which the United Church has clearly *followed* the call of women's groups, both within and outside of the United Church, were those that required a recognition of the systemic power imbalance between the genders and a departure from the accepted order. Only after the proliferation of women's organizations in wider Canadian society did task forces emerge in the United Church to address women's concerns and changing gender roles. It was largely at the urging of these task forces that the Church began to acknowledge and address gender-based power imbalances.

A Summary of the Factors That Blocked or Contributed to the Recognition of Violence against Women

Blocks and prods to the recognition of the issue of male violence against women can be summarized under the interconnected topics of human sexuality, the family and gender roles, critique, and solidarity.

▶ HUMAN SEXUALITY

As the United Church shifted from a primarily act-centred sexual ethic to a primarily relational ethic, the quality and purpose of sexual intimacy was explored and the goodness of sexual intimacy within the context of marriage could no longer be assumed. The understanding of the purpose of sexual intercourse, initially assumed to be for procreation and union—the strengthening of family life—expanded as the shift to a primarily relational ethic occurred. Pleasure and vulnerability slowly became accepted as parts of the purpose of sexual intercourse and intimacy. Although historically the United Church had insisted on the need for mutuality, it was not until a more critical analysis of marriage emerged that the norm of mutuality was no longer simply assumed.

In 1980, the study document *In God's Image* recognized human sexuality as "neither divine nor demonic." The authors of this study perceived the quality of the relationship, as distinct from sexual acts in and of themselves as most significant. While the two sexuality documents defined sexuality as neither good nor bad, both documents emphasized the giftedness of our bodies and sexualities. Most notably, the authors of *In God's Image* stressed the need for freedom and joy, and discussed limits in sexually intimate relationships, but these emphases neglected issues of accountability and sin. Neither document adequately explored or defined sexual sin.

▶ THE FAMILY AND GENDER ROLES

The United Church had assumed the goodness of the family under almost all conditions, and had upheld the preservation of the family as necessary to the preservation and salvation of the nation. Historically, the illusion of the picture perfect family has been implicitly valued above the well-being of individual family members. Not until the 1960s was this assumption of the good family challenged.[31]

Connected to the preservation of the family had been the maintenance of traditional gender roles. As women gained "new freedoms," the United Church experienced ambivalence towards these changes; on the one hand, many believed that women should exercise full agency, but on the other hand, did not want these changes to affect the traditional societal and familial order. The tension this paradox created manifested in United Church policy.[32] By the 1970s, however, United Church groups were criticizing gender stereotyping as limiting the development of God-given qualities and gifts.

Women gained more voice as gender task forces emerged and challenged the United Church to think about power imbalances and abuse as they relate to sexism as well as other systems of oppression including classism, racism and heterosexism.[33] The task forces were instrumental in getting the issue of sexism and its manifestation of violence against women onto the Church's agenda.

▶ CRITIQUE

As the concept of family became more critiqued, so too did the United Church family. During the early years of the social gospel movement, the Church saw itself as part of the solution to the country's problems.[34] Particularly with the advent of the second wave of feminism in the early 1970s, the United Church began to recognize that it could be part of the problem in relation to gender and family issues.

In the earlier years, the United Church (and other churches) assumed the role of the conscience of the nation. The Church saw itself as protecting the survival and salvation of the nation through its efforts to safeguard the family, and so embraced war with the evils of the public realm that threatened the sanctity of the home.

Some questioning of long-held beliefs concerning marriage and divorce began in the 1960s (for example, see ROP 1962:142) but it was not until the late 1970s that two particular changes occurred regarding the role of the United Church in areas pertaining to gender and human sexuality. First, a broadly based, internal critique evolved due largely to the greater emergence of women's voices; this challenged the Church to become more active in issues related to the status of women (ROP 1980:155). At least partially in response to this expressed concern, the General Council Executive approved the formation of the TFWM (ROP 1982:399), which became a critical force calling the United Church to account regarding women's experiences.

The second change regarding the role of the United Church in these issues was the emergence of a confessional response. The TFWM, in 1977, stated that "every area of life" was patriarchal and androcentric (ROP 1977:270-80). Soon afterwards, the 1984 General Council as a whole confessed the Church's "complicity in sexism" (ROP 1984:90).

The TFWM itself developed as it responded to the wider women's movements of the 1970s and 1980s; as more information became available and more stories told of violence against women, the task force heard these stories and began to challenge the United Church on a more radical level. For instance, by the early 1980s a liberal feminist push for reform within existing structures was no longer sufficient for the task force. Education, attitudes, networking and the critique of the very nature of Church structures became its more central concerns.

Other groups within the United Church took longer to understand the critical relevance of sexism to institutions such as marriage. One factor behind this was the tendency to demonize and sacralize particular structures and roles. Marriage and the family had been sacralized in the past as had traditional gender roles. Sex outside marriage and other deviations from the sacrosanct institutions and roles have been demonized. The authors of the two sexuality reports,—In God's Image... Male and Female and Gift, Dilemma and Promise, particularly the former, reacted to this demonization of human sexuality outside of the privacy of the heterosexual marriage by emphasizing the goodness and liberatory potential of sexuality. These reports did not lay an adequate foundation from which to approach such issues as violence against women; more open discourse was needed with regard to the complexities of human sexuality. In this area, the TFWM was more successful. (Certainly, they had advantages over the two teams who wrote the sexuality reports: the TFWM, although not without difficulty, functioned for a much longer period; the TFWM benefitted from the two teams' work, and from changes in the wider society brought about by the work of women's movements.) However, particularly in the TFWM's earlier years, use of the term "sexism," while seen as necessary to self-authorization and naming by the task force members, also shut down discussion at times. By collapsing power and equity issues into a general charge of sexism, moral and political discourse becomes very difficult. Since sexism is understood to be an evil, anything that is named as sexism is also immediately branded as evil and negotiation or discussion can be closed.

▶ Solidarity

The three contemporary case studies demonstrate the importance of working style and process. The writing teams for *In God's Image* and *Gift, Dilemma and Promise* were more task and consensus oriented (based on a common-good model) than was the TFWM. Partially because of this difference in focus, the TFWM was clearer regarding the type of discourse it used and its underlying orientation than the two sexuality writing teams. The TFWM devoted time at each of its meetings to reflection on group process, and its members also engaged in theological reflection on their experiences as a group, using the models of storytelling and the image of the dance. This process work was time consuming and sometimes frustrating, but it enabled the group to become more aware of the relevance of different factors to their discussions and encouraged the development of self-critique. As part of this attention to self-awareness, the task force recognized the importance of their history and the need to challenge and build on both the Church's past and their own particular pasts. For instance, as the TFWM began to recognize the complexity of sexism, their initial responses to the issue changed and developed. At first, anger at the injustices of sexism largely— and understandably—shaped the group's resonse. If not for righteous anger, this work may never have been initiated. As more stories were told, the initial anger began to subside, internal strength built, the group began to develop their critique, and the focus shifted to outreach and education through the opening of discussion. Furthermore, the complexity of the issues became more evident as the task force identified and explored connections with other oppressions.

On the other hand, for example, the two sexuality writing teams did not identify their own standpoints, and in the case of *In God's Image*, put little time into process. The discourse used in both reports was inconsistent; often a dominant discourse that failed to take into account the feminist experiences of women shaped the theology and ethical analyses presented in the reports. Further, though the 1984 report (*Gift, Dilemma and Promise*) was written with more input from other relevant United Church groups and reflected greater team dialogue, more discussion could further have clarified the approaches in the report.

Having said that, it is important to remember that the TFWM was not formed for only one specific purpose, unlike the two sexuality groups whose explicit purpose had been to write a report or study on human sexuality and the Church. Perhaps one lesson that can be gleaned is the possible benefit inherent in working groups that have some longevity and more than one particular task as their purpose.

As discourse opened up, violence against women was named. As more women's voices became heard, experiences of violence began to be articulated. Voices of dissent and experiences of exploitation challenged institutions and roles, and it became increasingly difficult to continue to demonize or sacralize. The common-good model, as defined by the status quo, began to crumble as it became more apparent that assumptions of common good often functioned to protect the powerful and silence the vulnerable. The TFWM increasingly focused on the development of a solidarity model based on the experiences of marginalized people.

Concluding Remarks

The needless suffering of many women can be overcome through communal resistance and hope, grounded in a belief that change occurs one step at a time—and sometimes when we cannot see it at all. Sharon Welch writes of an "ethic of risk" in which one chooses to work for justice even when there are "no guarantees of success."[35]

I have begun to reconstruct and analyze the work in gender and sexuality of those who have had power at the level of policy making and official reporting in the United Church. The purpose of this analysis has been 1) to generate a greater awareness of the Church's story in relation to gender and human sexuality, and 2) to ask how its official approaches to sexuality and gender have contributed to (a) the delay in naming the significant related ethical issue of violence against women as a concrete issue on the agenda of The United Church of Canada, and (b) the ways the Church has understood this issue. I have also identified some of the blocks to naming and understanding violence against women, as well as factors that have been helpful and necessary to getting the issue on the Church's agenda.

As well as containing many official statements of United Church policy, the *Records of Proceedings* are an important source from which to begin to reconstruct and analyze the evolution of Church's official thinking. Other sources from the United Church Archives have added to this picture and it has been possible to begin a reconstruction of the Church's approaches to gender, human sexuality and subsequently to related issues, including violence against women.

I want to be clear regarding the limitations of this book. This is a first but necessary step if we are to understand the United Church's roots and therefore the causal dynamics regarding its approach to issues related to gender and human sexuality. A next step, as stated earlier, would be to study the Church's history from the underside; particularly the relevant stories of women and marginalized men.

Theologians such as Marilyn Legge and James N. Poling argue that "the voices of victims and survivors must be given priority"[36] since "people who are disempowered can offer critical interpretations of our society and culture that must be acknowledged and applied to rectify the distortions of our partial perspectives."[37] Not only do the voices of women in the United Church need further study, but particular attention needs to be given to the experiences of women, whose voices are not recorded in official church records.

As we have seen, the symbols of sex as a source of sin, the traditional patriarchal family as source of salvation, and the Church as exemplary family and answer to problems have demonstrated tenacity and power over time. As this dissent has persisted, tension has mounted between the desire to maintain previously accepted symbols and norms and the recognition that many traditional understandings of institutions and roles were at the least limiting and at the worst destructive. The desire to maintain the traditional order has been juxtaposed with this recognition and the resulting dialectic has helped create a space in which alternative symbols have been emerging. As marginalized voices challenged the status quo, the United Church community engaged in a struggle to uphold its understanding of Christian principles including a long-standing commitment to radical inclusivity. In a world much battered by violence, such faithful witness is good cause for hope and celebration.

Notes

Notes to Introduction

1 Nicole Lacelle, "The Political Is Personal" in *The Montreal Massacre*, ed. Louise Malette and Marie Chalouh, trans. M. Wildeman (Charlottetown, PEI: gynergy books, 1991), 29.
2 All references to "Church," unless otherwise indicated, are to The United Church of Canada. The use of "church," in the lower case, will refer to the wider institutional Christian church.

Notes to Chapter 1

1 Sharon Welch, *A Feminist Ethic of Risk* (Minneapolis, MN: Fortress Press, 1990), 108.
2 Marilyn Legge, *The Grace of Difference—A Canadian Feminist Theological Ethic* (Atlanta, GA: Scholars Press, 1992), 26. As Legge points out, "Contextual and liberation theologies assume that social ethics is historically grounded; their social ethics, therefore, understand the world as transformable" (5). Also see Carol Robb, "A Framework for Feminist Ethics" in *Women's Consciousness, Women's Conscience*, ed. Barbara H. Andolsen, Christine E. Gudorf and Mary D. Pellauer, eds. (New York: Harper & Row, 1985), 214.
3 Albert Jonsen and Stephen Toulmin, *The Abuse of Casuistry—A History of Moral Reasoning* (Berkeley, CA: University of California Press, 1988), 40-44.
4 Elisabeth Schüssler Fiorenza, *Jesus Miriam's Child, Sophia's Prophet—Critical Issues in Feminist Christology* (New York: Continuum, 1995), 14.
5 Anthropologist Peggy Reeves Sanday argues this position very persuasively in a number of studies of different cultures and their respective experiences, or lack thereof, of male violence against women. See, for example, *Fraternity Gang Rape* (New York: New York University Press, 1990).
6 Elisabeth Schüssler Fiorenza, *In Memory of Her—A Feminist Theological Reconstruction of Christian Origins* (New York: Crossroad, 1983), 30, stresses the importance of context and the fact that it is always changing: "A feminist revision of Christian origins and biblical history must be achieved in and through a critical analysis of patriarchal-androcentric texts and sources by recognizing as a methodological principle that being human and being Christian is essentially a social, historical, and cultural process." Rita Nakashima Brock also sees history as being open-ended: "We must understand the roots of our suffering. We require some structure of meaning that empowers us to change our world to lessen suffering" (*Journeys by Heart—A Christology of Erotic Power* [New York: Crossroad, 1988] 1). Similarly, Rosemary Radford Ruether points to a need to know or identity our roots in order for justice to be a

hope (e.g., Rosemary Radford Ruether, *Sexism and God-Talk* [Boston, MA: Beacon,, 1983], chap. 3). Also see Legge, 5.

7 Legge, *(Grace)*, 13-16. Legge understands mutuality and justice to be included within these three central principles.

8 Margaret Farley, "Feminist Consciousness and the Interpretation of Scripture" in *From Christ to the World—Introductory Readings in Christian Ethics*, eds. Wayne G. Boulton, Thomas D. Kennedy and Allen Verhey (Grand Rapids, MI: Eerdmans, 1994), 53-54. Farley acknowledges the pluralism within feminism but points to certain "central convictions," one of which is "the conviction that women are fully human and are to be valued as such." Within this conviction, Farley suggests that there are two principles: equality, and mutuality. Farley points to what she understands as a further facet of the principle of equality: "equitable sharing…of goods and services necessary to human life and basic happiness" (*Feminist Consciousness*, 54). My understanding of justice is somewhat different from Farley's description of equality and equitable sharing; it is similar to Karen Lebacqz's understanding of justice as a "process of correcting what is unjust." Her contextual approach takes seriously the need to respond to historical and ongoing systems and patterns of "exploitation" ("Implications for a Theory of Justice" in *From Christ to the World*) 254-60.

9 See, for example, Ruether, *Sexism and God-Talk*.

10 Beverly W. Harrison, introduction to *Making the Connections—Essays in Feminist Social Ethics* by Carol Robb (Boston, MA: Beacon, 1985), xi-xxii.

11 James Newton Poling, *The Abuse of Power—A Theological Problem* (Nashville: TN, Abingdon Press, 1991), 31.

12 Karen Lebacqz and Ronald G. Barton, *Sex in the Parish* (Louisville, KY: Westminster/John Knox Press, 1991), 161.

13 Lebacqz and Barton, 162.

Notes to Chapter 2

1 An earlier version of this chapter entitled "A Social Ethical Analysis of The United Church of Canada's Historical Approach to Human Sexuality" is published in *Studies in Religion/Sciences Religieuses* 29, no. 3 (2000):325-39.

2 Beverly W. Harrison, "Sexuality and Social Policy" in *Sexuality and the Sacred—Sources for Theological Reflection*, ed. James Nelson and Sandra Longfellow (Louisville, KY: Westminster/John Knox Press, 1994), 245.

3 Harrison, "Sexuality and Social Policy," 253.

4 Lebacqz and Barton, 146-47. After examining both this female stereotype, and the "myth that men are 'out of control,'" the authors conclude that "with these patterns in place, 'taking' the woman who says no is not just an extreme form of sexual violence, but is normatively built into our expectations of sexual interaction and response."

5 Rosemary Radford Ruether, "The Western Tradition" in *Sexuality and the Sacred*, 32-33. Ruether argues that this tendency to blame the female victim of sexual assault is connected to the theology of the Fall. Eve is traditionally viewed as having generated the loss of paradise and thereby established the precondition for Jesus's death: "Woman's subordinate status, therefore, not only reflects her original inferior nature but also is a just punishment for her guilt in causing evil to come into the world, thereby leading to the death of Christ. Far from saving her, the death of Christ only deepens her guilt, while it absolves the male of his fault and allows him to represent the male savior." Ultimately, then, women could be held responsible for all suffering.

6 Rosemary Radford Ruether, *New Woman/New Earth* (San Francisco, CA: Harper & Row, 1975), 79. Or, to put the point more succinctly, regarding sexual dualism, the "alienation of woman culminates in the dehumanization of society" (23).

7 Many helpful resources provide a great deal more than is discussed in the preceding few pages. For instance, see Adrian Thatcher and Elizabeth Stuart, eds., *Christian Perspectives on Sexuality and Gender* (Grand Rapids, MI: Eerdmans, 1996) and Nelson and Longfellow, *Sexuality and the Sacred.*

8 Mariana Valverde, *The Age of Light, Soap, and Water—Moral Reform in English Canada, 1885-1925* (Toronto, ON: McClelland & Stewart, 1991), 18. Expanding on this definition, Valverde explains that "social purity was a campaign to regulate morality, in particular sexual morality, in order to preserve and enhance a certain type of human life" (24).

9 Valverde, *Age*, 44-58.

10 Valverde, *Age*, 68.

11 See Legge, *Grace.*

12 Part Two of this report on "Sterilization" was received and filed but not adopted. It recommended that sterilization be available for those with "mental defect and disease." The central difficulty the report addressed was whether or not such a person would be capable of giving consent to sterilization (*ROP* 1936:332). This concern with consent reappears in the early 1960s regarding marital sexual intercourse (*ROP* 1960:157). The United Church's concern with mutuality is manifest in this awareness of the importance and complicated nature of consent.

13 Regarding the impact of the fear of an unwanted pregnancy on the spousal relationship, the authors of the report reflect that "the elimination of this disturbing factor may release emotional life from more or less serious frustration and thus enrich and strengthen the family life" (*ROP* 1936:326).

14 Angus McLaren and Arlene Tigar McLaren, *The Bedroom and the State* (Toronto, ON: McClelland & Stewart, 1986), 120. When women's groups began to agitate publicly for birth control, their primary motivation came from social and economic pressures: "The leading Canadian women's organizations were slow in publicly defending birth control. They only did so in the 1930s when their moral misgivings were overwhelmed by evidence of the social and economic misery resulting from unwanted pregnancies" (70). Others were drawn to public support of birth control, also largely due to the economic and social hardships of the time: "The 1929 depression and the social fears that it kindled, precipitated the entry into the birth control discussion of clergymen, society women, and philanthropic businessmen who had heretofore remained aloof" (92). The social gospel movement, particularly in the Canadian West, supported these efforts and greatly helped to lend credibility to the voices of these women, mainly through reliance on experiential justice arguments (120).

15 James B. Nelson, *The Intimate Connection—Male Sexuality, Masculine Spirituality* (Philadelphia, PA: Westminster Press, 1988), 58.

16 Valverde, *Age*, 144-45.

17 Valverde, *Age*, 102-3.

18 As Harrison points out, "when women have been sexually active or self-initiating, society has defined them as 'whores or deviants'" (*Sexuality and Social Policy*, 245-46). There is no record indicating that the men involved experienced any institutional consequences connected with the United Church.

19 Both prostitution and white slavery were central concerns of the social purity movement. The fear of white slavery was tied directly, as Valverde persuasively argues, to contemporary racism and, tied to this, immigration (see, for example, *Age*, 103).

20 Both the Division of Mission in Canada and the Division of Communication were in the process of establishing such a task force (*ROP* 1977:143, 247).

21 See also The United Church of Canada, *Pornography Kit* (Toronto, ON: CANEC, 1985), 1.

22 For instance, the adhoc committee on pornography wrote a response to the report of the Fraser Committee (the federal government's Special Committee on Pornography and Prostitution).

23 An 1974 interim report of the task force defined sexuality as "the freedom to express all of the masculine and feminine qualities given in a person with joy, creativity, integrity and acceptance." Although this definition assumed gender stereotyped qualities, it was an attempt to dispel the hierarchical assumption that so-called masculine qualities are better than so-called feminine qualities (ROP 1974:243).

24 The United Church of Canada, *Contraception and Abortion* (Toronto, ON: The United Church of Canada, 1982), 2.

25 One of the men dissented from the conclusions of the others and authored a separate "minority report" which was included at the end of the document and received, as an important reminder of the range of views on the controversial subject, but not approved by General Council. The appended minority report argued strenuously against abortion except in extreme circumstances in which the life of the mother is threatened (ROP 1980:518).

26 The United Church of Canada, *Contraception and Abortion*, 11.

27 Carter Heyward, "Notes on Historical Grounding: Beyond Sexual Essentialism" in *Sexuality and the Sacred*, 14.

Notes to Chapter 3

1 It has been argued that this lack of critical attention to the private sphere was characteristic of the social gospel era in general. For instance, Marilyn Legge argues that although the Radical Christianity of the social gospel era propounded an "understanding of sin as that which breaks the bonds of relationship," this understanding was not extended to the private sphere of the family (*Grace,* 53).

2 Rev. George Dorey, "A Good Minister of Jesus Christ" in *The New Outlook*, The United Church of Canada, 18 November 1936, 1059.

3 Enforcement of these restrictions continued in the 1960s. A similar psychological test was not required for male candidates.

4 For instance, there is a brief item in the ROPs (ROP 1946:263) that reads: "A communication from the Committee on Deaconess Order and Women Workers, expressing disappointment that in the booklet recently published entitled 'The Christian Ministry' no reference was made to the fact that the United Church accepts women as ordinands and ordains them, was referred to the Board of Colleges and Secondary Schools."

5 Shirley Davy, Project Coordinator, *Women, Work & Worship in The United Church of Canada* (Toronto, ON: The United Church of Canada, 1983), 18.

6 Davy, *Women, Work and Worship,* 7.

7 Judith Vaughan, *Sociality, Ethics, and Social Change—A Critical Appraisal of Reinhold Niebuhr's Ethics in the Light of Rosemary Radford Ruether's Works* (New York: University Press of America, 1983), 117. Vaughan quotes from Niebuhr, "Some Things I Have Learned" *Saturday Review* (6 November 1965), 22. The reason Niebuhr believed this revolved largely around his belief that groups are more easily corrupted than individuals. Only individuals, and particularly women because they are associated mainly with the family, have the capacity for self-transcendence, and therefore the capacity for sacrificial, other-interested love: "Only individuals are moral agents, and group pride is therefore merely an aspect of the pride and arrogance of individuals.... The pretensions and claims of a collective or social self exceed those of the individual ego" (Reinhold Niebuhr, *The Nature and Destiny of Man—Vol. 1 Human Nature* [New York: Charles Scribner's Sons, 1964], 208). Niebuhr observed that groups tend to be more self-interested than individuals. Thus, unlike the family, within which grace is the operative tool that enables love to function, law must be relied upon as the force which creates room for "love" in society (Niebuhr, *Christian Realism and Political Problems* [New York: Charles Scribner's Sons, 1953], 152). Niebuhr's "realism" caused him to doubt

the possible existence of agapic love in the public sphere: "Law…accepts and regulates self-interest and prohibits only the most excessive forms of it" (*Christian Realism*, 171).

8 The general purpose of the Woman's Association is contained in its statement of purpose: "To administer and govern all matters of general policy for advancement, spiritually, educationally, socially and financially of 'The Woman's Association' in the homebuilding of The United Church of Canada" (*ROP* 1944:374).

9 For instance, see *ROP* 1944:345: "The financial history for 1943 was attended by much sunlight and some shadow, for, while there was substantial increase in income, it was insufficient to meet the greatly increased expenditures."

10 Shelagh Parsons, "Women and Power in The United Church of Canada" in *Women, Work & Worship*, 178.

11 The Board of Evangelism and Social Service reflected that "the family as the basic and essential association of human life has shown marks of impairment and threat of disintegration. Our conviction is that the Christian Family is vital to Christian civilization and the coming Kingdom of God" (*ROP* 1940:89).

12 Davy (*Women, Work & Worship*, 55) points out that those people at General Council in 1960 who gave unanimous approval to the formation of the UCW "consisted of 315 men and 72 women."

13 See *ROP* 1944:269, 307-8; *ROP*1948:123-25 concerning women and ordination; and *ROP* 1960:175.

14 In the words of the official record contained in the *ROP*, "Ordination for women is to be open only to those women who are unmarried or widows or at that time in life when they are no longer required in the home as mothers and if a suitable ministry can be arranged which does not interfere with the stability of the marriage and their positions as wives and therefore able to fulfil the vows of ordination.

The ordained woman, if she marries, should enter then her special calling of wife and mother, and cease to be eligible for settlement" (*ROP* 1962:394).

15 See *ROP* 1956:268. The Marriage Guidance Council observed that "although 90% of Canada's families are 'normal families' according to the census—that is, husband and wife are living together—the other 10% numbers 321,000 'broken families,' where one partner is dead, or there is a separation or divorce."

16 *ROP* 1962:154, 156. These references, respectively, conclude that "Christian conscience and humanitarian sensitivity agree that it is better for some married partners to separate rather than continue to abuse each other grievously, or to harm their children, or to demoralize their neighbourhood," and, "Where faithful and intelligent efforts to reconcile the partners and to heal the broken relationship are ineffective, and the marriage is apparently dead, we believe that it may be the will of God to recognize this fact in the church as well as in society."

17 The United Church of Canada, The Committee on Theology and Faith, *The Permanence of Christian Marriage* (Toronto, ON: The United Church of Canada, 1974), Preface.

Notes to Chapter 4

1 Donald G. Ray, Deputy Secretary of General Council, Letter to Robin Smith, The Division of Mission in Canada, 1 February 1974.

2 The task force members were: Robert Bater, Bonnie Bean, Donald H. Brundage (Chair), Marilyn Dyer, Oakley Dyer, R.M. Freeman, David Hallman, Louise Mack, Eileen Sinclair and Robin Smith (*In God's Image…Male and Female* [Toronto, ON: The United Church of Canada, 1980] vii). Since it is not clear whether one or more author(s) wrote any chapter, the chapter authors are referred to in the singular for the sake of simplicity.

3 Howard Brox, Secretary Division of Mission in Canada, "An Introduction to the Study on Human Sexuality by the Division of Mission in Canada," April 1980, 1.

4 For instance, both Dr Robert Bater, who authored the chapter on the Bible, and Robin Smith served on the committee that developed the 1978 United Church report, *Marriage Today*. As the task force for *In God's Image* began meeting the year *Marriage Today* was released, some material from *Marriage Today* was used in *In God's Image,* including verbatim segments in the section regarding intimacy and marriage.

   When asked about factors that influenced his theology in the 1980 study, Dr Bater pointed to his participation in the creation of *Marriage Today*, personal experience, and to the effect of the 1960s movement toward "sexual openness" (Robert Bater, Interview at Queen's Theological College, 18 October 1994).

   Another secondary source the task force members often used is James B. Nelson's *Embodiment—An Approach to Sexuality and Christian Theology* (Minneapolis, MN: Augsburg, 1978). Nelson was in correspondence with the task force and also participated in one of their meetings (James Nelson, Letter to Robin Smith, 8 March 1980).

5 Task Force, "Report of the Task Force on Human Sexuality," 30 January 1979, 1.

6 Roger Hutchinson, *Prophets, Pastors and Public Choices: Canadian Churches and the Mackenzie Valley Pipeline Debate*, Comparative Ethics, Vol. 3 (Waterloo, ON: Wilfrid Laurier University Press, 1992), 125.

7 *In God's Image...Male and Female.* Consistent with this emphasis on experience, storytelling was used throughout the study to communicate the complexities of human sexuality. As Nelson commented regarding this methodology: "The interweaving of evocative personal testimonies is powerful throughout" (James B. Nelson, Letter to Robin Smith, 8 March 1980).

8 Robin Smith, letter to Rev. James Hamilton, 10 June 1983, 2.

9 Howard Brox, Secretary DMC, "An Introduction to the Study on Human Sexuality," April 1980, 3.

10 Material from chapter 1, "Sexuality, What Is and What Might Be—An Introduction and Overview," chap. 3, "On Being Sexual Persons," and the conclusion of the study are analyzed in this subsection.

11 Robin Smith, in a letter to Rev. Morley Clarke, 20 October 1980 (2), lamented the fact that many of the responses to the study, including a letter from Clarke, did not recognize adequately "the value of what the study tries to say in affirming sexuality as essential to our humanity, a great deal more than genitalia."

12 James B. Nelson, letter to Robin Smith, 8 March 1980.

13 See the subsection on "Sexism" for further critique of this claim. Notably, the assumption that God is male, as expressed by the exclusive use of the male pronoun, was neither challenged nor critiqued.

14 Carol Robb, Introduction, xix. Ethicist Carol Robb echoes the argument that "mutual wholeness" must be a norm for human relationships: "Mutuality, rather than control, ownership, or paternalism, is a major moral norm for social, including sexual, communication."

15 Robin Smith, "'In God's Image...Male and Female—An Outline," 25 March 1980.

16 James B. Nelson, quoted in *In God's Image*, 46.

17 Jonsen and Toulmin, *Abuse of Casuistry*, 8, 15-16. Paradigmatic cases are necessary to the development of *"pattern recognition"* (40).

18 For example, see Canada, House of Commons, Sub-Committee on the Status of Women, *The War Against Women* (Ottawa, ON: Queen's Printer, 1991). Some interest groups assumed that education is necessary *and* sufficient to end all forms of violence against women, while others assumed that education is necessary but *not* sufficient.

19 Elly Danica, *Don't—A Woman's Word* (Toronto, ON: McClelland & Stewart, 1990), 10. As Elly Danica, a survivor of incest, reflected: after confiding in her teacher about her father's sexual abuse she was told to pray "to jesus for comfort....There is no comfort so I pray for martyrdom....I have begged the virgin mary for help. I know that whatever they say in school about her son, he is deaf to the pleas of children."

20 Lebacqz and Barton, "Implications," 61.

21 Lebacqz and Barton, "Implications," 62-63.

22 Interestingly, as explained in chap. 2, the Task Force on Pornography in 1984 argued that because pornography contributes to male violence against women, the "right of male gratification" is less important than the right of women and children to safety. If some sexual fantasies were recognized as contributing to the objectification of women and therefore to violence against women (pornography, it is argued, functions in a similar way), then, sexual fantasizing would in all likelihood, have been cautiously affirmed with serious critique of the dangers. However, such a connection was not drawn; focus remained on the perceived tendency of society and the church community, in particular, to sexual repression.

23 See Schüssler Fiorenza, *In Memory of Her*. Particularly since the writing of this study, feminist theologians such as Schüssler Fiorenza have engaged in biblical exegesis with particular attention to this principle. For instance, Schüssler Fiorenza notes that the dominant ideology at the time of the composition of the writings that constitute the Christian scriptures was androcentric in nature and the *Sitz im Leben* patriarchal (30-33). This has serious implications for the reading of the Bible. History is usually written from the point of view of the powerful. History, particularly the history of marginalized people, is often "prescriptive" not "descriptive" of the actual situation. Ending the silence regarding women's biblical experiences is necessary to the reconstruction or re-creation of the memory of these women's stories of joy, living, dying and suffering. The reconstruction of this memory begins the reclaiming of and the challenge to, triumphalist history. Monique Wittig recognizes the radical nature of the telling of stories by women and about women: "You say there are no words to describe this time, you say it does not exist. But remember. Make an effort to remember. Or, failing that, invent." (Wittig, *Les Guerilleres*, quoted in Anne Kent Rush, "The Politics of Feminist Spirituality" in *The Politics of Women's Spirituality—Essays on the Rise of Spiritual Power within the Feminist Movement* [New York: Anchor, 1982], 385.) The preservation and recreation of women's memories is important to the recognition and naming of women's experience of suffering and violence.

24 Gerald T. Sheppard, *The Future of the Bible* (Toronto, ON: United Church Publishing House, 1990). Perhaps Sheppard's thesis that some parts of the Bible may make no sense to us right now but may speak to us in the future, provides a starting point from which to address this problem.

25 Maxine Hancock, quoted in Joanne F. Houlden, "Fails to See Temptation" in *The Observer*, March 1982, 18.

26 Methodologically, questions arise regarding this chapter. Did Bater apply his own interpretive principles? He used a critical approach regarding the historical context of the Bible; this is taken into account in his interpretations. Did he allow the Bible sufficient distance from his personal experience and context? Although it is clear that Bater examined biblical passages in the context of the rest of the Bible and its message, it is not clear that Bater succeeded in satisfying his last two interpretive principles of setting the Bible "free" to illumine our present experience and of being "vulnerable" to the biblical message in order that it might critique our viewpoints and challenge us further. Of course, there is no indisputable interpretation of the Bible; rather we must acknowledge our own underlying orientation, the type of discourse in which we are engaging, and our method of interpretation. As ethicist Roger Hutchinson concluded regarding the "appeals to biblical teachings and religious convictions" made by various parties involved in the Mackenzie Valley pipeline debate: "In themselves they did not provide a certain basis for resolving disputes or choosing between stories. This does not mean that theology is not important. It simply means that theology, like ethics, is a practical rather than a theoretical discipline" (Hutchinson, *Prophets*, 134).

27 Also see Howard Brox, "An Introduction to the Study on Human Sexuality by the Division of Mission in Canada," 2.

28 Robb, Introduction, xvii-xviii.

29 For a more complete discussion on the ethics of self-sacrifice, see Barbara Hilkert Andolsen, "Agape in Feminist Ethics" in *Feminist Theological Ethics—A Reader,* ed. Lois K. Daly (Louisville, KY: Westminster John Knox Press, 1994), 146-59.

30 See Karen Lebacqz, *Professional Ethics—Power and Paradox* (Nashville, TN: Abingdon Press, 1985). As Lebacqz explains, rules and norms "develop because the human community has found that they facilitate good consequences" (18). Although our understanding of what is "good" changes, it is prudent to be self-critical as we evaluate social norms and values. Further, Lebacqz argues, the "question is not whether we should follow rules, but whether the rules have been well written" (23). In order to discern this, it is necessary to be aware of the community's story and of our own stories, as the task force had pointed out earlier . As Lebacqz clarifies, "part of discernment, then, is understanding structures and their meaning in our lives" (149).

31 Perhaps former theology professor Douglas Crichton's questions about the report could be best applied to this section: "Was the doctrine of creation sufficiently balanced with a biblical doctrine of sin and the fall? Does it take the selfishness and ruthlessness of even well-intentioned people seriously enough? Is there a sufficiently clear call for repentance? Is there an adequate theology of the cross?" (Muriel Duncan, "Human Sexuality to Be Long-Term Study" in *The Observer,* October 1980, 19.) This concern may have been *implicitly* present in the norms, but it was neither explicit nor consistently applied.

32 Gillian Cosgrove, "Church Sexuality report hasn't a hope, cleric says" in the *Toronto Star,* 18 March 1980.

33 Paul Sullivan, "The latest in morality—Maybe 'thou shalt not' was just a loose guideline" in the *Winnipeg Free Press,* 20 March 1980.

34 "Facing up to Human Imperfection" in the *Kingston Whig Standard,* 19 May 1980.

35 Accountability in this sense is discussed earlier in the study document (58) but it is important to draw these connections more explicitly.

36 Smith, "In God's Image...An Outline," 25 March 1980, 4.

37 See the Task Force on Marriage and Alternative Styles, DMC, *Marriage Today—An Exploration of Man/Woman Relationships and of Marriage* (Toronto, ON: DMC in The United Church, 1978), 89-93, and *In God's Image,* 63-66.

38 See (*In God's Image,* 66, 63), respectively. Intimacy was described as a dance: "the richness comes from the meshing, bonding and sharing of two lives, separated yet committed to each other, and part of the human community" (64).

39 The task force further clarified the meaning of exclusivity: "Exclusivity is the assurance that there is no one else who is going to take my place with you, not that there is no one else who has a place with you" (*In God's Image:* 65).

40 As Lebacqz and Barton contend, "recognizing the other as created in God's image sets limits on sexual behaviour..." (34).

41 Smith, letter to Rev. James Hamilton, 10 June 1983, 2.

42 The Interdivisional Task Force on the Changing Roles of Women and Men in Church and Society, "A Response to Chapter 5: Sexism of the Human Sexuality Report: 'In God's Image...Male and Female,'" (The United Church of Canada, November 1981), Introduction. This definition was cited as the "primary concern" of the TFWM.

43 The only place where the TFWM found that was not so was in the "affirmations'" section of the chapter. The TFWM contended that the chapter embraced a liberal individualistic view of the problem: "The overall effect of the vignettes, examples and questions used is to trivialize sexism by centring reflection on, for example, how individuals receive self-affirmation and support, or on the division of labour in the congregation" (1).

44 TFWM, 2. The members claimed that "women have much to acknowledge and confess, but along critically different lines. Sexism is not something for which they can be held primarily responsible."

45 TFWM, Minutes, 27-29 April 1981, 2. Feminist ethicists have since written more about women's involvement in sexism and other facets of patriarchy. It is recognized, gen-

erally, that women also need to take responsibility by claiming their power and persisting in the work of justice. While there is no doubt that men, especially those who fit the dominant male norms of whiteness, etc., benefit most from patriarchy, it is also clear that women participate in patriarchal culture. (See, for example, Mary Stewart Van Leeuwen, "The Christian Mind and the Challenge of Gender Relations" in *Sexuality and the Sacred—Sources for Theological Reflection*, ed. James B. Nelson and Sandra P. Longfellow [Louisville, KY: Westminster/John Knox Press, 1994], 120-30.)

46 See, for example, Legge, *Grace*, 206. As Legge notes, "If women are to become moral subjects and if we are to author our own lives, the importance of naming our own experience cannot be overestimated. An exploration of narrative can both tell the truth about the differences and commonalities of women's experience under varying power dynamics and keep our theological ethics accountable to women's lived-world experience" (206).

47 Marie M. Fortune, too, points out that restitution can be an important step after repentance if reconciliation is desired or if the perpetrator decides to manifest his repentance in concrete actions (*Sexual Violence—The Unmentionable Sin* [New York: Pilgrim Press, 1983]), 213.

48 Alberta Conference Division of Mission in Canada Caucus, "Feedback for the 1980 Study," 1980, 3. For instance, these members perceived the rule of sexual exclusivity within marriage as a good rule that benefited the community and relationships and followed God's intent.

49 Smith, "That Sexuality Report—Panel Discussion—Questions and Answers at Metropolitan United Church, London, Ontario," 30 November 1980, 5.

50 See my ethical analysis of the report's chap. 5 regarding intimacy and marriage.

51 Jonsen and Toulmin, *Abuse of Casuistry*, 10.

52 Relativism claims no rules; each case is completely distinct. Absolutism, on the other hand, claims that a set of rules and principles are absolute and that there can be no justification for deviation from these rules and principles. Casuistry takes a middle ground, arguing that general principles are relevant to each case but so are the specific contexts and circumstances characterizing each individual case (Jonsen and Toulmin, *Abuse of Casuistry*, 131).

53 Notably, there is some application of these dynamics in the chapters on biblical interpretation (especially) and sexism. There were also some attempts made at other points in the study but this needed to be a more consistent piece of the study.

54 The reception of *In God's Image* at General Council in 1980 was tumultuous; there was a lot of anger and dissension regarding the report's content. As a result of a "move towards reconciliation at the end of the [heated] debate," it was decided that another report would be written which reflected the "'range of theological and ethical opinion in this area'" (Muriel Duncan, "Human Sexuality," 18). Subsequently, in 1982 Council received such a report, entitled *Faith & Sexuality: A Spectrum of Theological Views in The United Church of Canada* (ROP 1982:160). However, not everyone on the committee that created *Faith & Sexuality* thought that this brief collection of personal views succeeded in balancing the views expressed in the study document; at least one member claimed that it "was just a reflection of the 'Playboy' philosophy of *In God's Image...Male and Female*" (Smith, letter to John Osborne, 9 March 1982). Meanwhile, responses to *In God's Image* were gathered and collated in preparation for the report on human sexuality. The feedback indicated displeasure with the document's approach to three issue areas: the authority of the Bible, sexual morality and sexual orientation. Unfavourable responses between 54% and 61% for all three areas. Significantly fewer cited "sexuality and self" or "sexism in society" as issues and there was a lesser degree of opposition indicated to the approach of the study to these two areas (*Gift*, 83-90).

Notes to Chapter 5

1 Both documents reflected on discrimination against those who express a sexual orientation other than heterosexuality. The authors call for an end to this pervasive prejudice and are clear that people, regardless of sexual orientation, are created in God's image. *In God's Image* went a step further and argued that homosexuality should not be a barrier to ordination or commissioning in The United Church (98). I do not explore the sections of either report regarding sexual orientation. I leave that subject for another writer since it would be a book in itself. The background material that I provide regarding sexuality and gender could, however, be applied to sexual orientation just as well as to violence against women.

2 General Council Executive, Minutes, 21 October 1981, 1. The General Council Research Office believed that for "quite a few…[of the respondents] the mere fact of raising a question in morality for discussion was tantamount to promoting a permissive viewpoint" (*Gift*, 83).

    The reasons given for the ethical positions of the respondents were analyzed by the Council Executive. The great majority of those who responded to the issues of "sexual morality" and "sexual orientation" were believed to have based their positions on "emotion." Regarding the issue of the "authority of the Bible," "emotion" was also the most common basis but "authority" and "reason" were almost as common. The criteria for assessing the "basis of stance" were unclear. For instance, what distinguishes an emotional response from a reasoned one? As feminists have pointed out, this distinction can be tenuous at best. Robb, for example, describes objectivity as not precluding "emotional disinterestedness" but, rather, including an acknowledgment of one's emotional commitment to the issue (Robb, Introduction, xv). Reason and emotion have traditionally been perceived as dualistic opposites; one precluded the other by definition. Moreover, reason as associated with the mind and maleness, has been valued above emotion, the mutable, the body, and women. Without an analysis regarding the meaning of reason, emotion and authority, these categories are not helpful tools for the clarification of the responses. Instead, they obfuscate and may trivialize many of the responses by attributing "emotion" as their motivating factor. (See also The United Church of Canada, *Gift*, 90.)

3 Dave Stone, United Church research officer, Memorandum to Robin Smith, 19 July 1983.

4 Only 15.2% of the responses were classified as "unfavourable." The rest were either "favourable" or "neutral."

5 David Stone, United Church research officer, Memorandum to The Working Unit on Sexuality, Marriage and Family, Division of Mission in Canada, 19 November 1981, 5. The working unit seemed to define the issue primarily as pressure to shape the Church's mind. They did not see the main issue as a need to try to discover what is behind this critical response. As Walter Brueggeman reflected, in a book published just before the study was compiled, we must be willing to travel through the pain and "penetrate the numbness," instead of silencing or trivializing those who disagree with or even attack us, before healing and transformation can occur. Walter Brueggeman, *The Prophetic Imagination* (Philadelphia, PA: Fortress Press, 1978), 111.

6 Orientation Meeting of Key Persons and Meeting of Working Unit on Sexuality, Marriage & Family, Minutes, 3-6 November 1980, 1.

7 Human Sexuality and Family Education, Minutes, 23 June 1980, 2.

8 Apart from the participation of some members of the latter group, the nature of their involvement in the development of the report is unclear. General Council, in 1980, had requested the Theological Perspectives Unit (TPU) to "monitor" the writing of the report and the TPU agreed to "enable the Sexuality, Marriage & Family Unit to reflect on the content of the original report, on the process, past and current, of helping the church to deal with it, and on their plans for using the feedback from the church." However, as is evident from the minutes of their meeting in December 1982, the TPU was

unclear regarding how to implement its role which seemed to be one of informal advisor. The unit's involvement also functioned to increase the accountability base, which was a problem that adversely effected both the writing of the 1980 studies and the task force's members who received the large bulk of critique and attack (Theological Perspectives Unit Meeting, Minutes, December 1982, 11).

9   Smith, memorandum regarding the Human Sexuality Study, 4 May 1982. Also see Smith, "Progress Report" to members of the Human Sexuality Study Team, 25 October 1982, 2.

10 Regardless of the motives behind the engagement with these different interest groups, the result was increased dialogue. The motive may have been to develop the United Church's understanding of human sexuality, to appease the critical voices of the 1980 study or a combination of these and other factors.

11 Smith, "Time Line," 25 October 1982, 1.

12 Seventh Meeting of the Writing Team, Minutes, 8-9 November 1983, 1.

13 DMC Executive Meeting, Minutes, 15-16 October 1983, 1.

14 "Calm Greets Sex Report" in *The Observer*, October 1984, 15. One group that reviewed the report before its endorsement by the DMC—the Hamilton Conference DMC caucus—predicted a similar response: "There will not be the dramatic outburst of anger which greeted its predecessor. By comparison this study is mild and its rejection will be more subtle: It will be ignored. "Hamilton Conference DMC Caucus, Memorandum to R. Smith Re: Draft Report on Human Sexuality, 1983, 1.

15 Sixth Meeting of the Writing Team, Minutes, 7-8 September 1983, 1.

16 Some reviewers of the 1984 draft report continued to think that too much emphasis was placed on science. For instance, the DMC caucus from Hamilton Conference claimed that this report was "an argument rooted in the scientific rather than the theological frame of reference." Furthermore, this group contended that many scientific factual claims in the report are unsubstantiated (Hamilton Conference DMC Caucus, Memorandum to R. Smith Re: Draft Report on Human Sexuality, 1983, 1).

17 DMC Executive Meeting, "Discussion of Human Sexuality Report," 15 October 1983, 1.

18 Naramata Pre-Writing Workshop, A-iii, A-iv.

19 Welch, *A Feminist Ethic of Risk*. As Welch argues, such an understanding is necessary to conversion and justice: "Without understanding the mechanisms of sin and its hold on themselves, conversion, the turn away from exploitative habits of action and thought, is impossible" (55).

20 Fortune, *The Unmentionable Sin*.

21 Smith, "Some General Questions" for the Human Sexuality Writing Team, 1.

22 Marvin M. Ellison, *Erotic Justice—A Liberating Ethic of Sexuality* (Louisville, KY: Westminster John Knox Press, 1996), 22-23. Ellison provides a good discussion of the limitations of liberalism's commitment to individual rights and neglect of communal accountability.

23 As Lebacqz argues, "Morality is not a question of choosing rules over situations, or consequences over duty....Both situations and rules are involved in every ethical decision." As a result, rules are not absolute but "binding"—"Any violation of the rule requires justification, but such justification is not impossible" (Lebacqz, *Professional*, 22, 26).

24 As participants at the Cedar Glen Pre-Writing Workshop claimed, "Popular morality seems to promote promiscuity rather than freedom in a society of fragmentation....In our society intimacy is equated with sexual intimacy" (3).

25 The writers reasoned that without at least this explicit intention of lifelong commitment, the marriage is "bound to fail." The second affirmation in this chapter reads: "We affirm that in Christian marriage a man and woman give themselves to each other in the full intention of a lifelong commitment" (36). The TPU critiqued this statement in their feedback regarding the draft report. They argued that the phrase "give themselves to each other" should be changed to "offer and receive" since the former "implies

ownership." The Marriage, Sexuality & Family Unit rejected this suggestion. No reason was recorded (TPU, Feedback to the Draft Report, 9 December 1983).

26 Judith Plaskow in *Standing Again at Sinai* (New York: HarperCollins, 1990), posits a feminist critique of the concept of God's *choosing* Israel. Plaskow sees this as a "hierarchical understanding of difference" (97) and rejects it in favour of the understanding of "distinctness" (105). Distinctness is not necessarily "rooted in hierarchy" as is "chosenness" (106). The ramifications of such a critique on this ethical argument for the nature of the marriage covenant, are profound. Based on this model, marriage would be understood as a distinct relationship but not necessarily better than or having precedence over, each person's other relationships. Faithfulness characterizes this relationship; commitment is paramount as is a deep and abiding love. There are characteristics of this relationship that set it apart from other relationships but not over them. An example of such a characteristic *may* be genital exclusivity. But the main difference between a marriage constructed on this model as distinct from the model interpreted by the writers would be the "precedence" the writers cite as a defining characteristic of the marriage covenant (*Gift*, 25).

27 Ginny NiCarthy, "Building Self-Esteem: Overcoming Barriers to Recovery" in *Abuse and Religion—When Praying Isn't Enough*, ed. Anne Horton and Judith Williamson (Lexington, MA: Lexington Books, 1988), 114, 117.

28 Fortune, *The Unmentionable Sin*, 64-65. Fortune recounts the story of the martyrdom of St. Maria Goretti, a twelve-year-old-girl who died while fighting off her would be rapist. Fortune quotes Pope Pius XII at Maria's canonization: "In 1902 she was stabbed to death, preferring to die rather than be raped....From Maria's story carefree children and young people with their zest for life can learn not to be led astray by attractive pleasures which are not only ephemeral and empty but also sinful." To suffer and die, rather than be raped and rendered impure, is glorified. Not only is sexual violence confused with pleasure, but the preservation of one's sexual purity is valued over life.

29 As theologian Pamela Dickey Young explains, "Women's experience can and should be used as one of the major criteria judging whether or not theology serves to exalt one group (men) at the expense of another (women) and is therefore practically incredible to women." By this, Dickey Young clarifies that if one cannot relate traditional theological claims to one's own life experience, then those claims are not credible to that person. *Feminist Theology/Christian Theology—In Search of Method* (Minneapolis, MN: Fortress Press, 1990), 64-65.

30 It must also be clearly stated that the church does not value permanence in marriage over one partner's ongoing pain. Instead of recognizing this experience, the report stressed that often we turn to divorce too quickly and we need to realize that "challenges, struggles, set-backs, misunderstandings, exploitations and hurts arise in all marriages" (*Gift*, 29). Although, the beginning of chap. 3 on marriage points out that "merely bolstering the institution of marriage does not necessarily ensure that love and commitment become real" (*Gift*, 23), this was not pointed out in the context of abuse. Instead, the focus was on the need to convince people that if a partner in a marriage covenant fails and breaks their intention to lifelong sexual exclusivity, "the relationship need not and should not end." (Robin Smith, memorandum to the writing team, 24 November 1982.) Rather, there should be room for "grace, forgiveness" and repentance (*Gift*, 29). See also the Naramata Pre-Writing Workshop, C-II. While this is certainly true in some contexts, it neglects the perspectives and experiences of abused people.

31 Ethicist Lebacqz argues that we need to discover an "*appropriate*" vulnerability. She appeals to scripture as an authoritative source for this norm. For instance, the *Song of Songs* "displays in glowing detail the immense passion and vulnerability of lovers....It is passion pure and simple. And it is graphic sex....From the *Song of Songs* we can recover the importance of sexual desire as part of God's creation." (Bater, in *In God's*

Image, also appealed to the *Song of Songs* as an example of a biblical celebration of sexuality in a context of mutuality.) Lebacqz argues that in the Genesis 2 passage, in which it is said that the man and the woman were "naked" and "felt no shame," "'nakedness' was a metaphor for vulnerability, and 'feeling no shame' was a metaphor for appropriateness." Therefore, as "the summation and closure of the creation story, the verse tells us that the net result of sexual encounter...is that there was to be appropriate vulnerability." This vulnerability demands that power be shared; power over is contrary to a norm of vulnerability: "The desire to have power or control over another is a hardening of the heart against vulnerability [and therefore] loss of vulnerability is paradigmatic of the fall" (Lebacqz, "Appropriate Vulnerability," 258-61).

32 Young, *Method*, 55.

33 Legge, *Grace*, 205.

34 See, for instance, Lebacqz and Barton's analysis of the relevance of a sexist context to women in ministry, 132-53.

35 Muriel Duncan, "Sexuality Report: Guides, Not Rules" in *The Observer*, March 1984, 11.

36 DMC Executive, "29th General Council Business Related to DMC—As Considered by Initiating Unit," 21-22 January 1983, 4.

37 Similarly, Lebacqz and Barton observe, "Because sexual intercourse is a symbol for our deepest intimacy, any relationship that moves us can stimulate desire for that deepest union and therefore can be sexualized" (43).

38 Lois Sweet, "Fidelity" in the *Toronto Star*, 19 March 1984.

39 Robin Smith, "Sexual Exclusivity," 21 October 1982, 1.

40 Cedar Glen Pre-Writing Workshop, 6. Lebacqz makes this point: "Morality is not a question of choosing rules over situations, or consequences over duty....Both situations *and* rules are involved in every ethical question" (*Professional Ethics*, 22). Jonsen and Toulmin point out that the issue is not a choice between rules and situations but rather a question of how well the process of discernment is carried out: "The practical choice is not between a high-minded ethics of pure principle and an inevitably debased morality of cases and circumstances: it is between *good* casuistry, which applies general rules to particular cases with discernment, and *bad* casuistry, which does the same thing sloppily" (*Abuse of Casuistry*, 15-16).

41 This view was expressed by participants at the PCTC Pre-Writing Workshop (15) in that they "affirmed the importance of the sense of ought-ness and of the necessity for giving due weight to basic principles" with the central criterion identified as "love" in relationship. Most desired the affirmation of the rule of genital exclusivity within marriage, understanding that "love" remained the overriding principle and if this central value could justify a departure from the rule of exclusivity, then that was acceptable, if difficult to imagine.

42 DMC Executive, "29th G.C. Business Related to DMC—As Considered by Initiating Unit", 21-22 January 1983, 4, and Robin Smith, letter to Members of the Human Sexuality Study Writing Team, 20 October 1982.

43 Robin Smith, letter to L. Mancell, 18 July 1984.

44 It should be noted that connections apparently were not made between this chapter of the report and the observation in the chapter on sexism that all oppression is linked and in order to pursue justice we must become aware of the ways in which we oppress others. While this general claim may have been realized, it was obviously not recognized that the association of "dark" with evil or sinfulness is a form of racism.

45 Lebacqz and Barton, *Sex in the Parish* 49.

46 While Peter Rutter, *Sex in the Forbidden Zone* (New York: Fawcett Crest, 1989) and Marie M. Fortune, *Is Nothing Sacred?—When Sex Invades the Pastoral Relationship* (San Francisco, CA: Harper & Row, 1989) both argue that sexual contact between a pastor and parishioner must never happen because of the power imbalance and the resulting "violation of trust," Lebacqz and Barton argue that under some conditions in

which the power imbalance is not so pronounced and in which certain steps are taken, sexual involvement, although problematic due to the power imbalance, is not impossible (*Sex in the Parish*, 126-31).

47 For instance, see Ruether, *Sexism and God-Talk*, 139-58; Diana Scully, *Understanding Sexual Violence—A Study of Convicted Rapists* (Boston, MA: Unwin Hyman, 1990), 81, 107; and Susan Edwards, "'Provoking Her Own Demise': From Common Assault to Homicide" in *Women, Violence and Social Control,* ed. Jalna Hamner and Mary Maynard (Atlantic Highlands, NJ: Humanities Press International, 1987), 153-64.

48 It would have been helpful to extend this critique of the "enshrinement of the nuclear family" to the discussion on marriage and, in particular, regarding the reasons why some marriage partners remain in lifeless unions (*Gift,* 23).

49 Robin Smith, letter to James Taylor, editor, 23 December 1983. The chapters on intimacy and sexism were the most difficult and time-consuming chapters for the authors to prepare.

50 PCTC Pre-Writing Workshop, 4.

51 Robin Smith, Meeting with Theological Perspectives Unit, 27 January 1984, 1.

52 Seventh Meeting of the Writing Team, 8-9 November 1983, 3.

53 Robin Smith, letter to Human Sexuality Writing Team, 13 January 1984.

54 PCTC Pre-Writing Workshop, 13.

55 The writing team corresponded with the TFWM and solicited information and advice (Karen Toole Mitchell, letter to Jeri Velnes—chairperson TFWM, 11 January 1983). However, not all of the TFWM's suggestions were accepted by the writing team. For instance, the TFWM wrote to the team "stating that we don't see sexism as a separate issue but that it is integral to the whole area of sexuality." (Minutes, February 1982). The PCTC Pre-Writing workshop echoed this concern: "We believe that sexism is an all-pervasive issue and should be addressed as a perspective in all discussions on sexuality." (2), as did participants at the Cedar Glen workshop: "The group's recommendation was that sexism should be built into each issue rather than being dealt with separately" (8). The TFWM were concerned that the issue of power be identified, in terms of sexism, in all issue areas (Minutes, June 1983). Although some gender analysis entered discussion in other chapters, it was not consistently applied and discussed. For example, see my analysis of the chapter on marriage, regarding explosive spousal episodes.

56 War imagery, such as "battle," can function to condone patriarchal militaristic activity.

57 Toole Mitchell originally wanted to avoid raising "needless red flags...as in the case of including a reference to inclusive language, [since] language change is in fact slow and real. The issue is important; the strategy chosen must not be counter-productive" (Seventh Meeting of the Writing Team, Minutes, 8-9 November 1983, 3). However, the TPU disagreed and argued that the chapter needed a fuller "theological rationale for dealing with it [sexism]. E.g., a discussion of how we use images of God should tackle whether or not Christianity is essentially sexist" ("Feedback," 9 December 1983, 1). In fact, largely because of what the TPU believed to be its theological weakness, they recommended to the writing team three options regarding this chapter: "1. Edit significantly, OR 2. Write a new chapter, OR 3. Delete for the present" (1).The writing team chose, instead, to do minor revisions. For instance, the reflection on inclusive God-language was added but what appears in my text is the extent of the analysis on this topic. The writing team elected to accept the edited version, although the TPU recommended more theological analysis.

58 For example see Writing Team, "'Sexism, Society, Self—Final Draft after Meeting with TPU," 13 January 1984, s-1, s-7.

59 B.J. Klassen, member DMC, "Revisions to Writing Team," 27 January 1984.

60 For instance, some of the feedback from the TPU was incorporated into the chapter on sexism and helped to expand its theological analysis.

61 Welch, *A Feminist Ethic of Risk*, 20

62 Later (1990), in an excellent study, professor of social work Gillian Walker made clear some of the dangers of reframing women's experiences of male violence in the language and structures of traditional male dominant discourse. In her analysis of the history of Ontario's response to the issue of male violence against women she articulated how women's experiences were appropriated, absorbed and redefined in terms of existing structures and ideologies. The same thing happened in parts of these two United Church reports, both of which explored "exploitative sexual behaviour" and other forms of violence against women through the use of traditional Euro-American theology developed largely through white male experience. The danger is that women's experiences become trivialized, excessively individualized, misinterpreted or absorbed and redefined as these experiences are retold and analyzed in terms of a dominant discourse, not through women's particular experiences of suffering. As Walker explained, "This process of referencing its own ideological framework forms an ideological circle, providing an interpretive schema cut off from the experienced world. The ideological circle keeps out any possible explanations or ways of knowing that do not conform to the framework" (Gillian Walker, *Family Violence and the Women's Movement—The Conceptual Politics of Struggle* [Toronto, ON: University of Toronto Press, 1990], 62-63).

63 I use the term "content methodology" as the title of this subsection in order to describe the ways in which the content of the report is connected or not and, generally, how the subject material is presented.

64 Young, *Method*, 55.

65 Young, *Method*, 67.

66 PCTC Pre-Writing Workshop, 13.

67 As Harrison argues, "No sexual ethic will be adequate unless it incorporates a full appreciation of the interstructuring of social oppression.…An adequate normative sexual ethic will be predicated on awareness that where people…are socially powerless, they are vulnerable to irresponsible and inappropriate—that is, nonvoluntary and/or nonmutual—sexual transactions" ("Sexuality and Social Policy" in *Sexuality and the Sacred*, 247-48).

68 For further discussion of the relevance of these theological issues to woman abuse, see, for instance, Joanne Brown and Carol Bohn, eds. *Christianity, Patriarchy and Abuse* (New York: Pilgrim Press, 1989).

69 As chapters 2 and 3 of this book show, self-critique had only recently begun to emerge in United Church documents and reports related to gender, family and sexuality; the role of the church had been changing from that of the nation's conscience to a recognition that the church could also be part of the problem.

70 Walker, *Family Violence*, 85. As Walker explains, "Power is the overriding issue to be addressed, within the specific historical context in which battering occurs. Oppressive power relations must be recognized if the situation is to be properly understood."

71 As Lebacqz and Barton argue, "Our 'normal' expectations around sexuality are not consensual and mutual, but involve male domination and even violence," *Sex in the Parish*, (146). Similarly, Fortune posits that generally we have a confused understanding of the difference between expressions of sexuality and violence (Fortune, *The Unmentionable Sin*, chap. 2, 14-41). See also Brown and Bohn, xiv.

72 Legge, *Grace*, 127.

73 Chung Hyun Kyung, "Following Naked Dancing and Long Dreaming" in *Inheriting Our Mothers' Gardens—Feminist Theology in Third World Perspective*, Letty Russell et al., eds. (Louisville, KY: The Westminster Press, 1988), 54.

Notes to Chapter 6

1 Task Force on Women and Partnership Between Men and Women in Church and Society (TFWP), Minutes, 20 June 1974, 1. The General Council referred this recommendation to the Committee on Union and Joint Mission (ROP 1974:11). Additionally, the United Church had recently participated in preparing and presenting a brief to the Royal Commission on the Status of Women. A United Church committee followed up this submission with study of the report and recommendations to General Council Executive.

2 Task Force on Women and Partnership, Minutes, 20 June 1974, 1.

3 Goals of the Task Force on Women and Partnership, 1974.

4 Task Force on Women and Partnership, Minutes, 20 June 1974, 1.

5 Carol Christ and Charlene Spretnak make this point regarding the expression of women's lives in narratives: "Since women have not told their own stories, they have not actively shaped their experiences of self and world nor named the great powers from their own perspectives.

   "As women become more aware of how much of their own experience they must suppress in order to fit themselves into the stories of men, their yearning grows for a literature of their own, in which women's stories are told from women's perspectives" (Carol Christ and Charlene Spretnak, "Images of Spiritual Power in Women's Fiction" in *The Politics of Women's Spirituality—Essays on the Rise of Spiritual Power within the Feminist Movement*, ed. Charlene Spretnak [New York: Anchor, 1982], 328).

6 For instance, the task force discovered that in 1972-74, 71 women as compared to 1,750 men had received educational grants from the United Church. About ninety percent of the recipients of "Investment in People" grants given to support the development of lay leadership during the same period were women (Task Force on Women and Partnership, Minutes, 4 November 1974, 1). This may reflect a continuation of the belief that women's ministry was more appropriately expressed in the private sphere; for instance, women tended to be discouraged from ordination and university education. Moreover, as women have been historically undervalued, lay ministry has also been undervalued; ordination has often been perceived as the fulfilment of lay ministry. It is no coincidence that women have been associated with lay ministry and lay ministry with women.

7 This was part of the concern expressed at the task force's third meeting regarding "the proportion of women to men on the Executive of General Council, Standing Committees, Divisions and Boards, and College Boards" (Task Force on Women and Partnership, Minutes, 25 September 1974, 1). As a first step, a letter was written to the Personnel Officer, Jim MacFadzean, to ascertain data on the representation of women on the national staff. His response indicated that the employees "at the clerical level (in the main people who are wedded to a typewriter) with one exception [are] all women." He claimed that the number of women employed "at the professional level" was increasing. Finally, he indicated that it was important to "identify and train interested and competent people in the clerical areas to *advance* into the Executive level" (Jim MacFadzean, Personnel Officer, letter to Task Force on Women and Partnership, 26 March 1975; emphasis mine). The hierarchical valuing of positions within head office was assumed.

8 Task Force on Women and Partnership, Minutes, 11 June 1975, 1. The criteria for assessing the value of work were not discussed.

9 Paul Deeth, Research Report, 7 October 1975, 1.

10 Task Force on Women and Partnership, Minutes, 20 June 1974, 2.

11 As the United Church's official magazine, *The Observer* communicates information, opinions and concerns throughout the Church. The task force was particularly interested in how the magazine presented women both in articles and advertisements, and in investigating the ways in which "articles/pictures reinforce or demolish stereotypes

of the place of women and the relationships between men and women" (Task Force on Women and Partnership, Minutes, 25 September 1974, 1).

12   Task Force on Women and Partnership, Minutes, 4 November 1974, 1.

13   Task Force on Women and Partnership, Minutes, 15 January 1975, 1.

14   Task Force on Women and Partnership, "Accomplishments," 20 March 1975, 1.

15   Task Force on Women and Partnership, Minutes, 18 February 1976, 2.

16   Task Force on Women and Partnership, Memorandum to the Committee on Worship, 3 April 1975.

17   At its fourth meeting, the task force passed a motion reading as follows: "That this task force urge and request the Divisions of the Church to keep in mind the women's movement as a matter of great social and theological concern for our time and society" (Task Force on Women and Partnership, Minutes, 4 November 1974, 1). This concern was reiterated in September 1975: "There is a need for the Church to...be alert and open to [the] women's movement in Canada" (Task Force on Women and Partnership, "Purpose and Direction," September 1975). Harriet Christie was the first representative to NAC, but died soon after in 1974. Since then, the national task group responsible for addressing women's concerns has appointed a woman as representative to NAC (Task Force on Women and Partnership, Minutes, 26 March 1975, 1).

18   Wilber Howard and Ferne Graham, letter to members of the order of ministry from the Moderator and the Secretary of the Task Force on Women and Partnership, respectively, 10 February 1975. Litanies and prayers written particularly for such a service were prepared and distributed in cooperation with the Worship Committee.

19   Task Force on Women and Partnership, "Purpose and Direction," September 1975.

20   Task Force on Women and Partnership, Memorandum to DMC Executive, June 1976.

21   Task Force on Women and Partnership, Memorandum to DMC, June 1976. A significant part of the reason why the task force had not accomplished as much as they would have liked, was the death of Harriet Christie in 1974. The task force went into a low year following Christie's death.

22   A consensus model does *not* tend to value the clarification of different perspectives, whereas, a model that develops "mutual critique lead[s] to more adequate understandings of what is just and how particular forms of justice may be achieved" (Welch, *A Feminist Ethic of Risk*, 129).

23   Howard Brox, Secretary DMC, "DMC's Response to Evaluation Memo from Task Force on Women and Partnership," 14 September 1976.

24   Committee to Clarify the Concerns Regarding Women, Minutes, 27 October 1976, 1.

25   Committee to Clarify the Concerns Regarding Women, Minutes, 27 October 1976, 1.

26   Sin is defined in this statement to mean "lusting after God's power." As many feminist theologians point out, women in this culture often do not sin by "lusting after God's power" but by accepting a lack of power and lack of self. (See, for example, Judith Plaskow, *Sex, Sin and Grace* [Washington, DC: University Press of America, 1980], 62-68.)

27   Committee to Clarify the Concerns Regarding Women, Minutes, 27 October 1976, 1.

28   Anthropologist Peggy Reeves Sanday has since presented evidence that there are cultures, albeit small and isolated, that are not androcentric (see, *Fraternity Gang Rape*).

29   Committee to Clarify the Concerns Regarding Women, Minutes, 27 October 1976, 1.

30   Rosemary R. Ruether, *Disputed Questions: On Being a Christian* (Nashville, TN: Abingdon, 1982), 50.

31   Committee to Clarify the Concerns Regarding Women, Minutes, 27 October 1976.

32   These theological convictions are as follows:
     " (a) All persons, both male and female, are created in God's image....
       (b) The intention of creation is that the created beings, male and female, should live in relationship with each other and with God.
       (c) Sin, lusting for God's power, leads to alienation from the earth, each other and God. This alienation manifests itself between men and women in patterns of domination/subjugation, hierarchy, separateness, exploitation and competition....

(e) Jesus's life expresses identification with a people who suffer under alienation and so calls us to become one with those who suffer oppression and injustice.

(f) While differences and similarities between male and female go beyond the obvious physical ones, they are not clearly or reliably definable at this stage of our experience, and we are called at this point to live with this ambiguity.

(g) It is critically important that we not assign specific roles or qualities by reason of sex alone....

(h) We live in a world where male is 'norm'....

(i) Likewise, we continue to suffer as Christians from living with a past whose patriarchal character is deeply embedded....

(j) The distortions of male as norm and patriarchalism pervade every area of life...."

33 The authors acknowledged that these views were relatively new. As with most changes that involve a redistribution of power, the tension between words and actions persisted. Importantly, the working group named this tension: "Our actions often negate and deny [these convictions]" (ROP 1977:281).

34 Specific tasks, in order to accomplish these goals, were delineated: the creation of a newsletter, workshops and the development of national networking with particular attention to building a closer relationship with NAC (Ferne Graham, for Working Unit with Adults, April 1978).

35 The first meeting, in 1978, discussed "ways of encouraging and supporting women's concerns in Conferences." No action emerged from this discussion. The second meeting occurred in November 1979. The topics were networking and a recommendation for the establishment of an interdivisional task force (TFWM, Minutes, 9-11 January, 1981).

36 One manifestation of the failure of the United Church to educate itself in terms of justice issues for women was the continued resistance in the pastorate to women clergy. The Division of Ministry, Personnel and Education reflected, regarding women in the ordered ministry: "Perhaps the most important and most underestimated issue in ministry these days focuses around WOMEN. The fact that about one-third of all candidates for the order of ministry are now women means that an increasing number of pastoral charges will have the opportunity of being led by women clergy in the near future....We are called to celebrate and grow in this situation—and to press for openness to change among those for whom feminism in the church seems to call forth resistance" (ROP 1980:136). Building on the base that women are made in God's image, women are as able as men to participate fully in the United Church's ministry, actions that subvert these claims are justice issues, and the church must be engaged in justice issues, the DMC found it necessary to create a group of people with a mandate to study and act on issues related to the changing roles of women and men. This task force would be accountable to the Council Executive through the executive of the DMC, although their "primary relationship" would be with the Ministry with Adults Working Unit of the DMC.

37 General Council Executive, description of the "Inter-Divisional Task Force on the Role of Women and Men in Church and Society," July 1980.

38 At this point, the TFMW did not yet indicate a recognition of the variety of male experiences. For instance, this claim did not take into account the power differential between heterosexual men and gay men.

39 Ministry with Adults Working Unit, Report to the DMC, January 1980.

40 General Council Executive, Minutes, March 1980.

41 TFWM, Minutes, 28-30 November, 1980.

42 TFWM, Minutes, 9-11 January, 1981. The task force echoed this belief at a meeting in 1983 when it claimed in the minutes that "the church tends to work with 'safe' women" and not feminist women who speak boldly and critically of the church (TFWM, Minutes, September 1983).

43 Jeri Velnes, chairperson of the TFWM, letter to United Church Moderator, Lois Wilson, 23 February 1981.

44 See Ruether, *Disputed Questions*, 104. In spite of Jesus's attempts, "the powers and principalities are not changed. They close in on him and string him up on the gallows of their false justice." Ruether, *Sexism and God-Talk*, 5-8, 170-72. See also Ruether, *New Woman/New Earth*, 99-107.

45 Ruether, *New Woman/New Earth*, 108.

46 TFWM, Minutes, March 1982. At the same meeting, the TFWM observed that "we are reaching a critical point in our understanding of the complexity of the issue whereby we can be more useful to the church" (1). The TFWM had been operating for two years at this point and had worked hard to establish an effective "working style." Furthermore, "The very existence of the task force is an important statement to other denominations that the...[United Church] is committed to the equality of women and men." For these reasons and others, the task force recommended: "That the mandate, membership and staff position of the...[TFWM] continue until the *Thirtieth General Council*, with a full report at that time."

47 One of the ways in which the TFWM indicated how strongly they felt regarding their name was the manner in which they named themselves in correspondence. For example, in a letter to the United Church Head Office, the opening line reads, "At a recent meeting of the National Task Group on Sexism (the Interdivisional Task Force on the Changing Roles of Women and Men in Church and Society)" (Betty Marlin for the Task Group, letter "To Friends at 85 St. Clair," 2 October 1981).

48 TFWM, "The Purpose and Work of the Task Force" in *The Observer*, May 1984, 47.

49 TFWM, "Faith/Purpose Statement," February 3-6 1984, 21.

50 As Poling explains, a systemic power imbalance provides the foundation for the exploitation of the disadvantaged: "Patriarchy, the unjust power relationships of men and women perpetuated by ideologies and institutions, is another structure of domination that creates the conditions for abuse of power" (*Abuse of Power*, 29).

51 See Roy T. Jacobs, Special Assistant Portfolio, Office of The Prime Minister of Canada, response to a petition organized by the Task Force re: the *Indian Act*, 9 November 1981, and TFWM, Minutes, March 1982. Also see Poling, for a discussion regarding the interconnectedness of systems of domination such as patriarchy, classism, heterosexism and imperialism. These systems and structures subvert God's intention for communion of all life: "Structures of domination mean that the power of creation is not being used to enhance communion and enlarged freedom for all persons." (30-31).

52 TFWM, Minutes, April, 14-15.

53 TFWM, Minutes, October 1982. The task force reiterated this goal in its February 1983 Minutes.

54 TFWM, Minutes, February 1983. As early as September 1981, the TFWM recorded discussion of homophobia in its minutes.

55 TFWM, Minutes, 16 January 1984.

56 Frederick Seller, on behalf of the TFWM, letter to AFFIRM, 27 June 1983. Sharon Welch understands solidarity to require: "(1) granting each group sufficient respect to listen to their ideas and to be challenged by them and (2) recognizing that the lives of the various groups are so intertwined that each is accountable to the other" (*A Feminist Ethic of Risk*, 133).

57 Walker, *Family Violence*, 34.

58 Mary Connor, staff person for the TFWM, quoted in *The Observer*, "Task Force Name May be Changed," October 1981, 20.

59 TFWM, Minutes, October 1982.

60 See TFWM, Minutes, October 1982 and 25-28 February 1983.

61 Discussion of other tasks, including inclusive language (and a reference to the task force's concern regarding the language of the trinitarian formula) and the relevance to male experience of a theology that takes sexism seriously as an evil appear in the sub-

sections of "Inclusive Language and Imagery" and "Pornography and Other Forms of Male Violence Against Women."

Because theology pervades so many of the areas that the task force addressed, this section is not confined to the following few pages; instead, the reader will find reference to theological reflection/questions throughout the task force's work in accordance with their hermeneutical understanding of theology.

62 This is also how Walter Brueggeman understands the task of prophetic ministry: "*The task of prophetic ministry is to nurture, nourish, and evoke a consciousness and perception alternative to the consciousness and perception of the dominant culture around us*" (13, emphasis in the original).

63 As Pamela Dickey Young states, "Women's feminist experience exposes a patriarchal theology for what it is, half a theology, and judges it accordingly....Women's experience provides the material for making half a theology a whole theology" (*Feminist Theology/Christian Theology*, 67).

64 To this end, the leadership of the group was shared: "We work in a circle, with each of us stepping into the centre from time to time to help direct and focus things....This way has to do with what we believe about shared gifts, equal opportunities, and mutual responsibility" (ROP 1982:560).

65 TFWM, Minutes, October 1982. The parts in square brackets were added to this goal in the minutes taken at a subsequent meeting in February 1983.

66 TFWM, Minutes, February 1983.

67 Mary Thompson Boyd (on behalf of the TFWM), "Ourselves Through a Rearview Mirror," prepared for General Council 1982.

68 TFWM, "Proposal for an Internal Audit," 1 March 1983.

69 Similarly, the great majority of people recognize that violence against women is wrong, but there is wide disagreement as to what constitutes violence. Language shapes our attitudes and vice versa. Moreover, the way in which this issue is defined influences the response to such violence. In the case of sexism at Church House, while the people who discussed the issue agreed that discrimination based on one's sex was wrong, they did not perceive that such discrimination existed in their context.

70 TFWM, "Proposal for an Internal Audit," 1 March 1983.

71 TFWM, Internal Audit, 1 January 1984. These statistics were based on payroll information available as of 1 January 1984. A further breakdown showed the following:

Women Employed at National Office, as a percentage of total staff:

21.7% of senior management staff (Division Secretaries, Department Heads, etc.);

24.2% of program staff and those in mid-level management and administrative positions;

63.6% of first-line supervisory and junior-level management and administrative staff;

90.0% of support staff.

Economically, as well as in terms of social status, those at the top of the hierarchy benefited most.

72 The responses fell into one of four categories: "1. [sexism is] not an issue, 2. some recognition that sexism is an issue, but do not understand it, 3. issue owned, but not clear (outside pressure greatly needed), or 4. issue owned, with some future direction" (TFWM, Minutes, 1-4 June 1984, 6).

73 ROP 1984:440. The percentage of women in the ordered ministry at this time was far lower than the percentage of women employed in the work force in Canada: "Today for every 100 men in the Order of Ministry, there are approximately 15 women (Ordained and Diaconal). In the total Canadian work force, there are about 70 women for every 100 men." This number had increased since 1978 when "only four percent of ordained clergy were women" (Mary Rose Donelly, "Still Unready for Women Clergy: Study" in *The Observer* [January 1984], 37). In the March 1986 issue of *The Observer*, Gillian Sniatynski wrote that women "now make up almost 10 percent of

ordained clergy, but they still have enormous difficulty getting jobs" ("After 50 Years, Still Barriers to Women in Ministry," 24).

74 TFWM, General Council Report, August 1984.

75 TFWM, Minutes, October 1984, 8.

76 Frederick Sellers on behalf of the TFWM, letter to General Council Executive, 23 March 1983.

77 Legge, among other feminist ethicists, affirms the importance of language to systemic justice issues: "Metaphorical images do not set out abstract ideals and doctrines but rather generate a worldview and infuse our lives with meaning and nourishment for empowered, fruitful lives" (*Grace*, 29). Walker's work also emphasizes the power of language to shape our perceptions and reactions to issues: "Concepts...are not simply descriptive linguistic conventions; they organize the social construction of knowledge: ways of thinking about, defining, and giving abstract and generalized meaning to our particular experience. Knowledge, thus produced, provides for particular ways of taking action" (*Family Violence*, 101).

78 Poling asserts that there is a "possible complicity of religion with sexual violence," based on several case studies of such violence against women in which the perpetrators "made explicit and implicit references to God to rationalize their abusive behaviors." These references to God were based on an understanding that a "father-God" sanctioned the "authority of men over women" (*Abuse of Power*, 154).

79 TFWM, Minutes, October 1982, 2.

80 TFWM, Minutes, October 1982, 1.

81 TFWM, Report to the Adult Working Unit, October 1981.

82 TFWM, Study Guide for *Killing Us Softly*, 1981, 5

83 As Brian Wren points out, based on his experiences as a white man in a North American context, men must be held accountable for any complicity and called to participate in a theology of repentance which "will be a theology of listening and self-critique and will lead to substantial changes in the way theology is done" (Brian Wren, *What Language Shall I Borrow?* [New York: Crossroad, 1991], 223). Various social groups have resisted and continue to resist such a call to repentance and accountability. For instance, many self-help movements of the 1980s and 1990s, such as the codependence and other addiction movements, have sometimes cast violent men as victims. Patrick Carnes has written one of the more influential books in this area, *Out of the Shadows—Understanding Sexual Addiction* (Minneapolis, MN: Compcare Publications, 1983). These medical models tend to reduce the issue to an individual problem.

84 TFWM, Presentation at General Council, August 1982, 4. This statement did not take into account the complexity created by the diverse experiences of power as held by men of different economic, racial and cultural backgrounds.

85 TFWM, Minutes, March 1982. The TFWM also had previously formed a "Men's Subgroup" that was mandated to explore "men's experience" and develop a network: "This group consists of the men on the Task Force whose task is to focus on men's experience and understanding of sexism. This group will be working on building and supporting a network of men in the church across Canada...recommending to appropriate bodies, committees resources for use with men's groups" (TFWM, Minutes, October 1981, 1).

86 TFWM, Minutes, October 1982, 5.

87 Through mutual concern regarding issues such as harassment, the TFWM and its successor had an increasing amount of contact with the Committee on Women in Ministry (WIM). In 1986, as a result of this increasing concern, General Council approved a policy statement on sexual harassment, as proposed by the Women in Ministry Committee. WIM was also responsible for the creation of the policy document on sexual abuse in the Church. Owing largely to their efforts, since 1992 the United Church has had a detailed policy regarding procedures to be followed in the case of an allegation of sexual abuse against people who are accountable to the Church. (United Church of

Canada, "Sexual Abuse: Harassment, Exploitation, Misconduct, Assault and Child Abuse" [Toronto, ON: Division of Ministry Personnel and Education, The United Church of Canada, August 1992], 1). In 1996 the General Council Committee on Abuse Policy was formed. This committee reviews the policy, proposes and/or implements changes, and educates Church members regarding the policy. The theological statement approved by the Executive reads in part: "Sexual harassment is a sin. We believe that women and men are equal before God and in creation. Sexual harassment is a violation of the integrity of persons based on unequal power relationships. Sexual harassment degrades persons and does not allow their gifts of creativity and wholeness to be used in the Church. Jesus emphasizes mutuality and respect in relationships. To harass is to misuse power and to distort relationships. It leads to alienation and distrust" (ROP 1986:221). WIM explained the importance of the power dynamics in sexual harassment cases: sexual harassment involves the "exploitation of a power relationship"; it is not "an exclusively sexual issue." Sexual harassment was defined to include anything from "verbal innuendo and subtle suggestions to overt demands and physical abuse." Thus, this type of sexual violence was defined primarily as an abuse of power. However, the policy was set forth in gender-neutral terms; the relevance of sexism was not discussed. The adopted "principles and assumptions" are printed as follows:

" • Sexual harassment is unacceptable within The United Church of Canada;
   • All complaints of sexual harassment need to be taken seriously;
   • The intent of these policies and procedures is to stop the violations of personhood resulting from sexual harassment and to attempt to heal the personal and corporate frailty that we share with all humanity;
   • All policies and procedures need to minimize further distress for the complainant;
   • Confidentiality needs to be assured;
   • Each stage in dealing with a case of harassment needs to involve as few people as possible;
   • Everyone dealing with a case should be familiar with the issues involved in sexual harassment;
   • At any stage prior to a decision to proceed with a Formal Hearing, the complainant has the right to decide not to proceed with the case;
   • Every effort needs to be made to stop the harassment without formal hearing procedures" (See ROP 1986:206-208)."

88 TFWM, Minutes, June 1983, 2.
89 Sheila Redmond, "Christian 'Virtues' and Recovery from Child Sexual Abuse" in *Christianity, Patriarchy and Abuse*, 76. Other United Church groups also began some work around harassment at about this time. The Women in Ministry Overview Group, of the Division of MP&E, conducted a survey in 1983 asking "women in ministry if they had ever been the victims of ['unwelcome verbal or physical behaviour related to sexuality']." The results indicated that "35 percent of the 238 women in United Church ministries surveyed, had been victims of sexual harassment" (Muriel Duncan, "Church Moves on Harassment Reports" in *The Observer* [May 1984], 35; and Mike Milne, "Council Passes Harassment Policy" in *The Observer* [May 1985], 9).
90 TFWM, Minutes, 18-21 October, 1984, 1.
91 TFWM, Minutes, October 1982.
92 One example of such contact between the United Church and a secular Canadian group was the connection between the Church and the National Action Committee (NAC). The United Church delegates to NAC, during the years of the TFWM, were typically women from the TFWM, although technically the connection was with the Adult Working Unit of DMC. The TFWM saw this as an important link and a good opportunity to introduce others to the significance, existence and meaning of feminist theology. (See TFWM, Minutes, April 1981, 29 January-1 February 1982, 12; and February 1983.)

93 TFWM, Letter to "Initial Contact People in Each Conference," 4 January 1982.

94 TFWM, letter to individuals re: network, May 1982.

95 TFWM, Minutes, June 1983, 24.

96 The groups that gathered in this space were: the Peace Office (An ecumenical program funded in part by the Manitoba and Northwestern Ontario Conference), the TFWM, AFFIRM (Gays and Lesbians of The United Church of Canada) and the National Native Ministry (TFWM, "An Invitation to Visitors and Commissioners in Morden," August 1984).

97 TFWM, Letter to Dr Allan McDougall, Chair Agenda Planning Committee for General Council 1984, 19 December 1983.

98 TFWM, "An Invitation...Morden," August 1984.

99 Standing Committee on Sexism, Minutes, 19-20 February, 9.

100 TFWM, Minutes, October 1984, 8.

101 TFWM, Minutes, September 1983, 10.

102 TFWM, Minutes, October 1984, 4, 13.

103 "Names Sexism Ills, Avoids Remedies" in *The Observer* (October 1984), 15.

104 As Ruether argues, Christians need to take their call to confession and repentance more seriously and engage in harsh self-critique in which any and all contradictions between how we act and what we are called to in the name of the liberating Christ will be exposed and our true identity restored. A recognition that confession was necessary regarding the Church's complicity in sexism was a *starting point* for such critique. (See, for example, Rosemary R. Ruether, *To Change the World* [New York: Crossroad, 1981], 24-25, and *Sexism and God-Talk*, 125.) Similarly, theologian Doris Dyke writes that confession regarding complicity in "structures and attitudes" that oppress women is the starting point of action directed toward the eradication of violence against women: "Women in our culture suffer *because* of their bodies. Caring about this can become action when we confess our personal and communal responsibility for violence against women, the sin of complicity in structures and attitudes that cause needless suffering" (*Crucified Woman* [Toronto, ON: The United Church Publishing House, 1991], 72).

105 Committee on Sexism, Report to the Thirty-Second General Council, August 1988, 6.

106 For instance, Ann Naylor, Secretary, Women In Ministry Committee, observed on the 50th anniversary of Lydia Gruchy's ordination that "women in ministry continue to experience discrimination" (ROP 1986:104).

107 Committee on Sexism, Report to 1988 General Council, 12.

108 For example, the TFWM perceived the confession of complicity in sexism at the 1984 General Council as an important, albeit ambiguous beginning to the United Church's journey regarding sexism as a justice issue.

109 In 1987, the Committee on Sexism recorded feedback from the Sexuality, Marriage and Family Unit: "It was suggested that the reason some units may be hesitant about meeting with us is because they suspect we have a monitoring function" (Committee on Sexism, Minutes, 5-7 March 1987, 3).

Notes to Chapter 7

1 Parts of this chapter have been published as "Prophetic or Followers? The United Church of Canada, Gender, Sexuality, and Violence Against Women" in *Violence Against Women and Children—A Christian Theological Sourcebook*, ed. Carol Adams and Marie M. Fortune (New York: Continuum, 1995), 187-313.

2 In 1990, the Committee on Sexism concluded, on the basis of a survey, that although progress had been made, sexism continued to be a problem in the United Church (ROP 1990:251).

3 See for example, *ROP* 1980:167ff; *ROP*1982:166ff; and *ROP* 1986:547ff.

4 Changing understandings of sexuality and sin also contributed to the naming of family sexual abuse. Previously, anything to do with sex had been taboo in the public realm; sex was not to be talked about.

5 The United Church of Canada, *Marriage Breakdown, Divorce, Remarriage: A Christian Understanding* (Toronto, ON: The United Church of Canada, 1962).

6 It is important to recognize the multifaceted nature of the women's movement in Canada. As Nancy Adamson et al. point out, particularly since the early 1970s, the women's movement has been characterized by diversity: "The women's movement has a shifting, amoeba-like character; it is and has always been, politically, ideologically, and strategically diverse. It is not, and never has been, represented by a single organizational entity; it has no head office, no single leaders, no membership cards to sign" (Nancy Adamson, Linda Briskin and Margaret McPhail, *Feminists Organizing for Change—The Contemporary Women's Movement in Canada* [Toronto, ON: Oxford, 1988], 7).

7 Adamson et. al., *Feminists Organizing*, 45.

8 Section 179(c) of the 1892 Canadian *Criminal Code* was changed accordingly (McLaren and McLaren, 136).

9 Adamson et al., *Feminists Organizing*, 46; Naomi Wall, "The Last Ten Years: A Personal/Political View" in *Still Ain't Satisfied—Canadian Feminism Today*, ed. M. Fitzgerald, C. Guberman and M. Wolfe (Toronto, ON: Women's Press, 1982), 19; and Kathleen McDonnell, "Claim No Easy Victories: The Fight For Reproductive Rights" in *Still Ain't Satisfied*, 32. Since the early 1970s, any popular attention to the abortion issue has focused largely on the court system. Aside from this attention to legal decisions, the issue has been relatively quiet in Canada, particularly compared with the United States, since then. In attempting to explain this relative silence, McDonnell observes, "In contrast to the United States where the Hyde amendment and the rise of the new right have thrown the abortion struggle into dramatic and highly visible relief, the situation in Canada is vague, much less polarized. Instead of a clearly visible threat to abortion rights, what we have is a complicated, slowly eroding situation whose impact is difficult to convey to the public" (33).

10 The United Church of Canada, *Contraception and Abortion* (Toronto, Ontario: The United Church of Canada, 1982).

11 *Healthsharing* Winter 1988, 27. Since then, a report of the Law Reform Commission, released in 1989, rejected this position and recommended a return to criminal legislation (*Healthsharing* Fall 1989, 24). Moreover, although such legislation has not been passed, as Joy Thompson, then spokesperson for the British Columbia Coalition of Abortion Clinics, stated: "Access to abortion has not improved one iota since January 1988" (quoted in *Kinesis* March 1991, 3).

12 For an in-depth explanation of the history and characteristics of these different types of feminist organizations, see Adamson et al., 62-71.

13 The Canadian Association of Sexual Assault Centres, "*Evaluation 1979-1982, to the Department of Health and Welfare*" (December 1986), 13.

14 Toronto Rape Crisis Centre, *No Safe Place: Violence Against Women and Children* (Toronto, ON: Women's Press, 1985), 67. This collective included as its goals the eradication of male violence against women, networking and support not only among the nation-wide crisis centres but also with other women's collectives who were struggling against oppression (CASAC report, 4).

15 *ROP* 1932:284. The 1932 report, *The Meaning and Responsibilities of Christian Marriage,* acknowledged that a marriage in which one spouse is "loveless" and "cruel" should not continue.

16 The Canadian Panel on Violence Against Women, *Changing the Landscape: Ending Violence—Achieving Equality—The Final Report* (Ottawa, ON: Minister of Supply and Services Canada, 1993), 49. Women Against Rape in British Columbia called for

5 November, 1977 to be a "National Day of Protest against Violence against Women." Women marched down Yonge Street in Toronto on this day and collected in front of a pornography cinema where "the demonstration became violent and some women were arrested" (Adamson et al., *Feminists Organizing*, 72).

17 *Kinesis* April 1992, 5.

18 *Kinesis* April 1992, 5.

19 Adamson et al., *Feminists Organizing*, 61, 83, 108-110.

20 Adamson et al., *Feminists Organizing*, 79.

21 *Pappajohn v R.* (1980), 111 D.L.R. (3d) 1 (S.C.C.).

22 The Canadian Panel on Violence Against Women, 17.

23 The Canadian Panel on Violence Against Women, 236.

24 This understanding is similar to that expressed by the authors of the sexism chapters in both *In God's Image* and *Gift, Dilemma and Promise*: sexism, and therefore violence against women, can be eradicated through education.

25 Walker, *Family Violence*, 57.

26 Walker, *Family Violence*, 132.

27 Walker, *Family Violence*, 191, and The Canadian Panel on Violence Against Women, 205.

28 Walker, *Family Violence*, 153.

29 Walker, *Family Violence*, 167.

30 For instance, the approval of contraceptives was due to the prevailing belief that the family was de facto good and because it was thought that the use of contraceptives would help preserve this institution. In 1960, mutual consent within marriage was named as necessary with the understood proviso that mutuality must not threaten the accepted gender roles. Divorce was justified if the physical safety of a spouse was threatened. This position was also taken in 1932 but not expressed as clearly. A concrete acknowledgment that women were at particular risk was not yet expressed.

31 We now know that the glorification of the nuclear family contributes to the perpetuation of male violence against women and children in the home. Because the maintenance of the private sphere continues to be bound up in many women's identities, the loss/destruction of the "good family" is often directly connected to a woman's sense of self-esteem. For this reason and because of the perpetuation of a theology that glorifies suffering, it continues to be more acceptable for an abused woman to present the appearance of "family bliss" and to be the longsuffering sacrificial victim for the sake of preserving the family. (See, for example, Joy M.K. Bussert, *Battered Women—From a Theology of Suffering to an Ethic of Empowerment* [Division for Mission in North America, Lutheran Church in America, Kutztown, PA: Kutztown Publishing, 1986], 28-30).

32 For instance, although the 1962 General Council received a report stating that working mothers were declared to be effective mothers who needed Church support, the same Council found that it was inappropriate for married women to be ordained.

33 As Lebacqz contends, to "put power into the central focus of ethical concern is to argue for the importance of the norm of justice" (Lebacqz, *Professional Ethics—Power and Paradox*, 129).

34 Richard Allen, *The Social Passion—Religion and Social Reform in Canada 1914-28* (Toronto: University of Toronto Press, 1971), and ed. R.B.Y. Scott and Gregory Vlastos, *Towards the Christian Revolution* (Kingston, ON: Ronald Frye, 1989, originally published in 1936).

35 See Poling, *Abuse of Power*, 33, and Welch, *Feminist Ethic of Risk*, 80.

36 Poling, *Abuse of Power*, 48.

37 Legge, *Grace*, 3-4.

Selected Bibliography

Adamson, Nancy, Linda Briskin and Margaret McPhail. *Feminists Organizing for Change: The Contemporary Women's Movement in Canada*. Toronto, ON: Oxford University Press, 1988.

Allen, Richard. *The Social Passion: Religion and Social Reform in Canada 1914-28*. Toronto, ON: University of Toronto Press, 1971.

The Anglican Church of Canada. *Violence against Women: Abuse in Society and Church and Proposals for Change*. The Taskforce Report to General Synod 1986 of the Anglican Church of Canada, 1987.

The Assembly of Quebec Bishops. *A Heritage of Violence: A Pastoral Reflection on Conjugal Violence*. Montreal, QC: The Assembly of Quebec Bishops, 1989.

Backhouse, C., and D. Flaherty, eds. *Challenging Times: The Women's Movement in Canada and the United States*. Kingston, ON: McGill-Queen's University Press, 1992.

Bjorge, Corinne. "Porn, Obscenity and the Supreme Court." *Kinesis: News About Women That's Not in the Dailies*. Vancouver, BC: Vancouver Status of Women (April 1992).

Boulton, Wayne G., Thomas D. Kennedy, and Allen Verhey, eds. *From Christ to the World: Introductory Readings in Christian Ethics*. Grand Rapids, MI: William B. Eerdmans, 1994.

Bowker, Lee H. "Battered Women and the Clergy: An Evaluation." *The Journal of Pastoral Care* 36, 4 (1982): 226-34

Brock, Rita Nakashima. *Journeys by Heart: A Christology of Erotic Power*. New York, NY: Crossroad, 1988.

Brooks Thistlethwaite, Susan. *Sex, Race and God: Christian Feminism in Black and White*. New York, NY: Crossroad, 1989.

Brown, Jackie. "Abortion Bill Defeated: Too Close for Comfort." *Kinesis: News about Women That's Not in the Dailies*. Vancouver, BC: Vancouver Status of Women (March 1991).

Brown, Joanne, and Carole Bohn, eds. *Christianity, Patriarchy and Abuse*. New York, NY: Pilgrim Press, 1989.

Brownmiller, Susan. *Waverly Place*. New York, NY: Grove Press, 1989.

Brueggemann, Walter. *The Prophetic Imagination*. Philadelphia, PA: Fortress Press, 1978.

Bussert, Joy M.K. *Battered Women: From a Theology of Suffering to an Ethic of Empowerment*. Division for Mission in North America, Lutheran Church in America, Kutztown, PA: Kutztown Publishing, 1986.

Canada, Report of the Standing Committee on Health and Welfare, Social Affairs, Seniors and the Status of Women. *The War against Women.* Ottawa, ON: Queen's Printer, June 1991. (Chair: Barbara Greene.)

The Canadian Association of Sexual Assault Centres. "Evaluation 1979-1982, to the Department of Health and Welfare." December 1986.

The Canadian Conference of Catholic Bishops. "To Live Without Fear." Ottawa, ON: CASAC, 1991.

The Canadian Panel on Violence against Women. *Changing the Landscape: Ending Violence—Achieving Equality: The Final Report.* Ottawa, ON: Minister of Supply and Services Canada, 1993.

Caplan, Paula. *The Myth of Women's Masochism.* New York, NY: New American Library, 1985.

Carnes, Patrick. *Out of the Shadows: Understanding Sexual Addiction.* Minneapolis, MN: Compcare Publications, 1983.

Carr, Anne E. *Transforming Grace: Christian Tradition and Women's Experience.* San Francisco, CA: Harper & Row, 1988.

The Church Council on Justice and Corrections and The Canadian Council on Social Development. *Family Violence in a Patriarchal Culture: A Challenge to Our Way of Living.* Ottawa, ON: The Keith Press, September 1988.

The Church Leaders' Submission to the Canadian Panel on Violence against Women. *And No One Shall Make Them Afraid (Micah 4:4).* 27 March 1992.

Cormie, Lee. "Revolutions in Reading the Bible." In *The Bible and the Politics of Exegesis.* Ed. David Jobling, Peggy Day, and Gerald Sheppard. Cleveland, OH: Pilgrims Press, 1991.

Daly, Lois, ed. *Feminist Ethics: A Reader:* Louisville, KY: Westminster John Knox Press, 1984

Daly, Mary. *Gyn/Ecology: The Metaethics of Radical Feminism.* Boston, MA: Beacon Press, 1978.

Danica, Elly. *Don't—A Woman's Word.* Toronto, ON: McClelland & Stewart, 1990.

Davy, Shirley, Project Coordinator. *Women, Work & Worship in the United Church of Canada.* Toronto, ON: The United Church of Canada, 1983.

Devaney, Sheila. "The Limits of the Appeal to Women's Experience." In *Shaping New Vision: Gender and Values in American Culture,* ed. C.W. Atkinson, C.H. Buchanan, and M.R. Miles. The Harvard Women's Studies in Religion Series, No. 5. London, UK: U.M.II. Research Press, 1987.

Dyke, Doris. *Crucified Woman.* Toronto, ON: The United Church Publishing House, 1991.

Ellison, Marvin M. *Erotic Justice: A Liberating Ethic of Sexuality.* Louisville, KY: Westminster John Knox Press, 1996.

Estrich, Susan. *Real Rape: How the Legal System Victimizes Women Who Say No.* Boston, MA: Harvard University Press, 1987.

Faludi, Susan. *Backlash: The Undeclared War against American Women.* New York, NY: Crown Publishers, 1991.

Fitzgerald, M., C. Guberman, and M. Wolfe, eds. *Still Ain't Satisfied: Canadian Feminism Today.* Toronto, ON: Women's Press, 1982.

Fortune, Marie Marshall. *Sexual Violence: The Unmentionable Sin, An Ethical and Pastoral Perspective.* New York, NY: Pilgrim Press, 1983.

———. *Keeping the Faith: Questions ad Answers for the Abused Woman.* San Francisco, CA: Harper & Row, 1987.

————. *Is Nothing Sacred?: When Sex Invades the Pastoral Relationship.* San Francisco, CA: Harper & Row, 1989.

Friedan, Betty. *The Feminine Mystique.* New York, NY: Dell Publishing, 1963.

Geertz, Clifford. "Religion as a Cultural System." In *Anthropological Approaches to the Study of Religion,* ed. Michael Banton, London, UK: Tavistock, 1965.

Gilligan, Carol. *In a Different Voice: Psychological Theory and Women's Development.* Boston, MA: Harvard University Press, 1982.

Glaz, M. and J.S. Moessner, eds. *Women in Travail & Transition: A New Pastoral Care.* Minneapolis, MN: Fortress Press, 1991.

Golding, Gail. *Hands to End Violence against Women: A Resource for Theological Education.* Toronto, ON: Women's Inter-Church Council of Canada, 1988.

Gordon, Linda. *Heroes of Their Own Lives: The Politics and History of Family Violence, Boston 1880-1960.* New York, NY: Viking, 1988.

Guttierez, Gustavo. *We Drink from Our Own Wells.* Trans. Matthew J. O'Connell. New York, NY: Orbis Books, 1984.

Hamner, Jalna, and Mary Maynard, eds. *Women, Violence and Social Control.* Atlantic Highlands, NJ: Humanities Press International, 1987.

Hampson, Daphne. "Reinhold Niebuhr on Sin: A Critique." In *Reinhold Niebuhr and the Issues of Our Times,* ed. Richard Harries. Oxford, England: A.R. Mowbray, 1986.

Harrison, Beverly. *Our Right to Choose: Toward a New Ethic of Abortion.* Boston, MA: Beacon Press, 1983.

————. *Making the Connections: Essays in Feminist Social Ethics.* Ed. Carol S. Robb. Boston, MA: Beacon Press, 1985.

Horton, Anne L., and Judith A. Williamson, eds. *Abuse and Religion: When Praying Isn't Enough.* Lexington, MA: Lexington Books, 1988.

Hurcombe, Linda, ed. *Sex and God: Some Varieties of Women's Religious Experience.* New York, NY: Routledge & Kegan Paul, 1987.

Hutchinson, Norah. "No New Law." *Healthsharing: A Canadian Women's Health Quarterly.* Toronto, ON: Women Healthsharing (Winter 1988).

Hutchinson, Roger. "Contextualization: No Passing Fad." In *A New Beginning,* Theresa Chu and Christopher Lind, ed. Canada China Program of the Canadian Council of Churches, 1983.

————. "Towards a 'Pedagogy for Allies of the Oppressed'." In *Studies in Religion/Sciences Religieuses* 13, 2 (Spring 1984): 145-50.

————. *Prophets, Pastors and Public Choices: Canadian Churches and the Mackenzie Valley Pipeline Debate.* Vol. 3 of *Comparative Ethics.* Canadian Corporation for Studies in Religion, Waterloo, ON: Wilfrid Laurier University Press, 1992.

————. "Social Ethics and Mission in a Post-Liberal Age." Unpublished manuscript. Emmanuel College, University of Toronto, Toronto, ON, 1992.

Hutchinson, Roger, and Cranford Pratt, eds. *Christian Faith and Economic Justice: Toward a Canadian Perspective.* Toronto, ON: Trinity Press, 1988.

Jonsen, Albert R., and Stephen Toulmin. *The Abuse of Casuistry: A History of Moral Reasoning.* Berkeley, CA: University of California Press, 1988.

Kaminer, Wendy. "Chances Are You're Codependent Too." Book Review, in *The New York Times.* 11 February 1990.

Kaufman, Michael. *Cracking the Armour: Power, Pain and the Lives of Men.* Toronto, ON: Viking, 1993.

King, Ursula. *Women and Spirituality: Voices of Protest and Promise.* New York, NY: New Amsterdam Books, 1989.

Kingston Rape Crisis Centre. Pamphlet. Kingston, ON: Kingston Rape Crisis Centre, 1987.

Larner, Christina. *Witchcraft and Religion: The Politics of Popular Belief.* New York, NY: Basil Blackwell, 1984.

Lebacqz, Karen. *Professional Ethics: Power and Paradox.* Nashville, TN: Abingdon Press, 1985.

Lebacqz, Karen, and Ronald G. Barton. *Sex in the Parish.* Louisville, KY: Westminster/John Knox Press, 1991.

Legge, Marilyn. *The Grace of Difference: A Canadian Feminist Theological Ethic.* Atlanta, GA: Scholars Press, 1992.

Livezey, Lois Gehr. "Sexual and Family Violence: A Growing Issue for the Churches." In *The Christian Century* (28 October 1987).

MATCH International Centre. *Linking Women's Global Struggles to End Violence.* Ottawa, ON: MATCH International Centre, June 1990.

McLaren, Angus, and Arlene Tigar McLaren. *The Bedroom and the State.* Toronto, ON: McClelland & Stewart, 1986.

Mellody, Pia. *Facing Codependence.* San Francisco, CA: Harper & Row, 1989.

Mennonite Central Committee, the Domestic Violence Task Force. *Broken Boundaries: Resources for Pastoring People—Child Sexual Abuse,* 1990.

———. *The Purple Packet: Wife Abuse,* 1990.

Metro Action Committee on Public Violence against Women and Children. "Women in Safe Enviroments." Toronto, ON: METRAC, 1987.

Metz, Johannes Baptist. *Faith in History and Society: Toward a Practical Fundamental Theology.* New York, NY: Seabury Press, 1980.

———. *The Emergent Church.* New York, NY: Crossroad, 1987.

Moller Okin, Susan. *Justice, Gender and the Family.* New York: Basic Books, 1989.

Morris, Roberta. *Ending Violence in Families: A Training Program for Pastoral Care Workers.* Toronto, ON: The United Church of Canada, 1988.

Niebuhr, Reinhold. *An Interpretation of Christian Ethics.* New York, NY: Harper & Brothers, 1935.

———. *Christian Realism and Political Problems.* New York, NY: Charles Scribner's Sons, 1953.

———. *The Nature and Destiny of Man: Vol. 1 Human Nature.* New York, NY: Charles Scribner's Sons, 1964.

———. *Leaves from the Notebook of a Tamed Cynic.* New York, NY: Da Capo Press, 1976.

Nelson, James B. *Embodiment: An Approach to Sexuality and Christian Theology.* Minneapolis, MN: Augsburg, 1978.

———. *The Intimate Connection: Male Sexuality, Masculine Spirituality.* Philadelphia, PA: Westminster Press, 1988.

Nelson, James B., and Sandra P. Longfellow, eds. *Sexuality and the Sacred: Sources for Theological Reflection.* Louisville, KY: John Knox Press, 1994.

Pappajohn v. R. (1980), 111 D.L.R. (3d) 1 (S.C.C.).

Piercy, Marge. *Living in the Open.* New York, NY: Knopf, 1976.

Plaskow, Judith. *Sex, Sin and Grace*. Seattle, WA: University Press of America, 1980.

————. *Standing Again at Sinai: Judaism from a Feminist Perspective*. New York, NY: HarperCollins Publishers, 1990.

Poling, James Newton. *The Abuse of Power: A Theological Problem*. Nashville, TN: Abingdon Press, 1991.

Radford, Jill, and Diane E.H. Russell, eds. *Femicide: The Politics of Woman Killing*. New York, NY: Macmillan, 1992.

Robb, Carol. "A Framework for Feminist Ethics." In *Women's Consciousness, Women's Conscience*, ed. Barbara H. Andolsen, Christine E. Gudorf and Mary D. Pellauer. New York, NY: Harper & Row, 1985, 211-34.

Ruether, Rosemary Radford. *Faith and Fratricide*. New York, NY: Seabury Press, 1974.

————. *New Woman/New Earth*. New York: Seabury Press, 1975.

————. "Women Priests." In *Women Priests: A Catholic Commentary on the Vatican Declaration*, ed. Leonard Swidler and Arlene Swidler. New York, NY: Paulist Press, 1977.

————. "Mothers of the Church." In *Women of Spirit*, ed. R. Ruether and E. McLaughlin. New York, NY: Simon & Schuster, 1979.

————. *To Change the World*. New York: Crossroad, 1981.

————. *Disputed Questions: On Being a Christian*. Nashville, TN: Abingdon, 1982.

————. *Sexism and God-Talk*. Boston, MA: Beacon Press, 1983.

————. "A Method of Correlation." In *A Feminist Interpretation of the Bible*, ed. Russell, Letty. Philadelphia, PA: Westminster Press, 1985.

Russell, Letty M. *Authority in Feminist Theology: Household of Freedom*. Philadelphia: Westminster, 1987.

Russell, Letty M., Kwok Pui-Lan, Ada Maria Isasi-Diaz, and Katie Geneva Cannon, eds. *Inheriting Our Mothers' Gardens: Feminist Theology in Third World Perspective*. Louisville, KY: Westminster, 1988.

Rutter, Peter. *Sex in the Forbidden Zone*. New York, NY: Fawcett Crest, 1989.

Saiving, Valerie. "The Human Situation: A Feminine View," in *The Journal of Religion* 40, 2 (1960): 100-12.

Sanday, Peggy Reeves. *Fraternity Gang Rape*. New York, NY: New York University Press, 1990.

Schüssler Fiorenza, Elizabeth. *In Memory of Her: A Feminist Theological Reconstruction of Christian Origins*. New York, NY: Crossroad, 1983.

————. *Bread Not Stone: The Challenge of Feminist Biblical Interpretation*. Boston, MA: Beacon Press, 1984.

————. *Jesus: Miriam's Child, Sophia's Prophet: Critical Issues in Feminist Christology*. New York, NY: Continuum, 1995, p. 14.

Scott, R.B.Y., and Gregory Vlastos, eds. *Towards the Christian Revolution*. Canada: Ronald P. Frye, 1989. Originally published in 1936.

Scully, Diana. *Understanding Sexual Violence: A Study of Convicted Rapists*. Boston, MA: Unwin Hyman, 1990.

Sharma, Arvind, ed. *Women in World Religions*. Albany, NY: SUNY Press, 1987.

Sheppard, Gerald T. *The Future of the Bible*. Toronto, ON: United Church Publishing House, 1990.

Sinclair, Deborah. *Understanding Wife Assault: A Training Manual for Counsellors and Advocates*. Toronto, ON: Publications Ontario, 1985.

Spretnak, Charlene, ed. *The Politics of Women's Spirituality: Essays on the Rise of Spiritual Power within the Feminist Movement.* New York, NY: Anchor, 1982.

Tanaka, Janet. "The Role of Religious Education in Preventing Sexual and Domestic Violence." In *Women's Issues in Religious Education,* ed. Fern M. Giltner. Birmingham, AL: Religious Education Press, 1985.

Taves, Ann, ed. *Religion and Domestic Violence in Early New England: The Memoirs of Abigail Abbot Bailey.* Indianapolis, IN: Indiana University Press, 1989.

Toronto Rape Crisis Centre. Pamphlet. 1990.

———. "Goals and Services." 1990.

———. *No Safe Place: Violence against Women and Children.* Toronto, ON: Women's Press, 1985.

Trible, Phyllis. *Texts of Terror.* Philadelphia, PA: Fortress Press, 1984.

Trothen, Tracy. "Prophetic or Followers? The United Church of Canada, Gender, Sexuality, and Violence against Women." In *Violence against Women and Children: A Christian Theological Sourcebook,* ed. Carol Adams and Marie M. Fortune. New York, NY: Continuum, 1995.

The United Church of Canada. *Records of Proceedings,* 1925-1968.

———. *The New Outlook.* Toronto, ON: The United Church of Canada, 18 November, 1936.

———. *Marriage Breakdown, Divorce, Remarriage: A Christian Understanding.* Toronto, ON: The United Church of Canada, 1962.

———. The Committee on Theology and Faith. *The Permanence of Christian Marriage.* Toronto, ON: The United Church of Canada, 1974.

———. The Task Force on Marriage and Alternative Styles, The Division of Mission in Canada. *Marriage Today: An Exploration of Man/Woman Relationship and of Marriage.* Toronto, ON: The Division of Mission in Canada in The United Church of Canada, 1978.

———. *In God's Image...Male and Female.* Toronto, ON: The United Church of Canada, 1980.

———. The Interdivisional Task Force on the Changing Roles of Women and Men in Church and Society, "A Response to Chapter Five: Sexism of the Human Sexuality Report: 'In God's Image...Male and Female.'" Toronto, ON: The United Church of Canada, November 1981.

———. *The Observer.* Toronto, ON: The United Church of Canada, January 1980-December 1986.

———. *Contraception and Abortion.* Toronto, ON: The United Church of Canada, 1982.

———. *Faith & Sexuality: A Spectrum of Theological Views in the United Church of Canada.* Toronto, ON: The United Church of Canada, 1982.

———. *Gift, Dilemma and Promise: A Report and Affirmations on Human Sexuality.* Toronto, ON: The United Church of Canada, 1984.

———. "Child Abuse." The Division of Mission in Canada, The United Church of Canada, February 1985.

———. *Pornography Kit.* Toronto, ON: CANEC, 1985.

———. "The Family." Toronto, ON: The Division of Mission in Canada, The United Church of Canada, 1987.

———. "Women in Abusive Relationships." The Division of Mission in Canada, The United Church of Canada, November 1987.

————. *Toward a Christian Understanding of Sexual Orientations, Lifestyles and Ministry*. Toronto, ON: The United Church of Canada, 1988.

————. "Abuse of the Elderly." The Division of Mission in Canada, The United Church of Canada, December 1989.

————. *Sexual Abuse (Sexual Harassment, Sexual Exploitation, Pastoral Sexual Misconduct, Sexual Assault) and Child Abuse*. Toronto, ON: Division of Ministry Personnel and Education, The United Church of Canada, 1992.

United Church of Canada Archives—files regarding various sexuality and gender reports. Toronto, ON: United Church Archives, 1970-1990.

Valverde, Mariana. *The Age of Light, Soap, and Water: Moral Reform in English Canada, 1885-1925*. Toronto, ON: McClelland & Stewart, 1991.

————. *Sex, Power and Pleasure*. Toronto, ON: Women's Press, 1985.

Van Wagner, Vicki, and B. Lee. "Legal Assault: A Feminist Analysis of the Law Reform Commission's Report on Abortion Legislation." *Healthsharing: A Canadian Women's Health Quarterly*. Toronto, ON: Women Healthsharing (Fall 1989).

Vaughan, Judith. *Sociality, Ethics, and Social Change: A Critical Appraisal of Reinhold Niebuhr's Ethics in the Light of Rosemary Radford Ruether's Works*. New York, NY: University Press of America, 1983.

Walker, Gillian A. *Family Violence and the Women's Movement: The Conceptual Politics of Struggle*. Toronto, ON: University of Toronto Press, 1990.

Warshaw, Robin. *I Never Called It Rape*. New York, NY: Harper & Row, 1980.

Webb, Judy. "Binding Up the Wounds." *Sojourners*. 26 November 1984.

Welch, Sharon. *A Feminist Ethic of Risk*. Minneapolis, MN: Fortress Press, 1990.

Winnipeg Presbytery. "Protocol on Child Abuse—as yet untitled—Draft." Winnipeg, MB: The United Church of Canada, 1993.

Winnipeg Presbytery and the Conference of Manitoba and Northwestern Ontario. "No Fear In Love..." Winnipeg, MB: The United Church of Canada, 1988.

Women's Inter-Church Council of Canada. "Report on the Theological Education Project on Violence against Women," May 1991.

Wren, Brian. *What Language Shall I Borrow?* New York, NY: Crossroad, 1991.

Young, Pamela Dickey. *Feminist Theology/Christian Theology: In Search of Method*. Minneapolis, MN: Fortress Press, 1990.

————. "Geertz Revisited: A Model for Feminist Studies in Religion." *Perkins School of Theology Journal* (January/April 1990).

Index

storytelling, 81, 98-99, 107-108, 120, 128
suffering, 7-8, 21, 37, 44, 71, 97, 123-24,
   129, 134, 137, 140, 145, 147
symbols, 4, 103, 122
systemic power imbalances, 19, 40, 44, 58,
   67, 82-83, 96, 117, 141
temptress, 12
tradition, 3, 13-16, 21, 27-28, 31-37, 45,
   47, 51-52, 54, 63, 66, 69-71, 73, 77-81,
   83, 91-92, 98-99, 104-105, 107-108, 112,
   118-19, 122, 132, 134
Valverde, Mariana, 17-18, 125
violence, 1-2, 6, 11-12, 20-22, 30, 36, 40,
   42, 50, 66, 70, 81-83, 97, 103-105,
   111-17, 122, 129, 136-37, 141-42, 146;
   against women, 1-4, 6-7, 12, 21-22, 39,
   41-42, 45, 58-9, 65-66, 72, 79, 83-84, 93,
   96-97, 103-105, 108-109, 111, 115-19,
   121, 123, 128, 129, 132, 137, 142-43,
   145-47

Walker, Gillian, 97, 116, 141
Welch, Sharon, 5, 133, 137, 141, 147
well-being, 25, 65, 111
white-slavery trade, 18, 125
wife, 3, 12, 19, 26-29, 35-36, 52, 77, 113-
   14, 127
Wittig, Monique, 129
Womanís Association (WA), 30
womenís groups, 13, 29, 97, 103, 113, 115,
   117, 125
Women's Missionary Society (WMS), 29
women's movements, 46, 54, 56, 89-90, 94,
   114-15, 119-20, 139, 146
worship, 89, 92, 126-27
Young, Pamela Dickey, 81, 134-35, 137, 142

Series Published by Wilfrid Laurier University Press for the Canadian Corporation for Studies in Religion/Corporation Canadienne des Sciences Religieuses

Editions SR

1. *La langue de Ya'udi : description et classement de l'ancien parler de Zencirci dans le cadre des langues sémitiques du nord-ouest*
   Paul-Eugène Dion, O.P. / 1974 / viii + 511 p. / OUT OF PRINT
2. *The Conception of Punishment in Early Indian Literature*
   Terence P. Day / 1982 / iv + 328 pp.
3. *Traditions in Contact and Change: Selected Proceedings of the XIVth Congress of the International Association for the History of Religions*
   Edited by Peter Slater and Donald Wiebe with Maurice Boutin and Harold Coward
   1983 / x + 758 pp. / OUT OF PRINT
4. *Le messianisme de Louis Riel*
   Gilles Martel / 1984 / xviii + 483 p.
5. *Mythologies and Philosophies of Salvation in the Theistic Traditions of India*
   Klaus K. Klostermaier / 1984 / xvi + 549 pp. / OUT OF PRINT
6. *Averroes' Doctrine of Immortality: A Matter of Controversy*
   Ovey N. Mohammed / 1984 / vi + 202 pp. / OUT OF PRINT
7. *L'étude des religions dans les écoles : l'expérience américaine, anglaise et canadienne*
   Fernand Ouellet / 1985 / xvi + 666 p.
8. *Of God and Maxim Guns: Presbyterianism in Nigeria, 1846-1966*
   Geoffrey Johnston / 1988 / iv + 322 pp.
9. *A Victorian Missionary and Canadian Indian Policy: Cultural Synthesis vs Cultural Replacement*
   David A. Nock / 1988 / x + 194 pp. / OUT OF PRINT
10. *Prometheus Rebound: The Irony of Atheism*
    Joseph C. McLelland / 1988 / xvi + 366 pp.
11. *Competition in Religious Life*
    Jay Newman / 1989 / viii + 237 pp.
12. *The Huguenots and French Opinion, 1685-1787: The Enlightenment Debate on Toleration*
    Geoffrey Adams / 1991 / xiv + 335 pp.
13. *Religion in History: The Word, the Idea, the Reality / La religion dans l'histoire : le mot, l'idée, la réalité*
    Edited by/Sous la direction de Michel Despland and/et Gérard Vallée
    1992 / x + 252 pp.
14. *Sharing Without Reckoning: Imperfect Right and the Norms of Reciprocity*
    Millard Schumaker / 1992 / xiv + 112 pp.
15. *Love and the Soul: Psychological Interpretations of the Eros and Psyche Myth*
    James Gollnick / 1992 / viii + 174 pp.
16. *The Promise of Critical Theology: Essays in Honour of Charles Davis*
    Edited by Marc P. Lalonde / 1995 / xii + 146 pp.
17. *The Five Aggregates: Understanding Theravāda Psychology and Soteriology*
    Mathieu Boisvert / 1995 / xii + 166 pp.
18. *Mysticism and Vocation*
    James R. Horne / 1996 / vi + 110 pp.

6. *The Rhetoric of the Babylonian Talmud, Its Social Meaning and Context*
   Jack N. Lightstone / 1994 / xiv + 317 pp.
7. *Whose Historical Jesus?*
   Edited by William E. Arnal and Michel Desjardins / 1997 / vi + 337 pp.
8. *Religious Rivalries and the Struggle for Success in Caesarea Maritima*
   Edited by Terence L. Donaldson / 2000 / xiv + 402 pp.
9. *Text and Artifact in the Religions of Mediterranean Antiquity*
   Edited by Stephen G. Wilson and Michel Desjardins / 2000 / xvi + 616 pp.
10. *Parables of War: Reading John's Jewish Apocalypse*
    by John W. Marshall / 2001 / viii + 262 pp.
11. *Mishnah and the Social Formation of the Early Rabbinic Guild:*
    A Socio-Rhetorical Approach
    by Jack N. Lightstone / 2002 / xii + 240 pp.
12. *The Social Setting of the Ministry as Reflected in the Writings of Hermas,*
    Clement and Ignatius
    Harry O. Maier / 1991, second impression 2002 / x + 234 pp.

The Study of Religion in Canada /
Sciences Religieuses au Canada

1. *Religious Studies in Alberta: A State-of-the-Art Review*
   Ronald W. Neufeldt / 1983 / xiv + 145 pp.
2. *Les sciences religieuses au Québec depuis 1972*
   Louis Rousseau et Michel Despland / 1988 / 158 p.
3. *Religious Studies in Ontario: A State-of-the-Art Review*
   Harold Remus, William Closson James and Daniel Fraikin / 1992 / xviii + 422 pp.
4. *Religious Studies in Manitoba and Saskatchewan: A State-of-the-Art Review*
   John M. Badertscher, Gordon Harland and Roland E. Miller / 1993 / vi + 166 pp.
5. *The Study of Religion in British Columbia: A State-of-the-Art Review*
   Brian J. Fraser / 1995 / x + 127 pp.
6. *Religious Studies in Atlantic Canada: A State-of-the-Art Review*
   Paul W. R. Bowlby with Tom Faulkner / 2001 / xii + 208 pp.

Studies in Women and Religion /
Études sur les femmes et la religion

1. *Femmes et religions**
   Sous la direction de Denise Veillette / 1995 / xviii + 466 p.
2. *The Work of Their Hands: Mennonite Women's Societies in Canada*
   Gloria Neufeld Redekop / 1996 / xvi + 172 pp.
3. *Profiles of Anabaptist Women: Sixteenth-Century Reforming Pioneers*
   Edited by C. Arnold Snyder and Linda A. Huebert Hecht / 1996 / xxii + 438 pp.
4. *Voices and Echoes: Canadian Women's Spirituality*
   Edited by Jo-Anne Elder and Colin O'Connell / 1997 / xxviii + 237 pp.
5. *Obedience, Suspicion and the Gospel of Mark: A Mennonite-Feminist Exploration*
   of Biblical Authority
   Lydia Neufeld Harder / 1998 / xiv + 168 pp.
6. *Clothed in Integrity: Weaving Just Cultural Relations and the Garment Industry*
   Barbara Paleczny / 2000 / xxxiv + 352 pp.
7. *Women in God's Army: Gender and Equality in the Early Salvation Army*
   Andrew Mark Eason / 2003 / xiv + 246 pp.
8. *Pour libérer la théologie.* Variations autour de la pensée féministe d'Ivone Gebara
   Pierrette Daviau, dir. / 2002 / 212 pp.
9. *Linking Sexuality & Gender: Naming Violence against Women in The United Church*
   of Canada
   Tracy J. Trothen / 2003 / x + 166 pp.

*Only available from Les Presses de l'Université Laval

SR Supplements

1. *Footnotes to a Theology: The Karl Barth Colloquium of 1972*
   Edited and Introduced by Martin Rumscheidt / 1974 / viii + 151 pp. / OUT OF PRINT
2. *Martin Heidegger's Philosophy of Religion*
   John R. Williams / 1977 / x + 190 pp. / OUT OF PRINT
3. *Mystics and Scholars: The Calgary Conference on Mysticism 1976*
   Edited by Harold Coward and Terence Penelhum / 1977 / viii + 121 pp. /
   OUT OF PRINT
4. *God's Intention for Man: Essays in Christian Anthropology*
   William O. Fennell / 1977 / xii + 56 pp. / out of print
5. *"Language" in Indian Philosophy and Religion*
   Edited and Introduced by Harold G. Coward / 1978 / x + 98 pp. / OUT OF PRINT
6. *Beyond Mysticism*
   James R. Horne / 1978 / vi + 158 pp. / OUT OF PRINT
7. *The Religious Dimension of Socrates' Thought*
   James Beckman / 1979 / xii + 276 pp. / OUT OF PRINT
8. *Native Religious Traditions*
   Edited by Earle H. Waugh and K. Dad Prithipaul / 1979 / xii + 244 pp. / OUT OF PRINT
9. *Developments in Buddhist Thought: Canadian Contributions to Buddhist Studies*
   Edited by Roy C. Amore / 1979 / iv + 196 pp.
10. *The Bodhisattva Doctrine in Buddhism*
    Edited and Introduced by Leslie S. Kawamura / 1981 / xxii + 274 pp. / OUT OF PRINT
11. *Political Theology in the Canadian Context*
    Edited by Benjamin G. Smillie / 1982 / xii + 260 pp.
12. *Truth and Compassion: Essays on Judaism and Religion in Memory of
    Rabbi Dr. Solomon Frank*
    Edited by Howard Joseph, Jack N. Lightstone and Michael D. Oppenheim / 1983 /
    vi + 217 pp. / OUT OF PRINT
13. *Craving and Salvation: A Study in Buddhist Soteriology*
    Bruce Matthews / 1983 / xiv + 138 pp. / OUT OF PRINT
14. *The Moral Mystic*
    James R. Horne / 1983 / x + 134 pp.
15. *Ignatian Spirituality in a Secular Age*
    Edited by George P. Schner / 1984 / viii + 128 pp. / OUT OF PRINT
16. *Studies in the Book of Job*
    Edited by Walter E. Aufrecht / 1985 / xii + 76 pp.
17. *Christ and Modernity: Christian Self-Understanding in a Technological Age*
    David J. Hawkin / 1985 / x + 181 pp.
18. *Young Man Shinran: A Reappraisal of Shinran's Life*
    Takamichi Takahatake / 1987 / xvi + 228 pp. / OUT OF PRINT
19. *Modernity and Religion*
    Edited by William Nicholls / 1987 / vi + 191 pp.
20. *The Social Uplifters: Presbyterian Progressives and the Social Gospel in Canada,
    1875-1915*
    Brian J. Fraser / 1988 / xvi + 212 pp. / OUT OF PRINT

Series discontinued

Available from:

Wilfrid Laurier University Press

Waterloo, Ontario, Canada N2L 3C5
Telephone: (519) 884-0710, ext. 6124
Fax: (519) 725-1399
E-mail: press@wlu.ca
World Wide Web: http://www.wlupress.wlu.ca